To
the

The Case for an Earth Ethic

Robert F. Harrington

hancock
house

ISBN 0-88839-242-7

Cataloging in Publication Data

Harrington, Robert F., 1926–
    To heal the earth
    The case for an earth ethic

    Includes bibliographical references.
    ISBN 0-88839-242-7

    1.   Human ecology — Moral and ethical aspects.
2.   Environmental protection — Moral and ethical
aspects.   3.   Man — Influence on nature.   I.   Title.

GF80.H37 1990   179'.1   C90-091110-7

Edited and designed by H. W. Bryce
Production by Lorna Lake

Printed in Hong Kong

Published simultaneously in Canada and the United States by

HANCOCK HOUSE PUBLISHERS LTD.
19313 Zero Ave., Surrey, B.C. V3S 5J9

HANCOCK HOUSE PUBLISHERS
1431 Harrison Ave., P.O. Box X-1, Blaine, WA 98230

Dedicated to the healing of the earth.

Contents

Acknowledgments

Inasmuch as a good portion of this book is a history of thoughts and ideas of many philosophers, scientists and other individuals, I wish to acknowledge their contributions. Our cultural heritage is vast, and I have sought an aspect of it that pertains to the earth and the attitudes that have been expressed about it. Appreciation is extended to the many authors, publishers and copyright holders for permission to use various quotes throughout the text.

I am indebted to a number of individuals who have read portions of this book and made valuable comments. These include John Oxley, Dan Gagnier, Ray Travers, Caren Olsen, and Rodney Ehl. I have also enjoyed constructive discussions with Joe Rickert.

Individuals who have helped in special ways are Karen and Len Gagnier, Shelese Gagnier, Eugene McDonald, Olive and Brian Winter, Robert Mathews, Mary MacMillan, Fred Marshall, Karen Switzer Howse, Marilyn Taylor, Henning von Krogh, Jack Gregson, Mary O'Brien, Cathy Smith, and Wayne Peppard. Assistance has also been received from Agriculture Canada, Soil Conservation Canada, the United States Soil Conservation Service, The Journal of Pesticide Reform, Glenbow Archives, and Western Canada Wilderness Committee.

Special thanks are extended to the Canada Council for a grant which facilitated the research and writing of this book.

Special thanks also to Herb Bryce, Senior Editor, Hancock House Publishers, for his meticulous attention to detail and his unfailing good humor.

My greatest help has come from my wife, Linda, who has discussed most of the points in this book with me, and who has been unflagging in her assistance at every step along the way, from notes to rough copy, through revisions and to final copy.

Preface

In the world of today, truly conservative individuals who have genuine concern for the earth and for future generations, are often referred to as radicals. They are considered to be radical because they disagree with the commonly held view that the purpose of life is profit and the acquisition of material goods. The word "environmentalist" is a convenient categorization for these individuals and sometimes efforts are made to devise more opprobrious terms such as "tree-huggers," "dickey-birders," or whatever else might seem sufficiently scathing.

To me, the foregoing play on words, and the virtual fanaticism with which the status quo is upheld, are quite interesting. They may be strong signs that the general vested interest in materialism will be defended unto doom. Nevertheless, one really has to go no farther than to some of our modern scientific literature to see that environmentalists are not the only ones worried about the future of the world.

Because of my own interests and because of job experiences in geology, in the nuclear industry, and in field work with pesticides I found myself seeking knowledge that would give me a better understanding of life. I was drawn to studies in ecology and related sciences and also began delving into classical literature and philosophy.

I pondered upon statements made by Margaret Mead and other individuals about the need for "generalists" in a world which relies increasingly on specialists. The more I studied, the more apparent it became that our focus was on taking the world apart piece by piece, exploiting it in the same piecemeal fashion, and at the same time ignoring the underlying truth of the adage that it is easier to break a dozen eggs than to put them together again.

At some point I began to appreciate the truth of a statement by Columbia University president and Nobel Peace Prize holder Nicholas Murray Butler. In addressing a Columbia University graduating class, he said: "An expert is one who knows more and more about less and less." I also recognized Butler's insight in another matter. When he founded Teachers' College at Columbia (1889), it was based on the adjustment of humanity to the new conditions of an expanding industrial society. Troubled by the direction of society after 1900, however, the realization grew upon him that "eternal truths" are a better foundation for human development than "practicalism."

The focus on expertise, with the concurrent rejection of historical example and experience that has accrued through the ages, has left us in the predicament we are in today. We live in a world of frenzied activity and little purpose, a world reminiscent of an old description of the Mississippi River, which referred to that river as "a mile wide and an inch deep," a world where the marketplace is filled with goods which will sell in a society that has been conditioned to "shop" and "buy" and to spontaneously think it "needs" whatever it sees.

Somewhere in a life that became involved in teaching, both in secondary schools and in universities, as well as in a life in which I have chosen to live in out-of-the-way places to be close to the natural world, the idea of this book emerged. I have thought seriously about the rather strident times in which we live and conclude that they are but a poor facsimile of true civilization. It seems that we are as rootless in our deepest thoughts as we are prone to move from job to job, from community to community, and from continent to continent—always, I think, in search of ourselves.

The purpose of this book is to try to lay the foundation for a worldview that is different than the one commonly held today. The new worldview is one which would allow us to focus on more enduring things than the accumulation of goods or the acquisition of wealth.

In attempting to construct such a foundation, I have drawn from material which readers may wish to study more extensively for additional depth and breadth.

Initially the book peruses ancient history to get a sense of the impact of civilization upon land. The historical record is written plainly on the face of the earth and we find that in many places where there were once majestic forests, lush pastures, and fertile meadows, there is now only desolation.

From the examination of continents other than our own, we move to North America and see what has happened to Canada and the United States in the short period they have been subjected to exploitation. The bison and Atlantic salmon are considered as species subjected to the influence of civilization; and to stress the urgency of our need for a land ethic, we take a brief look at five environmental problems: air pollution, pesticides, soil erosion, water pollution, and deforestation.

We next turn to the thoughts of individuals who date from ancient Chinese philosophers to modern times, and find that many renowned thinkers have held the earth to be a sacred manifestation of a Divine mind. Ecological insight is part of the awareness of such classical figures as Lao-Tzu, Plato, Aristotle, Theophrastus, Pliny, Thales, and Marcus Aurelius. Indeed, in his *Meditations,* Marcus Aurelius (pp. 121-180) advises us to, "Always think of the universe as one living organism, with a single substance and a single soul." Environmental awareness and concern, it seems clear, dates back to very early writings and includes some of the most prominent names in history. This review of thoughts and statements continues through the Romantic poets, the New England naturalists, the introduction of the idea of conservation to North America by Theodore Roosevelt and Gifford Pinchot, and looks at individual perceptions of deforestation in the United States and Canada in the late 1800s.

As a starting point in construction of a worldview that might enable us to develop some proper respect for earth, it is hypothesized that a composite philosophy could be developed from the thoughts of Henry David Thoreau, George Perkins Marsh, and Dr. Albert Schweitzer. These men, in their wholeness, express an ethical and intellectual foundation for a worldview that is realistic and is the bearer of much hope in the development of a sustainable, civilized world. Thoreau is examined as the austere defender of nature and of life lived according to the highest principles of which one is capable. George Perkins Marsh is seen as the traveled scholar who examined the damage caused by human occupation in Europe, and as an intent man who studied the history and causes of the visible effects of man's habitation of the land. From observation, research and reflection, he proposed ecological solutions more than a century ago which are still valid in our own time. Schweitzer, with his broad background in theology, philosophy, music and medicine, is the visionary who drew from Scripture the conviction that the principle, "Thou shalt love the neighbor as thyself," should be extended to include all living things.

A new worldview will come about through reflection upon our true relationship with nature and through use of our new understanding to make and implement decisions that will lighten the burden we place on the planet. There are already some attempts being made, at various places throughout the world, to mend the torn fabric of ecosystems and assist earth's restorative processes. Though these efforts are small in comparison to the damage that has been done, they are a sign of the emergence of a new awareness and concern.

Only when we succeed in awakening and in shedding the presently held conviction that we are superior to the rest of nature will we be ready to forge the restraints upon our own behavior that will enable us to save ourselves and our planet. To think that this can be done without major changes to our lives is simply to deceive ourselves. An earth ethic must become the very pivot around which all our future actions revolve. Love of and respect for the earth and its needs is the only foundation for any true love of humanity, simply because the future of all life depends on the viability of the life support systems of the planet.

Throughout the text, I have focused on the reckless abandon with which we are destroying forests. We are doing this in spite of long awareness that deforestation is the primary cause of degradation of land. So much evidence exists, and so much comment has been made on the folly of continuing our present course of forest destruction, that it should be apparent our economic single vision has brought us to the brink of disaster.

In the final analysis, my motive for writing this book is the simple fact that I love this beautiful and productive earth. Unless conscientious humans rise in defense of the living earth, it will succumb, perhaps sooner than we think, to the unbalanced demands of an industrial society.

Our great hope, perhaps our only hope, depends upon a revolution in character. Substantial signs of this revolution appear throughout the world. We are now in a race with time.

We are now faced with the fact that tomorrow is today. Over the bleached bones and jumbled residues of numerous civilizations are written the pathetic words, 'Too late.' There is an invisible book of life that faithfully records our vigilance or our neglect . . . This may well be mankind's last chance to choose between chaos and community.

Martin Luther King, Jr. 1967

1

1 Out of the Earth

The Earth sustains us. It is our home. Not only that, but we are literally "of the earth." If you could trace the history of a single atom (perhaps one that now occupies your body), it might at various times have been found as part of a mountain, as part of a blade of grass, a flower, a fish, or a man. The materials on the planet are exchanged in never-ending cycles. The world of the Carboniferous era, complete with the giant tree ferns and varied reptile life, contained the same atoms as the world of today. These building blocks of mountains, icebergs, polar bears, or people, are like numbers on a spinning wheel. When the wheel stops at a particular number, the atom is "tied up" in some living or nonliving form. Eventually the wheel spins again, the atom moves on, until it is once more stopped as part of another material. The movement of essential material of life from one form to another is something of which man has long been aware. Shakespeare's Hamlet marveled at this phenomenon, saying: "A man may fish with the worm that hath eat of a king, and eat of the fish that hath fed of the worm." (Act IV, Scene 3, Line 29.)

For billions of years the spinning atoms moved from one form to another. From random atoms, compounds emerged. The ebb, flow, and interplay of compounds in a design beyond our comprehension, produced cells; and a new condition called "life" became part of our planet. Life struggled in the harshness of a geologically raw environment, gradually building a foothold from which mind and personality could emerge. Suddenly, with the advent of mind, in the form of human intelligence, a new sort of energy was unleashed on earth. Ever since, humans have made relentless efforts to subjugate the forces of nature solely for their own use. We have but to look at our own claims of "taming rivers" behind dams, "conquering mountains" by tunneling through them, or "developing wilderness" by logging forests, or building roads and recreational facilities, to see that we are quite intent on controlling nature.

In many ways, human efforts at controlling nature have had apparent success. Where mixed grasslands and virgin forests once stood in many areas, there may now be orderly rows of fruit trees or vast acreages of grain. If we think carefully about less eye-catching panoramas, we may begin to realize that where once forests and grasslands flourished, there are now, also, large areas of desert or savagely eroded wastelands. In place of once beautiful, clear streams, there are now murky, turbid flowages that may be little more than open sewers. Man's conquest of nature has exacted a severe price from Earth. The seriousness of the human predicament has been acknowledged by author Robert Ardrey. In *African Genesis,* he suggests that nature may yet deem the experiment with intelligence "a failure." Another author, Dr. Paul Ehrlich, writing of the possible death of the oceans from toxic chemical substances, warns that man may be at bat in his half of the ninth inning, but also reminds us that "Nature Bats Last."[1]

We already know that environmental problems can continue to be ignored only at great risk. Prestigious scientists, research organizations, United Nations' reports, and growing worldwide awareness are forcibly calling the declining health of the planet to the attention of everyone, including those who were surest that nature could be manipulated at will.

Although there is much evidence that if we are serious about survival we will be forced into a new relationship with nature, we bend

12

only grudgingly in that direction. Thus far we have ignored the necessity of calling ourselves to full account for the heedless way in which we have ravaged the planet. We fight a delaying action with more and more "studies," hoping for some interpretation that will relieve us of any necessity of changing our wasteful ways. Political systems built on expediency and short-term benefits are singularly unfitted to cope with our current crises. On the one hand we have enough knowledge to realize that once the thresholds of biological systems are violated, decline can be rapid and summary; on the other we are lulled by the faith of our times, that science and technology can solve all problems. Any hypothesis that science and technology may have created more problems than they have solved is seen as a heretical violation of our belief that nature is a thing to be conquered.

The conquest of nature cannot be achieved without serious, often irrevocable destabilization of the integrity of the living system that is being "conquered." The definition of "integrity" that is meant here is "the quality or state of being complete; wholeness; entireness; unbroken state."[2]

To understand the integrity of a living system such as a forest more easily, it is often convenient to look at it in terms of its biological composition, function, and structure.

The composition of a forest, whether it be a Mediterranean or a boreal forest, has to do with the proportional arrangement of component species. On a rolling acreage in southeastern British Columbia, with wet and dry areas, perhaps with a swampy portion and coarser, drier soil on ridges, the composition might involve western red cedar, western hemlock, western white pine, Douglas fir, and white spruce. A number of "old settler" cottonwood trees might be found in the moister ground, and birch and aspen poplar might thrive before being shaded out. Shrubby growth might include willow, alder, hazelnut, and other species. Certainly Devil's club would be found in the moist places and on slightly higher ground, huckleberry, dogwood, thimbleberry, and honeysuckle would be common. Ground cover might include Prince's pine, wintergreen, twinflower, bunchberry, wild ginger, and many other species. Similarly, there would be indigenous animals, including white-tailed mice, short-tailed meadow mice, species of shrews, red squirrels, an occasional white-tailed deer, coyote, black bear, pine marten (at least in winter) and others. Varied thrushes would trill in early spring and, in May, Swainson's thrushes would sing their evening songs. Veeries, chickadees, downy woodpeckers, a few pileated woodpeckers—these and many others would make up the forest composition, along with indigenous amphibians, reptiles, and invertebrates.

The function of the forest involves the processes that make the forest work, the capture of the sun's energy for photosynthesis, the uptake of moisture and nutrients, fixation of nitrogen by suitable species, the storage and slow release of moisture, modifications of climate, evapo-transpiration, storage of carbon, and provision of macro- and micro-habitats.

Structure has to do with how the parts of the forest are assembled. It involves the large old trees and the smaller trees and the way in which they are arranged. It includes the old, rotting logs on the ground and the habitat they may provide for mice or for a nest of wasps. It has to do with dead snags which may provide nesting sites for woodpeckers or for flycatchers. It includes the dense thickets of brush that may shelter or provide food for grouse or other species. It has to do with the mushrooms which provide food for squirrels or pack rats, and which scatter spores for the mycorrhizae that keep tree roots healthy.

It is important to remember that structure, function, and composition are parts of the overall integrity of the forest. When the forests are removed in their entirety, as has happened in many European, Asian, and African countries, great changes come about. Species vanish, moisture regimes change, the reduction of evapo-transpiration affects the formation of clouds and of precipitation, the roots and rootlets that held soil in place decompose, and erosion, often massive erosion, may occur.

To be sure, all things are interrelated. We live by holding hands. In a symbolic sense, we hold hands with species we could not name even if we saw them. The more we know, the more we understand that our fate is linked to the fate of many other organisms. Also, the more we learn, the more evident it becomes that nature is a vast, intricate complexity whose secrets we are only beginning to discover.

History records the exploits of kings and queens, the rise and fall of ideologies and governments, but very little of our recorded history is intended to teach us of the impact of humanity on the earth. Yet, interwoven in the pages of countless history texts, are records of unthinking assaults upon the planet. Progress is glorified as a human achievement, isolated from all else, and history passes lightly over the substantial direct destruction that we have caused to the land base which supports all life. The truth of the matter is that we can call the

14

conditions we create by the name Progress only as long as we continue to practice legerdemain in our bookkeeping and never attempt to strike a balance between Gross National Products and Gross National Disasters. Our focus on short-term values guarantees the corollary that we are, wittingly or unwittingly, running our course as a short-term species. The one factor we seem unable to recognize is that we are running out of time in which we have any option to change our ways.

In the following pages we will examine enough of the effect that humans have had on land, particularly in long-settled areas, to show that the earth has received very little consideration from people. At the same time we will become aware of the fact that there have always been a few voices crying in the wilderness, questioning our heedlessness and suggesting that what we have been doing is wrong. It is certainly not surprising that these voices would not have been heeded when resources stretched from horizon to horizon and pristine lands were within easy reach. Now, however, the water and air of earth have become thin, toxic soup, and soil and subsurface waters are becoming impregnated with chemicals inimical to health. The entire historical record offers strong evidence that we must develop an ethical attitude toward the planet. There must be some limitation on human freedom to poison the planet with impunity. The barren moon, visible in our skies, is silent testimony of what the earth can become if we continue to nourish the illusion that we can heedlessly manipulate the good, good earth.

Along with some awareness of the history of man's relationships with land, we must consider the double-value system which humanity has applied to life. There is the well-professed but seldom followed recommendation of "storing up riches in Heaven," which must be contrasted with the far more evident quest to garner material goods and affluence on earth. No talk of patterns of sustained yield, harvest of the surplus, or conservation of the earth's resources has yet seemed to stand in the way of the search for an ever-increasing Gross National Product, a favorable trade balance, and a maximization of profit.

We are already at an impasse. The progress-as-usual viewpoint dominates the information networks. But there still is a great awareness of our sick planet. There is also great bafflement. Nobody knows where to begin. The so-familiar attitude is a shrug, and "What can I do?" Since blind faith in technology's ability to save the day is about the only hopeful alternative, many people grasp at this straw.

15

But technology cannot save the day. It's mail-clad foot and miracle elixirs only further serve to sicken the patient. Only by putting the most suitable technology together with great human concern, human effort, and human decision to live lightly, can we restore the planet to health.

We have thus far lacked the humility and, perhaps, the courage to demote ourselves from central position in the universe and recognize ourselves as part of nature. We are utterly dependent on the earth. Our declining health and multiple neuroses are but symptoms of the declining health of the earth. Our task is to forge a compact with our planet, protecting it from ourselves that it may continue to support life.

A Different Sort of History

In about 500 B.C., Heraclitus made an observation that seemed so sensible we remember it today: "There is nothing permanent except change."

When you sit beneath a cedar tree and hear a pileated woodpecker prospecting overhead for ants, change is taking place. Ants are being eaten, the woodpecker is getting food, the tree is being excavated by the woodpecker's beak, fine fragments of wood are raining down to be converted into humus, perhaps nestlings are being fed. The changes taking place range from minute to visible, but each is important in its own way. The same is true when a bee sips nectar or gathers pollen from a flower, when a weasel seizes a mouse, when a mink pounces on a fledgling in a thicket alongside the stream where it hunts, or when an aspen leaf miner works its way through a succulent leaf.

Change! Change! Change! Rivers fertilize their floodplains and build deltas at their mouths. Avalanches carry away growing forests on a steep mountainside. Waves batter shores and grind rocks into sand. Trees topple before a howling wind and begin the long process of moldering into nutrient to support the forests of the future.

There is no question that every species produces change in an ecosystem. Providing that change is gradual and not too severe, there is sufficient environmental flexibility to accept modification. Fluctuating, dynamic change is the norm, not the exception.

Human activities offer an example of what happens when change introduced into the environment is too rapid and too traumatic. Soil, air, water, the ozone layer, isostatic balance, electromagnetic radiation, nuclear radiation: these are all areas in which the rapid changes we are seeing are of serious concern.

Robert Service once wrote a poem with a strangely prophetic title: "The Men That Don't Fit In." It was his intent to describe a particular kind of human, but in a larger sense, part of his poem seems to describe the quest of humankind for changes which involve the novel, the new, and often the unnecessary.

> If they just went straight they might go far;
> They are strong and brave and true;
> But they're always tired of the things that are,
> And they want the strange and new.
> They say: "Could I find my proper groove,
> What a deep mark I would make!"
> So they chop and change, and each fresh move
> Is only a fresh mistake.[3]

Far back in history, people developed tools to make significant change in their environment. By means of change they intended to make life more secure and comfortable. So change was brought about, but the problem arose early in history that the employment of the means of change was excessive—and that is probably the root of the problem, even today.

In this chapter we will take a brief tour through the historical record of a number of countries. The need for a land ethic is demonstrated early in the affairs of our species, and increases rapidly with the advent of new technologies used to shape its environment.

Fire

The earliest evidence of human agriculture in Europe, as determined by carbon-14 dating, occurred between 5000 B.C. and 4000 B.C., and was located in the areas of present-day Czechoslovakia and Holland. As far as can be determined, the people were semimigratory and moved from one area to another at intervals of about ten years. These moves were probably made as a result of the decline in local soil fertility. After a period of years, certain areas would be reoccupied, the interval of absence having served as a rest period for the natural restoration of the fertility of the land.

The expansion of agricultural efforts in Europe was aided by the widespread use of fire as a means of clearing land. In Neolithic times, between 3000 B.C. and 2000 B.C., northwestern Europe was covered by mixed-oak forests. Many countries, including present-day Denmark, Norway, Germany, Switzerland, and the British Isles, showed a marked change in species of trees comprising the forests during this period. Pollen studies have revealed that elm and ivy trees decreased while a species of ash tree increased. The alteration was not brought about by natural causes such as temperature change or drought. Charcoal deposits found in the soil profile, just beneath the level of the decline in elm pollen, offer substantial evidence that large areas of forest were cleared by fire, and that the fire was employed by humans clearing the land for agricultural and grazing purposes.[4]

Pakistan and India

From its headwaters in southwestern Tibet, the Indus River snakes its way through western Tibet, the Indian states of Jammu and Kashmir and Pakistan to the Arabian Sea. On its 2,000-mile (3,200 kilometer) journey to the sea, it drains about 372,000 square miles (963,480 square kilometers).

The earliest major civilization of the Indian subcontinent was located in the valley of the Indus and flourished between 2500 and 1500 B.C. Two great cities, Mohenjo Daro (a present-day archeological site on the Indus River in Sind, Pakistan) and Harappa, some 400 miles north, were the cultural centers of this civilization.

Irrigated agriculture was practiced and agriculture was a settled, rather than a nomadic operation. Through the centuries both vegetational and climatic changes took place. The region, which was forested in ancient times, is now semiarid and covered by tamarisk and scrub.

Why did these changes take place?

As the Indus civilization developed, much building construction was undertaken, and baked bricks were used as the principal building material. Soil historian Edward Hyams suggests that the fate of the forests was to provide the vast quantities of fuel needed for baking bricks. Over a period that stretched to about 30 generations, these people of the Indus "were steadily destroying the one sure stabilizer (the forests) of their precariously equable climate, as were the

Chinese a thousand years later (and) the Americans 3,500 years later."[5]

We might add that the Canadians have been doing this at an accelerated rate in the late nineteenth and through the twentieth centuries.

Hyams explains that changes in the abundance and diversity of animal species which occupied the area prior to settlement can be accounted for by changes in temperature difference resulting from clearing of the forests. Since forests affect the amount of rainfall, a general decline in moisture would also occur. As long as agriculture flourished and the ground was covered with vegetation, desiccation of the area was controlled. However, "since 1500 B.C., race after race has overrun India . . . the desiccation of Sind has been man made, but over a vast lapse of time."[6]

An additional cause of man-made deserts, in India and elsewhere, was the mismanagement of livestock. The pastoralist Aryan invaders of India, about 1500 B.C. or earlier, measured their wealth in livestock and took cattle and sheep with them. The tropical agriculture existent beforehand had developed without intensive grazing. Interestingly enough, those animals were not taken into the country to enhance the agricultural economy as much as they were to be used in religious rituals. Allowed to roam and multiply unchecked, cattle and sheep did increasing damage to the land they ranged. Although India, if undisturbed, would be a forested country, "from the mismanagement of cattle and other livestock, there is no shortage of desert in India today."[7] Even today the cow in India is considered sacred, and is allowed to roam unchecked, often destroying precious vegetation.

The magnitude of the changes mentioned in these examples is such that no simple solution can be suggested to restore the land. Even at present there is no reduction of human demands made upon the already damaged land. Increasing population alone means greater impact on environment, and any search for a higher standard of living means still further land damage. Historian R. O. White suggests that regeneration of forests is prevented not only by the fire, grazing, and cutting that has taken place but also by general deterioration of the soil as a result of these events.[8]

For example, in 1972 alone, 5.9 billion tons (5.37 billion tonnes) of soil eroded in India. With the eroded soil went more nutrient than was provided by all the inorganic fertilizer applied in 1980. Urgent soil conservation measures are needed on more than two-thirds of the land which is under cultivation.[9]

Soil degradation in India is not a recent phenomenon for it also took place when commercialized forestry was introduced by the British during the colonial period. Traditional land management in India had preserved communally managed village forests, wood lots, and commons. Under the British, these village resources became the property of new landlords and were destroyed for lumber. This forced villagers to exploit nearby natural forests which, in their turn, were logged commercially on a large scale. Management focused on earning revenue rather than on long-term forest stability. This was a blow to the village economies which depended on the forests for fuel for cooking fires and fodder for animals whose dung provided their only fertilizer.

Following the passage of forest laws that severely limited the right of villages to forest products and even to forest access, nonviolent protests (satyagrahas) were carried out by the villagers. These protests were suppressed by the British. In one village (Tilari) in 1930, dozens of unarmed villagers were killed and hundreds were injured.

The Chipko (tree-hugging) movement, an extension of Gandhian satyagrahas in India, began in 1973 and continues to this day. Villagers hug trees to prevent them from being felled (chipko = to embrace). Combining this action with fasting, the villagers have served public notice that they are against the overexploitation of Indian forests. Alarming ecological destabilization in the hills, major landslides, and floods lend impetus to the movement.[10]

To the forest industry slogan:
What do the forests bear?
Profit or resin and timber.

The Chipko movement has responded with:
What do the forests bear?
Soil, Water and Pure air.

This is a new public response, substituting obvious long-term values for the short-term values of the forest industry. The fact that the movement has surfaced recently is more understandable when we realize that sixty percent of India's forests have been cut down in the last forty years.

As a result, many "forest dwelling communities" and marginal populations dependent on forest resources have been displaced.[11]

Afghanistan

An extreme climate and inadequate rainfall have combined to make Afghanistan a land to test the strength of its people. It is believed that in early times the harsh winters led to indiscriminate cutting of forests in order that the people might have fuel.

Prior to 1220 A.D., a Muslim civilization had endured the climatic rigors and developed an agricultural economy based on irrigation. Underground irrigation channels, called kanats, were constructed to supply water to the ripening crops.

In 1220 A.D., Afghanistan was invaded by the Mongols. In his history of Afghanistan, Sir Percy Sykes gives us some idea of the extent of the damage that took place: "Bamian had been captured . . . and to avenge the death of one of his grandsons, Chenghiz destroyed every living creature, including animals and plants, and the site remained desolate for a century."[12] History bears out the fact that Attila expressed the rapacity of many military conquerors when he boasted that "no grass grew where his horse's hooves had trod."[13]

At Herat, a city destroyed by Genghis Khan in 1226 A.D., the destruction was so merciless and thorough that it is still visible in the twentieth century. The entire population of Herat was massacred. The

---

War Against the Earth

An article from Science Action Coalition reports, "Man's Great War . . . the war against earth and life continues unabated. During the Vietnam War the U.S. Defense Department delivered an average of thirty tons of explosive per square mile in Vietnam. From 1965 to 1975 strip-mining operations in Appalachian coal fields detonated thirty-five tons of explosives per square mile."

Meanwhile, a report from UNEP says that in South Vietnam, chemical herbicides "completely destroyed 1,500 sq. kilometers of mangrove forest, and caused some damage to about 15,000 sq. kilometers more."

destruction of the peasantry led to neglect of the land and a shortage of people to carry on the work necessary to hold back the constantly encroaching desert. Desert sands blew in over the plowed fields. The kanats collapsed, and to this day there are kanats which have not been repaired since the Mongol invasion. Without the life-giving water provided by irrigation, the entire agricultural prospect of Afghanistan rapidly declined.

In the 1930s, a development program was begun in the valley of one of the four major rivers, the Helmand. But the wonders of modern technology failed to take into account a people unused to adequate water supplies. Thousands of acres, unfit for irrigation, were overirrigated. This caused water tables to rise and the soil to become salinized. Expensive reclamation projects thus had to be undertaken to make the soils arable once again.

It was a Mongol intent, when they invaded, to lay waste a large area of land, thus protecting themselves by creating an inhospitable, artificial "No-Man's Land" around their own country. That a military strategy to devastate land can be successful has been proven time and again through history. But only now are large numbers of people becoming increasingly aware that damage to the land, while perhaps aimed at only a single conquest, can lead to a poorer life for untold generations of people who will live long after the folly of the military victories has become apparent. This may well be the case with herbicides developed for chemical warfare in Vietnam. Their long-term effect on soil microflora and microfauna cannot be predicted at this time. For example, the herbicide Hoegrass (diclofop methyl mixture) destroys as much as 80 percent of soil algae. About 25 percent of nitrogen naturally fixed in soil is produced by algae. Any interference with algae is serious, especially in spring, which is the peak season of algal growth.[14]

Syria

Early agricultural civilization in ancient Syria waxed and waned from 2400 B.C. until the Pax Romana brought political stability and a period of prosperity for the first three centuries A.D. The semiarid nature of the cultivable land would likely have assured soil depletion earlier in history if it had not been for warring armies that interfered with agriculture and left long periods in which natural vegetation could help restore the land. This seems to be one of the few cases in which military activity produced a beneficial side effect.

That substantial forests once guarded the upslope water courses was pointed out by the ancient Greek naturalist-philosopher Theophrastus, who gave a word picture of Syrian forests about 300 B.C.:

> . . . in Syria and on the mountains, cedars grow to surprising heights and thickness: . . . sometimes so large that three men cannot embrace the tree . . . any tree, if it is left alone grows to a remarkable height and thickness.[15]

Where possible, irrigated agriculture was practiced and if water supplies were inadequate, dry land farming and grazing took place. During the Roman occupation, most of the arable land was kept under cultivation and produce was exported.

The most productive area was the Plain of Antioch, about 200 square miles of relatively level land which grew excellent crops without irrigation. The city, for which the plain was named, provided water to most homes, had lighted streets, and a main avenue paved with granite. Between the fourth and twelfth centuries, the city was conquered by invading armies and was heavily damaged by an earthquake. It was finally destroyed in 1258 A.D. during the Crusades.[16]

Deforestation by overcutting of the highlands and the subsequent erosion completed the destruction of the Plain of Antioch. Of the 175 towns once found on the plain, only seven still survive. Archaeologists excavating the ruins of the city of Antioch had to dig through twenty-eight feet of silt that had washed off the once forested mountains.

In 1943, Walter Clay Lowdermilk described the ruins of hillside towns resting on skeleton rock, from which three to six feet of topsoil had been swept away. Rather than being buried, the settlements in these areas had sometimes been left elevated by soil erosion. He summarized what had happened, saying that soil erosion in Syria had been so thorough that the country is a man-made desert, lacking vegetation, water, and soil. In his words: "The cities . . . will remain dead forever . . . their soils are gone beyond hope of restoration."[17]

Dr. J. V. Thirgood of the Faculty of Forestry, University of British Columbia, notes that the boundaries of modern Syria do not coincide with its boundaries during Roman, Crusader, or Ottoman times and that some observations about Syria may include Lebanon, Jordan, and

Israel. He speaks hopefully of the "remarkable powers of recovery" of the natural forest, "when goats are excluded and grubbing of roots prevented." Action now may prevent final destruction of forests in the cradle of civilization.[18]

Mesopotamia

Present day Iraq occupies much of the area once known as Mesopotamia, a land that was blessed with several million acres of level, fertile soil. To compensate for the dryness of the area, the Tigris and Euphrates rivers made irrigated farming possible.

Silt loads are known to vary from river to river. The Tigris and Euphrates have their headwater in the Armenian Hills and early in the history of Mesopotamia, these hills were stripped of timber and then overgrazed. The result was that tremendous silt loads resulting from erosion led to the irrigation ditches being continually laden with silt. The ditches had to be frequently cleaned if the life-giving water were to be available to farmers. As a result, a never-ending supply of slaves was needed to keep the irrigation canals open.

As was typical of ancient (and modern) civilizations, invasions and warfare were a common occurrence. A portion of the area called Mesopotamia was once known as the Elamite Empire. Its territory included the Tigris Valley, a large portion of the Persian Gulf shore, and the Zagros Mountains. Elam fell to the Assyrian conqueror, Ashurbanipal, about 642 B.C. A scribe, who faithfully kept a yearly record of Ashurbanipal's deeds, records in the first person, Ashurbanipal's war in the land of Elam:

> For a distance of one month and twenty-five days' march I devastated the districts of Elam. I spread salt and thorn-bush there (to injure the soil). Sons of the kings, sisters of the kings, members of Elam's royal family young and old, prefects, governors, knights, artisans, as many as there were, inhabitants male and female, big and little, horses, mules, asses, flocks and herds more numerous than a swarm of locusts—I carried them off as booty to Assyria. The dust of Susa, of Madaktu, of Haltemash and of their other cities, I carried it off to Assyria. In a month of days I subdued Elam in its whole extent. The voice of man, the steps of flocks and herds, the happy shouts of mirth—I put

an end to them in its fields, which I left for the asses, the gazelles, and all manner of wild beasts to people.[19]

In time, Mesopotamia became part of the empire of Alexander the Great, of Greece. Babylon's fame remained undiminished, but the never-ending dependency on slave labor continued. Alexander's empire dissolved in 323 B.C. Later conquerors neglected the canals, which began to choke up with silt. The area gradually declined until the Mongols invaded the region in the thirteenth century A.D. The Mongols disdained agriculture. They destroyed cities and massacred much of the population and wrecked irrigation systems that had functioned to at least some extent for five millennia. Their destruction of the major Nahrwan Canal and a diversion dam that fed it led to loss of control of floodwater of the Tigris. This water periodically surged out of control and dissected the land, eroding much of the fertile soil.

Basically the whole irrigation system, that had made the area highly cultivable, disintegrated. Deforestation and overgrazing continued and the food supply for the area was dramatically reduced. Today, in the twentieth century, the land feeds fewer than a quarter of the people it hosted in ancient times.

Palestine

In the Holy Bible, one may read Moses' description of Palestine: ". . . a good land, a land of brooks of water, of fountains and springs, flowing forth in valleys and hills, a land of wheat and barley, of vines and fig trees and pomegranates, a land of olive trees and honey, a land in which you will eat bread without scarcity, in which you will lack nothing, a land whose stones are iron, and out of whose hills you can dig copper."[20]

By now the story should be familiar: typical acts such as the cutting of trees from slopes and overgrazing enabled erosion, unchecked by normal vegetation, to accelerate.

Let us consider a recent description of Palestine:

The 'Promised Land' which 3,000 years ago was 'flowing with milk and honey' has been so devastated by erosion that the soils have been swept off fully half the area of the hill lands . . . the finer particles are swept out in floodwater to change the beautiful blue of the Mediterranean to a dirty brown as far as the horizon; the coarser particles are spread out on former alluvium where they are still cultivated, but in a progressively reduced area. Accelerated run-off from barren slopes continues to cut gullies through the alluvial valleys and to choke up the channels of streams flowing through the coastal plain.[21]

As we shall continue to see, human action has varied little from one country to another. By extending this brief tour through land history, we are bound to arrive at the conclusion that, even though it is late, there remains an absolute need of a guiding ethic in land use.

Lebanon

At one time Lebanon was primarily a heavily forested country. Its lowlands, when cleared, were very fertile, but the amount of lowland was limited to a coastal strip a few miles wide, abutted by steeply rising mountains. Originally, a Phoenician civilization developed in Lebanon. The Phoenicians found a market for lumber and as the population of laborers rose, more land came under cultivation. The demand for lumber by King Solomon and other wealthy Hebrews kept a work force of 150,000 laboring to supply their needs.[22] As forests were cleared on the hillsides, cultivated fields appeared where there had been timber. Some of the slopes were as steep as 30 degrees, and winter rains immediately caused sheet erosion and gullying.

Along with crop farming, goat herds were important to the Phoenician agricultural economy. If it had not been for the goats, there is a possibility that natural forest succession might have cloaked some parts of the hillsides with protective vegetation, thus retarding erosion. Eupolis, one of the poets of the Greek, *Old Comedy,* in his play *The Goats,* introduces these animals, boasting of the variety of food they enjoy: "We feed on all manner of shrubs, browsing on the tender shoots of pine, ilex, and arbutus, and on spurge, clover, and fragrant sage, and many-leaved bindweed as well, wild olive and Lentisk and ash, fir, sea oak, ivy, and heather, willow, thorn, mullein, and asphodel, cistus, oak, thyme, and savory."[23]

26

During the Phoenician civilization, most of the topsoil was stripped from the hills. Drainage patterns were altered, pestilential marshes were created on river deltas, and the lowlands were mantled with eroded materials from the hills.

Both World War I and II saw additional strains placed on the remaining timber resources. Lebanese timber was used as fuel for railways operated by the Ottoman authorities during World War I. It is estimated that 60 percent of the remaining forests in Lebanon were used for this purpose during the first three years of the war.[24] During World War II, British and French military forces used timber from the still forested highlands to build a coastal railway.

Now, of the original 1,000 square miles (2,600 square kilometers) of forest, only a few groves of the famed Cedars of Lebanon are left.[25] One, the Tripoli grove, contains about 400 trees . . . a church protects it from human vandalism and a stone wall guards it from goatherds. Most of Lebanon is so heavily eroded that only through geological processes of long duration is there hope of producing new soil.

Crete

A famous civilization known as the Minoan kingdom flourished on the island of Crete some four thousand years ago. Although seapower made Crete a wealthy trading nation, the condition of the island soil steadily deteriorated. However, the ability of the people to import goods kept the lifestyle lavish. About 1300 B.C., Crete was invaded

Harry Emerson Fosdick, in one of his sermons, vividly illustrated the difference between giving and getting in "The Meaning of Service" written in 1920. As he said: "The Sea of Galilee and the Dead Sea are made of the same water. It flows down, clear and cool, from the heights of Hermon and the roots of the cedars of Lebanon. The Sea of Galilee makes beauty of it, for the Sea of Galilee has an outlet. It gets to give. It gathers in its riches that it may pour them out again to fertilize the Jordan plain. But the Dead Sea with the same water makes horror. For the Dead Sea has no outlet. It gets to keep."

from the mainland sixty miles away, its rich cities burned, and the people enslaved.[26] Forced by this defeat to live on their own diminished resources, the population was reduced to poverty.

Nearly two-thirds of the island is now a barren, rocky wasteland. The decline of the Minoan kingdom is attributed to neglect of conservation practices which might have enabled Crete to continue to support a healthy, prosperous civilization. By 500 B.C. it was common for the Greeks to use the word "Cretan" to describe a person of inferior mentality. Although time has obscured the exact causes of the decline of the Minoan kingdom, it has been suggested that one of the specific reasons was deforestation of the land, which made it impossible to maintain the large wooden fleets of military and commercial vessels.

Greece

Plato (427 to 347 B.C.) today, is still renowned for his philosophical observations. It would be wrong, though, to assume that he had no time for practical observations as well as those of a more abstract nature. In Critias, Plato reflected on the changes that had taken place in the soils of his native land:

> And of its goodness a strong proof is this: what is now left of our soil rivals any other in being all-productive and abundant in crops and rich in pasturage for all kinds of cattle; and at that period, in addition to their fine quality, it produced these things in vast quantity. . . . What now remains compared with what then existed is like the skeleton of a sick man, all the fat and soft earth having wasted away, and only the bare framework of the land being left. But at that epoch the country was unimpaired, and for its mountains it had high arable hills, and in place of the 'moorlands' (with stony soil) . . . it contained plains full of rich soil; and it had much forest-land in its mountains . . . there are some mountains now which have nothing but food for bees, but they had trees no very long time ago. . . . Moreover, it was enriched by the yearly rains from Zeus, which were not lost to it, as now, by flowing from the bare land into the sea; but the soil it had was deep, and therein it received the water.[27]

It is not surprising that Plato, in his Laws, advised that the state should take measures to control deforestation in order to keep the water pure and to assure that there was constant flow from the forested hills.

But it is surprising that 2,300 years later, we are ignoring history and are now clear-cutting watersheds with the ruthless efficiency made possible by modern machinery. We do this in spite of studies such as the one conducted by Abel Wolman Associates, Johns Hopkins University, for the Select Committee on National Water Resources of the U.S. Senate which indicated that the greatest public benefit of the National Forests "is for their watershed value and not for grazing, timber, wildlife, or recreation."[28]

In British Columbia, groups of citizens dependent on small mountain streams for their domestic and irrigation water supply have banded together in watershed alliances in an attempt to protect their watersheds from clear-cutting, industrial pollution, and avalanche hazard.

As for the politicians and industrialists, it appears that unlike Plato, they have "eyes to see, and see not; they have ears to hear, and hear not." (Ezekiel, 12:27). We can only hope that these people are not so besotted with the monomania of economic growth that the shingle plains of British Columbia will be their legacy to posterity.

At least part of the soil damage done to Greece was done deliberately as a result of the worldwide human tendency to engage in warfare. Some of this unthinking behavior (toward the earth) was described by Thucydides (471-401 B.C.), in the following brief quotes which illustrate the assault that took place upon the land itself, as well as upon the enemy.

> . . . Making a halt they proceeded to ravage, first of all the territory of Eleusis and Thriasian plain . . . until they came to Acharnae, the largest of the demes of Attica, as they are called. Halting in the town they made a camp, where they remained for a long time ravaging the country.

How did they ravage the country? The following excerpt gives us an idea, as Thucydides describes a battle:

> The battle took place at Tangara in Boetia, and in it the Lacedaemonians and their allies were victorious, and there

was much slaughter on both sides. The Lacedaemonians then entered the Megarian territory, cut down the trees, and went home . . .

That ruination of land was standard practice during the wars is indicated from another account, later in the war . . . in 413 B.C.:

At the very beginning of the next spring, earlier than ever before, the Lacedaemonians and their allies invaded Attica . . . at first they ravaged the plain of Attica and then proceeded to fortify Decelia . . . the purpose of the fort . . . was to dominate the plain and the most fertile parts of the country *with a view to devastating them* . . . [29]

After reading Thucydides' comments, it is obvious that wars between people have often turned out to be wars against the land as well. This is not surprising, as commanders of armies were aware that their enemies could not continue to function without the land that supported them. Biologists too, have long acknowledged that the surest way to destroy a species is to destroy its habitat.

The following facts may help clarify how damage occurs to the land from acts such as those committed by the Lacedaemonians when they cut down the trees in Megarian territory. In his book on water, Thompson King offers information about water-holding capacity of soils under various sorts of vegetative cover; this in turn indicates the difficulty of restoring trees once the land has been ravaged.[30] Bare soil, he says, may retain as little as 5,500 gallons per acre per hour of rainfall. If soil is protected by grass or shrub growth, it may absorb more than 25,500 gallons per acre per hour.

Ground litter, such as dead grass or leaves, helps absorb and hold water, and leafy growth enables rainfall to drip gently to earth rather than to splash violently. But good forest land is even better, and is capable of absorbing four or five inches of heavy rainfall, which is more than 100,000 gallons per acre. Such forest soils may store up to 17 inches of gentle rainfall, which is more than 400,000 gallons per acre.

Thus the aridity noted by Plato, and the erosion which carried away the soil, would be greatly accelerated by the Lacedaemonian war on the land.

The deforestation would speed up runoff, cause gullying, and wash topsoil into rivers where it would be carried toward the sea and at the same time cause the siltation of the rivers, increase the threat of floods, and bury spawning beds. One marvels at the interrelatedness of natural systems and at the far-reaching effect of what seem to be simple, isolated events.

(The long-term effect of forest removal is explained in a recent statement by Lester Brown, Director of Worldwatch Institute. Speaking of Ethiopia, Mr. Brown made reference to public and media impressions that the famine problems in Ethiopia will end once plentiful rain occurs and leads to good harvests. Mr. Brown expresses the view that both the days of plentiful rain and good harvests have ended.

The reason is simple. Before large areas of Africa were cleared, the great forests stored and released moisture, acting like beneficent

---

Taking Root!

The extent to which roots serve to hold soil together is amazing. Observation of roots and root hairs in one single cubic inch (15.6 cubic centimeters) of soil present some imposing figures.

There has been detected, in a single cubic inch of soil planted to oats, 110 roots, 150,000 root hairs, and a combined length of roots and root hairs of 630 feet (192 meters).

Kentucky bluegrass is even more important in soil-binding qualities. Two thousand of these roots may be found in a single cubic inch of soil and as many as a million root hairs. The combined length of both would be as great as 4,000 feet (1,219 meters). Studies have determined that a square meter of prairie sod may contain five miles (8 kilometers) of roots.

The effect of roots on erosion control is significant. It has been estimated that a fallow field, ploughed four inches (10 centimeters) deep and cultivated regularly, would lose seven inches (17.5 centimeters) of top soil in a period of 34 years. Under continuous growth of corn, it would take 50 years for the top seven inches to erode. But, under bluegrass sod continuously, the estimated time for erosion of the first seven inches of soil would be an impressive 3,043 years.

Addition of organic matter, in any of the above cases, would obviously slow the rate of erosion or possibly result in a net increase of soil.

"rain machines." When the forests were still alive they transpired two-thirds of the rainfall back into the atmosphere, producing clouds and rainfall for thirsting soil.

Now that the forests have been cut, two-thirds of the rainfall runs directly to the ocean, and only one-third remains to evaporate to the atmosphere. The result is that the entire African continent is drying out, and other nations in Africa will experience consequences similar to those Ethiopia is experiencing.[31]

Rome

Still another example of environmental degradation can be found in the history of the famed Pontine Marshes, from which brigands launched nightly forays against Roman citizens. In pre-Roman days, sixteen cities existed in the mountainous area later called the Pontine Marshes. Cultivation of the mountain slopes, without regard for conservation of soil, actually resulted in formation of the marshes. The area consisted of mountain ranges bordering a broad coastal plain. Farming on the slopes resulted in a serious erosion problem. The eroded material blocked stream channels in the coastal plain, resulting in the formation of a series of marshes. As a result, inhabitants of the area were severely afflicted by malaria, which was caused from the formation of a suitable habitat for hordes of malaria carrying mosquitoes. Attempts to drain the marshes began in the fourth century B.C., but were unsuccessful. In 1931, an expenditure of $500 million corrected the health problem by draining the marshes, but this did not restore the soils to the uplands from which they had been stripped.[32]

Roman history offers evidence that not only invading armies destroyed land, but sometimes residents of the land themselves destroyed anything that would be useful to the arriving invaders. In Edward Gibbon's *The History of the Decline and Fall of the Roman Empire,* there is a description of the scene that met a Roman army marching into the Julian Alps to quell an uprising. The seasoned army veterans were terrified by the desolation and silence of a region vacated by its inhabitants. Livestock had been driven away and anything that could offer shelter or nourishment for an army had been taken away or destroyed. Possibly the inhabitants were quite wise, at that. Gibbon describes the practice of the Roman invaders: "The naked country was ruined, the rivers filled with the slain and polluted with blood."[33]

own land that of Rome, founded by King Romulus. . . .

· Now if it is admitted that Thebes was founded before the deluge . . . its age is not more than about 2100 years: and if that period is compared with the lapse of time since men began to cultivate the land and to live in huts and hovels, knowing naught of city walls and gates, it is evident that life in the country preceded life in town by a tale of immemorial years. Nor is this to be wondered at since 'God made the country and man made the town.' While the tradition is that all the arts were invented in Greece within a thousand years, there never was a time when the earth could not be cultivated. And as life in the country is the more ancient, so it is the better life: for it was not without good reason that our ancestors were wont to plant colonies of citizens in the country, because by them they were both fed in times of peace and protected in times of war: nor was it without significance that they called both the Earth and Ceres by the common name of Mother and esteemed that those who worshipped her lead a life at once pious and useful and were the sole representatives left on earth of the race of Saturn. A proof of this is that the mysteries of the cult of Ceres were called Initia, the very name indicating that they are related to the beginning of things. . . . At first agriculture was conducted on so small a scale that it had little distinction, since those who followed it, being sprung from shepherds, at once sowed their corn and pastured their flocks on the same land, but as later this art grew in importance, the husbandry of livestock was separated and it befell that some men were called farmers and others shepherds.

"God Made the Country, and Man Made the Town"

Varro, the Roman historian and agriculturist, (B.C. 116-28), referred to agriculture of his time in "Rerum Rusticarum Libri Tres," his manual on agriculture, in the following manner:

There are two modes of human life . . . which are manifestly as different in the time of their origin as they are in their habitat, that of the country and that of the town. Country life is much more ancient, for time was when men lived altogether in the country and had no towns; indeed the oldest town in Greece, according to the tradition, is the Boeotian Thebes, which was founded by King Ogyges, and in our

Added to other reasons why war-making should cease is the age-old "all is fair in war" idea that could now be used as an excuse to destroy an enemy's nuclear power reactors, major hydroelectric dams, and other installations. Such destruction would very likely cause irreparable damage to our environment.

Africa

Following the defeat of Carthage at the battle of Zama (202 B.C.), the Romans made heavy demands on Algeria's fertility. For nearly six centuries, they sought maximum productivity of grain, oil, and livestock. Fertility declined, crop yields diminished, overgrazing took place, and cultivation was extended more and more toward the arid south. After A.D. 429, there was a series of conquests by the Vandals, the Byzantine Empire, and the Arabs and Berbers. Heavy overgrazing followed. The remaining forests were cut, and the grazing lands were burned to control brush.

As stabilizing vegetation disappeared, severe wind and water erosion followed.

Such extensive erosion took place that the city of Thamugadi, established about 100 B.C. by Emperor Trajan, was buried in dust and lost to knowledge for 1,200 years. Later, archaeological reconstruction of Thamugadi provided evidence of both wind and water erosion on the site of the city. Erosional debris from the hills, which are now devoid of soil, covered the valley plains. Rainstorms followed and caused large gullies to form. One of these gullies, which cuts through the city, had exposed an aqueduct which carried water from a large spring three miles away.[34]

Once again lack of protective vegetation promoted rapid runoff, lowering water tables and leaving aridity behind. Algeria, as so many other Mediterranean countries, still bears testimony to the words of French diplomat and literary celebrity Francois René de Chateaubriand, "Forests precede civilization and deserts follow them."

Although agriculture was once profitable there, this portion of Africa is now a barren land. Depleted as the land was by the Roman quest for high production, expert opinion holds that it might still have recovered had it not been for the desert nomads, with their herds of livestock. Overgrazing was the straw that broke the camel's back and led to accelerated soil erosion and subsequent degradation of the land.[35]

As has been pointed out by Belgian botanist Raymond Boullienne, some of the more recent land practices in Africa are also little short of disastrous. When soil becomes unproductive in one area, cultivation is abandoned and the land is taken over by herbaceous plants. It is then used for pasture. Periodic burning of pastureland is carried on to prevent crowding in of forest trees. The regular fires encourage the survival of pyrophilous (fire-loving) grasses, many of which are hardly palatable to livestock. Besides this, the numbers of animals pastured are often excessive. Overgrazing and compaction bares the soil, either forming brick-like laterite or predisposing it to erosion.

Studies by agronomists in the Congo have concluded that during a six-year period, 30,000 square kilometers (11,500 square miles) of soil were ruined. In Madagascar, there is now "an ocean of tough grasses, ravaged by fire and unsuitable even for the feeding of herds."[36] Bouillienne summarizes:

> In short, we are in the throes of an apparently irreversible progressive reduction of the surface of cultivable lands. It is estimated that the area of such lands on the earth has decreased by 20 percent in the last hundred years. Of the 40 billion acres remaining today, at least 20 million disappear irretrievably each year.[37]

France

Spectacular erosion caused by floods in the Alps illustrate an extreme problem in France between the close of the fifteenth century and the year 1800. The provinces of Dauphine, Avignon and Provence, an area of about 15,000 square miles (39,000 square kilometers), were particularly affected. Following the clearing of forests, it was found that the increased violence of torrents from the mountains swept away or buried more land beneath sand and gravel than had been cleared for agriculture. Soil degradation was so great that the land was gradually deserted by the starving population. George Perkins Marsh gives an itemized account (from Charles de Ribbe) of the gradual abandonment of towns and of the occurrence of slides and floods.[38]

French political economist J. A. Blanqui vividly described the desolation caused by erosion: "Vast deposits of flinty pebbles, many feet in thickness, which have rolled down and spread far over the plain, surround large trees, bury even their tops, and rise above them, leaving to the husbandman no longer a ray of hope."[39]

In 1800 floods destroyed property, drowned livestock and piled rocky wastes in fields. The French government was forced to attempt reforestation in the hills over the protests of those who grazed herds on the decreasing forage. (Marsh quotes an estimate of the Marquis de Mirabeau's which indicated that deforestation between 1750 and 1850 in France took place at the rate of 200,000 acres per year.)[40]

In May, 1856, such violent flooding occurred that most of the river basins in France were flooded to a great depth. In the Loire valley and its tributary valleys, about a million acres were flooded and many towns and villages were inundated. The need for reforestation was so apparent that, in spite of objections, 190,000 acres (76,000 hectares) were planted with trees. Levees, check dams, and storage basins were built and 7,000 acres (2,800 hectares) in the Hautes-Alpes were turfed. Many ravines were improved by grading and by the construction of barriers. Objections to mandatory afforestation were continued by private interests until these interests were silenced in 1882 by the passage of new legislation strengthening and stabilizing the forest service program. Conservation efforts continue to this day.[41]

The necessity of developing behavior styles reflecting a greater environmental awareness did not escape the attention of the French novelist, poet, and playwright, Victor Hugo (1802-1885). It is probably best summarized by his own observation in Les Misérables that the only thing more grief-provoking than a body agonizing for want of food is a soul dying for enlightenment. It was his observation that life itself is a quest for illumination in a world where darkness is more common.

In Les Misérables an entire chapter, entitled "The Intestines of Leviathan," is devoted to the wasteful practice of pouring the sewage of Paris into the sea. In commanding prose, he indicated the irony of sending convoys of ships to gather up the droppings of penguins and petrels at the South Pole while pouring human waste into the sea. "There is no guano comparable in fertility to the detritus of a capital. A great city is the most powerful of dung producers. To employ the city to enrich the plain would be a sure success. If our gold is manure, on the other hand, our manure is gold."

The use of manure to keep the land fertile would prevent in his words, "Hunger rising from the furrow and disease rising from the river." In regard to disease, he also pointed out that "It is well known ... the Thames is poisoning London."

Well aware of the need for a new code of behavior toward the earth, Hugo wrote in En Voyage, Alpes and Pyrénées: "In the relations of humans with the animals, with the flowers, with the objects of creation, there is a whole great ethic scarcely seen as yet, but which will eventually break through into the light and be the corollary and the complement to human ethics." Admitting the necessity to first civilize humans in respect to their behavior toward one another, he nevertheless contended: "It is also necessary to civilize humans in relation to nature. There, everything remains to be done."

St. Helena and Tahiti;
Islands are Changed too

When St. Helena was discovered in 1501, it was luxuriously forested. The precipices along the ocean were overhung with vegetation and every portion of the island was cloaked with greenery. But in 1513, goats were introduced by the Portuguese and, by 1588, there were uncounted thousands of them. When the English naturalist Alfred R. Wallace visited the island in the late nineteenth century, he wrote: "The rich soil . . . could only be retained on the steep slopes so long as it was protected by the vegetation to which it in great part owed its origin. When this was destroyed, the heavy tropical rain soon washed away the soil, and has left a vast expanse of bare rock or sterile clay."[42] The specific cause of the deforestation of St. Helena was suggested by A. H. Emsmann: "It was the goats which destroyed the beautiful forests that, three hundred and fifty years ago, covered a continuous surface of not less than two thousand acres in the interior of the island (of St. Helena), not to mention scattered groups of trees."[43]

On the other side of the world, Tahiti has long been hailed as an island paradise, but it too, has felt the heavy hand of change. Years ago, Tahitians began using fire in their hunts for wild pigs. Large upland areas were burned, and these now support North American weeds rather than the natural forest growth.

Still other islands, mainly in the Pacific, once had their soil fertility maintained by droppings from huge colonies of resident sea birds. As these colonies diminished, or were destroyed, a natural system in which nitrate and phosphate were added to the soil from the excreta, was altered. Change often seems slight in appearance, but cumulative effects of small changes can alter natural systems greatly.

New Zealand and Australia

New Zealand was originally heavily forested, and from earliest times was noted for its rich and varied bird life.[44] As there were no native mammals in New Zealand, a large population of flightless birds had developed, the largest of which—a moa (*Dinornis robustus*)—stood twelve feet high. It is not strange that the first colonizers, known as the Moa-hunters, depended heavily on the birds to supply food and other needs. The Moa-hunter economy was closely associated with the use of fire and the effect of fires set by men has had great impact on the ecology of New Zealand.

Fire altered the landscape so much that by the beginning of the seventeenth century, eight million acres (3.2 million hectares) of forest had been replaced by grass and shrubs and additional large areas had been partially modified. Soil erosion quite naturally followed burning and normal soil-forming processes were greatly altered. Many species of birds, including the moa, became extinct.[45]

Additional "fire-clearing" was done when European settlers arrived in great numbers. Farmers sought to replace forest cover with grasses and clovers, and the period 1890 to 1900 saw forest destruction of not less than nine million acres (3.6 million hectares). Problems resulting from declining soil fertility and weed invasion created impediments to agricultural development.

When brought to date, New Zealand's problems become even more magnified. Mammals in number and variety were introduced to the bird world of New Zealand. The economy rests heavily on sheep; but goats, several species of deer, opossums, kangaroos, rats, cats, rabbits, and hares have also been introduced. In a land of steep topography, thin soil, and high rainfall, the effect of grazing animals is being felt. Forests are changing in species composition and watersheds are losing storage capacity. Intensive aerial poisoning and hunting campaigns have been unleashed against deer, as their economic value is considered less than that of sheep. The eventual fate of New Zealand is still in the making, but here too we see evidence that mankind is more intent on economic, short-term gain than on the long-term well-being of the earth.

In neighboring Australia, a vivid description of the land before and after early settlement is given by Henry W. Haygarth in a book of recollections published in 1848. Before colonization: "plains and open forests, untrodden by the foot of the white man, and, as far as the eye can reach, covered with grass so luxuriant that it brushes the horseman in his saddle." But after settling the land and making it suitable for sheep farming: " . . . Anglo-Saxon energy at last triumphs over every obstacle. But nature, as if offended, withdraws half her beauty from the land; the pasture gradually loses its freshness; some of the rivers and lakes run low, others become wholly dry."[46]

Australia offers an interesting example of what can be produced by introducing an exotic animal species to a country. Wildlife biologist Durward Allen tells the interesting story of what happened after a consignment of twenty-four wild rabbits from Europe arrived in Hobson's Bay in southeastern Australia in 1859. Four days later the rabbits were released by Mr. Thomas Austin, near Geelong, Victoria.

With no natural enemies in Australia, the rabbits reproduced "like rabbits." Within six years, Mr. Austin had killed 20,000 of them and estimated his breeding stock to be 10,000.

In short order the rabbits spread northward into pasture lands of New South Wales, and in ten years had extended their range to Queensland, occupying thousands of square miles. With monotonous regularity, they mowed down vegetation, five rabbits being said to eat the equivalent of one sheep. In wet years they girdled woody growth and ate all available greenery. When dry years followed wet years, sand drifted on the scourged land.

Expenditures ran into the millions of dollars in an effort to control the rabbits. Thousands of miles of wire netting were erected and the rabbits were poisoned, hunted and controlled in every manner possible.

Not until the virus disease myxomatosis was introduced from America was a semblance of control established. The disease was introduced repeatedly and in 1950 swept through the rabbit population. Now that the disease is well established it helps keep the rabbit population in check, but the introduction of species to habitats in which they can reproduce without substantial checks is a serious problem and the rabbits still thrive in Australia. Starlings and English sparrows, knapweed, plantain, and halogeton are relocated species which have become problems in some areas. As a result, many North Americans have become familiar with these species.[47]

Central and South America

Edward Hyams refers to the Inca civilization in South America as one that was dedicated to the creation of soil rather than to its exploitation.[48] The Incas displayed an attitude of reverence toward fertile soil and made careful use of vegetable and animal matter, including human excrement, as fertilizers. He refers to them as the first people to discover the value of dead fish as fertilizer as they commonly planted fish heads with maize. They also pioneered the use of the white hills of guano, found at the immense rookeries on the islands off the Chilean and Peruvian coasts. Through careful use of these fertilizers and appropriate irrigation practices, highly fertile soils were developed. The arrival of Spanish invaders, however, led to the eventual destruction of the Inca's agricultural successes.

From Mexico southward, slash-and-burn agriculture was practiced by various civilizations. Ecologist, Raymond F. Dasmann refers to the Mayan civilization in Mexico as one that developed on the transient slash-and-burn system, having no permanent farms which were cultivated year after year.[49] Large numbers of people lived around the temple cities until the tropical soils in these areas were exhausted. New areas were periodically cleared and older areas allowed to return to wild growth. Eventually all the soils around temple cities were exhausted because the intervals of rest between croppings were too short to restore fertility. This led to abandonment of the cities, their ruins often being found again after centuries had elapsed. Historians Tom Dale and Vernon Carter, speaking of Central America and Mexico, referred to severe erosion that had already taken place before modern times, topography and climate both being conducive to these effects.[50]

Researchers Moser and Taylor visited several Colombian tribes and made observations on their farming practices.[51] One tribe, the Tukano, grew their crops in forest clearings called chagra. Every year or two the Tukano men would cut down a forested area and burn the fallen trees to make a new chagra. This area would be farmed until its soil showed signs of exhaustion and until weeds threatened strangulation of crops. As new chagras became more distant from villages, the villages would be moved closer to them.

One might expect that a tropical forest, being exceedingly lush, would be based on deep, highly fertile soil. This concept, though, is far from the truth. Most of the nutrients in tropical forest ecosystems are tied up in the standing vegetation. Heat and humidity favor rapid recycling of fallen leaves, branches and trunks of trees. The soil itself, because of high rainfall, is incapable of storing large quantities of nutrient minerals such as calcium, magnesium, and phosphorus. Indeed, there is no need for nutrients to be concentrated in soil because of the speed at which they can be recycled to living vegetation. Most of the jungle vegetation is evergreen and as a result this recycling process continues throughout the year.

When tropical forests are cleared for farming, a new situation of instability is created. The high rainfall quickly dissipates nutrients through runoff, iron and aluminum oxides remaining to the last. Five to ten percent of tropical forest soils are iron-rich lateritic soils which, through erosion and baking in the sun, change chemically into a brick-like substance called laterite. It is very difficult for forest regrowth to take place on laterite. (Paul Ehrlich et al refer in their Ecoscience study to the likelihood that the Khmer civilization in Cambodia may have disappeared due to laterization).[52]

Modern widespread clear-cutting of tropical forests along with compaction of soils by bulldozers leads to rapid leaching of minerals and to the denuded land being covered with unpalatable grasses such as Imperata. The loss of nutrient is indicated by studies such as one conducted by biologist Rafael Herrera in the Amazonian rainforest at San Carlo de Rio Negro in Venezuela.[53] On these poor tropical podzols he found that up to 92 percent of magnesium, 90 percent of potassium, 74 percent of calcium, 66 percent of phosphorus, and more than 60 percent of nitrogen are in the plant biomass. Removal of the standing crop, therefore, substantially removes forests nutrients as well.

Climatologists express grave concern over current forest removal inasmuch as deforestation on a large scale may substantially change global climate. Deforestation of the tropics is expected to alter the transfer of heat from the equator toward the poles and will likely lead to the expansion of deserts in the subtropics of both hemispheres. (Because deforestation in the tropics will result in less rainfall and faster runoff of water from land that has been stripped of moisture-retaining and moisture-recycling vegetation, rising air will be drier than at present. This air is pulled to the northeast and southeast by the earth's rotation, forming the winds known as the westerlies. As long as there are tropical forests, transpiring and evaporating moisture, the air rising from these forests is moist and warm due to the latent heat of evaporation. Drier air will carry less moisture and heat toward the poles.)

The incredibly complex diversity of the tropical forests (hundreds of thousands of plant species and more than a million animal species) is now undergoing destruction before its flora and fauna are completely classified and before its benefits are even partially comprehended.

On Reflection

The preceding pages are but a sample of the detailed evidence available which indicates that human civilizations have had severe impact on the lands that support them. George Perkins Marsh, nineteenth century historical geographer, lawyer, and diplomat, with a mastery of twenty languages, was one of those who assiduously sought out the causes of land degradation during his extensive travels. His studies led him to the conclusion that restoration of the planet is "one of the most obvious" of the duties which we owe to posterity. He commented on the need, not only to restore forests in particular, but to extend them beyond their present boundaries. While he recognized the human reluctance to plant a forest which would not mature in one lifetime, he warned of the terrible consequences that would result if this were not done. He pointed out that there were already parts of Asia Minor, North Africa, Greece, and Alpine Europe where human actions had set in motion such erosive processes that one can see desolation on parts of the earth which are nearly as complete as that on the moon.

We have seen that heavy damage of land has been a result of long occupation of Mediterranean countries, and that island ecosystems have been disrupted in relatively quick order as well. Evidence from

South America, Australia, and New Zealand also indicates that the change inflicted by people in these countries has been substantial. The next chapter, which will explore some of the same sort of changes that have taken place in North America, indicates that we are repeating history. Considering the relatively short duration of settlement in Canada and the United States, one would not be far amiss in deducting that we are as improvident today as people have been at previous times in history. Modern technology enables us to undo natural systems at a rate which was never possible before. Yet, the fact that a change in global climate looms as an extremely serious problem has caused no slackening of the rate at which we are undoing the ecology of the planet. Human consciousness, shallowly rooted in the immediate culture, seems unable to sink a taproot of comprehension into the reality of planetary ecology.

We have seen how composition, structure, and function of ecosystems have been destroyed. In many instances, when forests were destroyed, a domino effect followed. With the loss of forests, unprotected mountain soil was washed away and erstwhile fertile valley soils were littered and buried with erosional debris. Unchecked water, no longer absorbed by vegetation, poured off the mountains, dissecting the valley soils and leaving little but a wasteland in its wake. The destructive effects of overgrazing, overuse of fire, and of the malice of invading armies has, in many cases, hastened land degradation.

Fortunately, not all land has been affected so grievously. Many parts of Europe, for example, have thrived under careful husbandry. China, after four thousand years of farming, has likewise benefited from attentive care of the land. In spite of overcutting of forests and severe flooding on major rivers, the land is still productive, and now China has launched a serious program of reforestation as well.

If to be forewarned is to be forearmed, Social Studies, from its first appearance in the curriculum of schools, should devote some attention to the history of land abuse. It is one thing to say that "He who ignores history is doomed to repeat it." It is another thing entirely to omit an important aspect of education that can lead people to repeat mistakes, simply because they have never been acquainted with them. As French author Jean Rostand said, "the obligation to endure gives us the right to know." The child who is not taught that the abuse of land can lead to the downfall of nations has been deprived of one of the most valuable lessons that history can teach. Some knowledge of both the resilience and the fragility of the earth is as much a part of basic education as reading and writing. Attention to the history of ecology could well provide a taproot for educational institutions throughout the world.

Economist Kenneth C. Boulding lends credence to this thought in describing our present "cowboy economy" as one that is "associated with reckless, exploitative, romantic and violent behavior" and claims that it is necessary to shift to a "spaceman economy" in which a new understanding of extraction and pollution develops and in which "consumption must be minimized." Boulding suggests that future generations of economists may be weaned away from models of high production and consumption and learn to evaluate economic success as the "nature, extent, quality and complexity of the total capital stock, including in this the state of the human bodies and minds" that are part of the system.[54]

Boulding's implication that our economic views stand in need of change should be acceptable in light of what we already know about the constancy of change as it is manifested throughout nature. We have given quite consistent allegiance to an economic model which is now tattered, worn, and inadequate. New realizations about the waning health of the earth must finally convince us that some of our patterns of behavior need to be modified or even eliminated because of their serious consequences to life-support systems.

Civilization, we can now see, is something more than material progress. Perhaps there has never been a time until now when we needed to work as diligently for a true harmony among nations and for harmony between human societies and the rest of the natural world.

Possibly Mahatma Gandhi held some such view of a harmony toward which we must strive when he responded to the question, "What do you think of civilization?" with the reply, "It would be nice."

Mighty River

A few days ago, I wandered, musing, in a country that few people have yet seen. It was an area that had once experienced a mining boom; and an abandoned road, impassable to vehicles, led to a ghost town where a huge and out-of-place ore concentrator kept lonely vigil over a series of sagging and collapsed houses. Progress had come and gone, as one could note in what was once a settling pond and is now a graveyard of skeletal dead trees waving their frail bones in the winter winds that sweep the valley.

How many years, I wondered, will it be before the inexorable tides of nature can make vegetation grow in the acid sterility of the pond?

Along the road, old bridges, condemned for use by vehicles, looked down on a roaring river a hundred or more feet below. Rock bolts held the bridges against the canyon walls, and where planks were missing one could look beneath his feet into the maelstrom below.

The river itself was worth the visit. Greenish in hue from glacial silt, it surged through the canyon; intent on its own business and uninterested in the Fabulous Forties, the Frantic Fifties, the Soaring Sixties, the Sad Seventies, and Euphoric Eighties. How many millennia had it taken the river to carve the canyon? Unconscious of the fact that this was an election year, as it was unconscious of Caesar's rule in Rome, it goes about its business smoothing the rock, plucking boulders from the canyon wall as a child picks pebbles at his feet. Its business is leveling, bringing the mighty mountains down to the sea. Unchecked in its pace, it works at its task. Perhaps, I pondered, it may be tamed by a dam someday, a dam that will last a geologic moment or two, and then will be silted in, flowed over, and removed from the path—for what is a dam in reality, to a river that will eventually level mountains?

As the canyon widened, the old road descended from its fragile hold and paralleled the river a few feet above water level. Although the current was slower, I could see the suck and gurgle of the water around large rocks, and noted it nibbling patiently away at the banks where huge cottonwoods already were starting to lean toward their watery fate. A riot of thimbleberry, huckleberry, and saskatoons grew in the open area along the edge of the river, while up the slope marched sentinel cedars and hemlocks, raising lofty heads to better observe the march of the river to the sea.

In this valley people once lived, feverishly extracting mineral wealth from the rock. Hopes and dreams lived here, and now a rushing river was the only sound occupying terrain where once the rumble of ore wagons, the sound of blasting, even the sound of laughter made momentary impact on the valley. At a sandbar, a set of grizzly tracks showed that an occupant still roamed the land—hopefully he may stay there forever, as the steep mountain terrain and extremely heavy timber would tax the patience of the most devoted Nimrod.

Like many a mountain valley, it had its residents who stayed on after the mining boom had passed. One old-timer remained there for many years, long after everyone else had left. He had cleared fields and built a good bachelor cabin and a sturdy barn. In winter he was a solitary resident, and one winter he snowshoed out, stopping overnight to rest in one of the abandoned cabins of an old trapper. It was his last long sleep, for he passed on to other valleys during his night of rest. Over seventy when he died, his choice of the isolated life makes one realize that he had insights that gave him reason to choose to remain as a watchman in the valley—perhaps we all need to pause a moment to reflect on the love that man can have for a land, that will cause him to say, "Here I will remain for all of my time."

It is an interesting place, back of the modern beyond, back of the places where the cars must stop. I am grateful for such places, and must go there again and again, to follow out all the old mining trails leading to the memories of man that are gradually being erased by the growing vegetation. It is a nostalgic place, but not a tragic place, for it tells one many things about the recuperative powers of nature.

"If seven maids with seven mops,
Swept it for half a year,
Do you suppose," the Walrus said,
"That they could get it clear?"
"I doubt it," said the Carpenter,
And shed a bitter tear.

                    Lewis Carroll

We Stand on Guard for Thee?

It was a rich country beyond the dreams of men. When Cartier's two ships sailed slowly down the west coast of Newfoundland, the crews found it no hardship to catch a hundred large cod in an hour. They were astonished to find great beasts "like large oxen, which have two tusks in their jaw like elephant's tusks and swim about in the waters."[1] Along with these walruses, they saw "many whales and belugas (white whales),"[2] both rare sights in these waters today. On a later voyage up the St. Lawrence River, Cartier found fertile lands covered with magnificent trees: oak, ash, elm, walnut, cedar, yew, and other fine specimens of the same species found in France.

North America was a magnificent country everywhere. Along the Allegheny River travelers encountered wild turkeys running on the trails, some of them so fat they could hardly rise from the ground in flight. "It frequently happens that after shooting one on a tree, you will find him bursted by falling on the ground."[3] Elk mixed freely with the herds of settlers' cows. One fisherman in 1823 lamented that though a single cast of his net caught thirty barrels of fish, he was able to land only ten barrels because the net broke from the weight of the catch.

A Spanish officer amused himself by riding his horse into a cavity in a redwood tree near Watsonville, California, (where there are no redwoods today) commenting that now he had a house in case it should rain.[4]

But there has been a smugness involved in living in Canada and the United States. Both countries are large, enabling people to have ample room in which to lead their lives. Both countries enjoy high standards of living, available to their people as a result of an abundance of resources. Both countries, likewise, have given their people opportunity to study the history of other nations, and to avoid the mistakes, carelessness, ignorance, and lack of concern that have led one civilization after another to sadly deteriorate the land which provided its sustenance. Unfortunately, this opportunity hasn't prevented repetition of many mistakes made in older nations.

As stewards of the land, we have been unsuccessful. The remnants of massive forests are now being mopped up, their rich diversity established over thousands of years being replaced by fast-growing supertrees of unproved merit. Freeflowing waterways are contaminated with refuse, burdened with eroded soil, and often tainted with toxic pesticides shot-gunned against some agricultural or forest pest which would be better handled by natural predators and by more merciful management of resources. Acid rain threatens the life of forests and the health of soil.

We are in a dire predicament, but so estranged have we become from nature, so cushioned in our artificial world, so infused with the infallibility of technology, that we have become nations of Neros fiddling blithely while the foundation of our society, the natural world, succumbs to the blindness of our ways.

Never has there been such opportunity to see and realize what is happening. North America's population has mobility that was undreamed of at any previous time in history. Perhaps the speeds at which people move hamper perception or perhaps people are too preoccupied with the technological world that has been offered as an enticing substitute for the natural world. As George Perkins Marsh once commented, "Sight is a faculty, seeing is an art." Possibly Thoreau was prescient in observing that "The perception of beauty is a moral test," and our inability to see how we have transferred order into chaos is a reflection of our substitution of materialism for higher values.

Drivers stream along highways, apparently unaware of the carnage that surrounds them. Signs of erosion are commonplace and in forested areas the highways pass through unsightly clear-cut littered with charred wastes from slash-burning. Towns are announced by junkyards at their edges and by a yellow pall of smoke heralding one of the sites where the Great God Profit is being relentlessly worshipped. If we were less sophisticated but better educated, such sights might cause us to suspect that Dante's Inferno was materializing. No tear is shed for man's degradation of majestic forests, pristine streams, wild meadows and swamps that once graced our continent. We are too eminently practical a people to feel remorse.

A serious conservation ethic would be the first lonely sign that true civilization has entered the conscious thought of humanity. We are beginning to hear a strong call for renewed ethics in government, in finance, in business, in personal conduct, and in education. All of those things are vital parts of our society; but our society draws its health from the land. Just as a poor and uncared-for tree cannot produce good fruit, so a neglected and ravaged land cannot produce a healthy and gracious people. A code of ethical values towards the land will be repaid a thousandfold, and this should not be surprising if we remember the parable of the sower.

The following pages will focus on some of the impact humans have had on North America. The treatment of certain subjects, rather than being exhaustive, is merely intended to offer us ample evidence that we should formalize an earth ethic which will put boundaries on our aspirations for change. For centuries, the wisdom of the Latin maxim "Festina lente" (make haste slowly) was recognized; but the enormous haste for change that exists today creates series of precarious situations that leave us in last-ditch endeavors to protect species and sites before they are utterly destroyed. While we recognize the necessity of governors on engines, we do not yet recognize that we must govern the rate at which technology is applied. We have had too much already of "sinning in haste and repenting at leisure." An ethic might help to lock a few barns or corrals before all the horses have disappeared over the hill.

Destruction of the Bison

It was my custom in those days to pick out a herd that seemed to have the fattest cows and young heifers. I would then rush my horse into them, picking out the fattest cows and shooting them down, while my horse would be running a-longside of them. . . . I have killed from twenty-five to forty buffalo while the herd was circling, and they would all be dropped very close together; that is to say, in a space covering about five acres. . . . I killed buffalo for the railroad company for twelve months, and during that time the number I brought into camp was kept account of, and at the end of that period I had killed 4,280 buffalo. . . . [5]

So wrote Buffalo Bill Cody, recounting his experiences of the plains.

The systematic destruction of bison in North America is a saga of ruthlessness that has been repeated again and again as human technological prowess has outstripped the development of ethical behavior toward other life forms on the planet. In fact, it is estimated that every day the world loses three species of wildlife, and this rate is increasing.[6] Estimates have placed the original number of bison at seventy-five million, their range extending from Lake Erie west across the plains and prairies.

Although they were killed regularly as land was cleared from the mid 1700s onward, they were not endangered until about 1830 when their extermination was directed at the starvation of Sioux and other Indian tribes which were impeding continental takeover by the whites. The slaughter was in high gear by the 1870s and between 1870 and 1875 from two to five million buffalo were killed each year on the Great Plains. Five years later, the last lone survivor of the southern herd was killed at Buffalo Springs, Texas.[7]

What was left of the northern herd was trailed to the Cannonball River in North Dakota and destroyed by cutting off the herd's access to water. A remnant population of the northern herd was more inaccessible and now receives protection in Wood Buffalo National Park in northern Alberta. Another remnant, some twenty animals in Yellowstone Park, has slowly increased and is now protected on the National Bison Range in Montana.[8]

In his classic account of the extermination of the American bison, William T. Hornaday, an American zoologist who worked to establish reserves for protecting bison and other wildlife, included a table which showed, by best estimate possible, the number of bison running wild and unprotected on January 1, 1889, after the great slaughter:

In the Pan-handle of Texas 25
In Colorado 20
In southern Wyoming 26
In the Musselshell Country, Montana 10
In western Dakota 4
      Total number in the United States 85
In Athabasca, Northwest Territory (estimated) 550
      Total in all North America 635

"Add to the above the total number already recorded in captivity (256) and those under Government protection in the Yellowstone Park (250), and the whole number of individuals of Bison americanus now living is 1,091."[9]

In the foreword to his text, Mr. Hornaday wrote: "If his (the bison's) untimely end fails even to point a moral that shall benefit the surviving species of mammals *which are now being slaughtered in like manner,* it will be sad indeed."

Killed for sport from shooting cars on trains, killed for their tongues, killed for their hides, killed to dispossess the native people of the continent, killed to encourage the agricultural potential of the plains: the huge herds of bison that stretched to the far horizon and shook the earth when they moved have disappeared into history.

As Peter Mathiessen states: "The bison herds were almost certainly the greatest animal congregations that ever existed on earth, and the greed and waste which accompanied their annihilation doubtless warrants some sort of superlative also."[10]

Atlantic Salmon

When Europeans first began settling on the east coast of North America, almost every stream from north-central Labrador to the Hudson River hosted spawning populations of Atlantic salmon. Counting the feeder streams in the St. Lawrence system, there were several thousand spawning streams for these fish. Their numbers may well have exceeded the numbers of the various species found on the Pacific Coast.

Those who camped along the Miramichi River in the early 1700s told of such a volume of salmon that one could not sleep at night from the resounding splashes made as these fish hurled themselves into the air repeatedly when migrating over the river flats. The immediate response of people was to exploit the resource to the maximum extent, and a ready market for salted salmon was soon found in Europe.[11]

A vivid picture of the decline of the sensational Atlantic salmon fishery is given by Anthony Netboy. He refers to the amazement of Richard Nettle, newly arrived in Quebec from England in 1840. Nettle was "appalled that salmon were being slaughtered freely on their upstream journey"[12] before they had had time to spawn. He and other individuals raised a storm of protest that led to the appointment of a superintendent of fisheries for Upper and Lower Canada. Nettle received this appointment and was severe in prosecuting those who violated laws passed to protect the salmon; and as is so often the case, his impartial prosecution of rich landowners along with people of lesser means led to his removal from office.

By the 1880s declining salmon stocks were being observed even in the better streams. By 1886, an article in the *American Salmon-Fisherman* identified a number of poorly stocked or ruined Canadian rivers. These included the Quelle (blocked by four mill dams), the Rimouski (run down), and the Matane (badly poached). A north-shore stream, the Grand Escoumains, was identified as once having been very good, but now destroyed by logging.

Anthony Netboy cites a Newfoundland Department of Fisheries' annual report (1902) which explained the decline of catches as mainly due to nets, mill dams, and pollution by mill refuse. The Gander River is referred to as an object lesson in the ruination of a great fishery, with annual catches having been reduced from 400,000 pounds (182,000 kilograms) to less than 6,000 pounds (2,700 kilograms).[13]

The causes of the rapid decline of the salmon fishery were listed as the higher water temperatures in summer which resulted from the removal of vegetation, the heavy siltation caused by deposits of material eroded after forest removal, the pollution which resulted from the dumping of sawdust and other waste material directly into the rivers, and the barricading of many streams with dams.

The decline of salmon took place even more rapidly in the U.S.A. One New England river after another was blocked by dams in the early 1800s. By the 1880s salmon regularly entered only the St. Croix, Dennys, East Machias, Machias, Penobscot, Sheepscot, Kennebec, and

Androscoggin rivers. By 1925, only the Dennys and the Penobscot had regular salmon runs with a few fish entering the St. Croix. The fish found in the St. Croix were due to the decline in logging along that river which resulted in a lowering of the amounts of sawdust in the water.

In 1952, a new threat presented itself to the Atlantic salmon in New Brunswick. This took the form of spraying of pesticides in an effort to control populations of spruce budworms which were attacking spruce and fir forests. Between 1952 and 1960, millions of acres of forest land were sprayed with one-half pound (227 grams) of DDT per acre (roughly one-half kilogram per hectare). This dosage killed nine-tenths of the salmon fry, three-fourths of the small parr, and one-half of the larger parr.[14]

In 1964, biologists concurred that the spraying of New Brunswick forests had been a major cause of severe reductions in salmon catches.

Atlantic salmon are now identified as "among the most threatened creatures in northern marine and freshwater eco-systems."[15] In the United States, fisheries analysts fear that unless a huge effort is made to revive some of the northern rivers of New England, the Atlantic salmon will be gone for good. The combinations of industrial pollution, negligent forestry and overfishing have left only remnant populations in a few northern streams.

Added to the other threats to this species is the unfortunate increase in fishing pressure that resulted from discovery of the principal feeding area of the salmon in the high seas off western Greenland.[16] Since 1960, when this area was discovered, the western Greenland catch has soared by 5,000 percent with a record 5.8 million pounds (2,900 short tons or 2,630 metric tonnes) in 1971.

Today many efforts are being made to assure survival of the species. For example, in April, 1988, the Ontario Ministry of Natural Resources released 30,000 salmon smolts into the Credit River and Wilmot Creek in an effort to reintroduce fish that will reproduce in Lake Ontario. In the late 1800s the salmon were plentiful in this lake, but habitat destruction and overfishing led to eradication of the species from the lake. Biologists differ in their views as to whether the restocking will succeed but the effort is certainly worth making.[17]

Also, the formation of the North Atlantic Salmon Conservation Organization (NASCO) has led to some success in the attempt to develop a unified approach to sustaining the species. Dr. Frank E. Carlton, a U.S. commissioner to NASCO, contends that two serious problems must be overcome before a workable international effort can be made to assure survival of *Salmo salar*. One is that nations must give up their reluctance to provide true catch statistics from which the total international catch can be determined. The second problem has to do with the fact that Atlantic salmon are now being reared in cages, and about ten percent of these fish escape. Dr. Carlton's concern is that the escaped fish may ascend natural rivers to spawn and introduce genetic changes to the indigenous stocks. He states that the genetic changes "need not be great to bring total destruction to a stock or regional group of stocks."[18]

The number of fish escaping from artificial rearing situations is substantial. Dr. Carlton states that in 1987, approximately 50,000 tons (45,350 tonnes) of salmon were reared in cages. The 10 percent of fish estimated to escape, in this instance, would amount to approximately 1.3 million fish or 5,000 tons (4,535 tonnes). Dr. Carlton expresses his fear that Atlantic salmon will become extinct within the next 40 to 50 years unless the gravity of the situation is recognized and leads to the solution of political problems that must be solved to assure an international effort to preserve the species.[19]

Only a true realization of our ethical responsibility to all life can now save this magnificent species from ultimate extinction.

Air Pollution

Unlike the bison and Atlantic salmon, which were continental resources (although the salmon is a high seas migrant), the quality of air is important to all the world's people. Now, the pollution of the air has become a global problem.

Air pollution is not a recent phenomenon in a qualitative sense. Lead was mined and smelted by the Romans in Britain and the locations of these smelting operations are purportedly still recognizable from the scraggly vegetation that grows on the poisoned soil.[20]

In the twelfth century there were references to the "poisonous vapors" of Rome and to the "lethal waters" of the Rhine.

Intensive pollution of air took place in Britain about 700 years ago when sea-coal began to be used in London for industrial purposes. An insufficient knowledge of the principles involved in combustion led to the production of dense smoke and choking odor produced by the inefficient burning of bituminous coal. Severe discomfort led to widespread protest, and royal ordinances in 1273 and 1306 attempted, without success, to ban its use.[21] Finally in the 1600s, Queen Elizabeth banned the burning of coal in London.[22]

Along with burgeoning industrialization, the odors emanating from large concentrations of population led Samuel Taylor Coleridge (1772-1834) to write a descriptive poem entitled: "The Smell of Cologne."[23]

> In Koln, a town of monks and bones,
> And pavements fanged with murderous stones,
> And rags and hags, and hideous wenches,
> I counted two and seventy stenches,
> All well defined, and several stinks!
> Ye nymphs that reign o'er sewers and sinks,
>
> The river Rhine, it is well known,
> Doth wash your city of Cologne;
> But tell me, Nymphs, what power divine
> Shall henceforth wash the river Rhine?

The condition of our air has not improved with the passage of time. Today, as part of our obsession with profit at any price, we accept the fact that death rates rise above normal in places where air pollution concentrations are sufficiently high. There have been well-known disasters caused by smog as in London in December, 1952, when 4,000 deaths resulted from a sudden increase in sulfur dioxide in the air. During that emergency, solids in suspension increased by three to ten times normal. In 1948, dense smog in Donora, Pennsylvania, caused a score of deaths and about 42 percent of the population of 12,000 people developed cardiac and respiratory problems.[24]

In 1968, 60 faculty members of the UCLA medical school assembled a statement which advised the people who lived in smoggy areas of southern California to move away from "smoggy portions of Los Angeles, San Bernardino, and Riverside counties to avoid chronic respiratory diseases like bronchitis and emphysema."[25] This advice was given to all those who did not have compelling reasons to continue living there.

Acid rain is now a well-known, and unfortunately well-accepted, phenomenon. When fossil-fuels containing sulfur are burned, sulfur dioxide is formed, some of which oxidizes further to form sulfur trioxide. This compound can react with moisture to form sulfuric acid, which then precipitates as acid rain. While we may be concerned with damage done to marble statues and even to granite structures, and with corrosion of metal, canvas, and clothing, its most serious effects may be on photosynthesis in plants and on increasing acidity of the soils in which they grow. Also, its effect on freshwater lakes is now well-known, with thousands of lakes in Scandinavia, the eastern United States, and eastern Canada already having suffered high mortality of fish, some species having been totally extirpated.[26] In Nova Scotia for example, nine out of twenty-seven rivers are so acidic that they can no longer support salmon fry or trout.[27]

Forests in the path of acid precipitation show reduced growth and are more prone to disease. It is acknowledged that the famed Black Forest of Germany is dying from acid rain, that reproductive capacity of some species of trees is diminished in many areas, and that acidification of some soils is reaching alarming proportions.

In general, the impact of air pollution on crops is of disturbing significance. A field experiment in Riverside, California, in 1974 revealed that crops exposed to pollution showed reduced yields compared to control crops. Crop losses ranged from 32 percent for black-eyed beans to 72 percent for sweet corn. California crop losses to air pollutants are estimated to amount to $25 million per year.

Dr. Samuel S. Epstein, M.D., points out the alarming rise in U.S. production of synthetic organic chemicals, from one billion pounds (500,000 tons or 453,500 tonnes) in the early 1940s to 400 billion pounds (200 million tons or 181.4 million tonnes) in the 1980s. Most of these chemicals, he says, have never been adequately tested, if tested at all, "for chronic toxic, carcinogenic, mutagenic, let alone ecological effects, and much of the limited available industrial data is at best suspect." He claims that living near petrochemical and certain other types of industries in highly urbanized communities increases the risk of cancer. This is borne out by local clustering of excess rates of cancer. He also states that high levels of toxic and carcinogenic chemicals are "deliberately discharged by a wide range of industries into the air of surrounding communities."[28]

Burning of garbage poses yet another concern to those who would solve the problem of disposal. Cynthia Pollock-Shea points out that some materials which are burned, such as paper and plastics, contain chlorine compounds. During combustion, these compounds regroup chemically to form dioxins and furans, some of the dioxins being the most toxic compounds known. These toxic dioxins suppress the immune system, increase proneness to cancer, affect fetal development, and cause chloracne.[29]

Other chemicals are also known to impair the human immune system and thin the ozone layer, as well as cause skin cancers and impair crop growth.

The air in cities is known to contain high populations of live germs. Jean Dorst refers to a comparison of microbe populations in France. A concentration of 0.3 microbes per cubic foot was found at Ballon d'Alsace in the Vosges Mountains. On the Champs Elysees, there were 25,000 microbes per cubic foot, and in a Paris department store, 1.1 million per cubic foot. Much, obviously, is to be said for open country air, even today.

All protestations to the contrary, it seems that we are overdue in initiating significant changes in the values we hold, lest T. S. Eliot be totally correct in predicting that the world will end "Not with a bang but a whimper."

Pesticides

Pesticides have moved to first place among environmental hazards. At least the U.S. Environmental Protection Agency (EPA) now contends that pesticide pollution is the *most urgent* environmental problem in the United States. Steven Schatzow, head of the Pesticide Division of the EPA, has stated:

> Pesticides dwarf the other environmental risks the agency deals with. The risks from pesticides are so much greater because of the exposures involved. Toxic waste dumps may affect a few thousand people who live around them. But virtually everyone is exposed to pesticides.[30]

It is important to fully understand the term pesticide, for there are many products which fit broadly under that label. We hear of many types of pesticides and each time the suffix "cide" is used at the end of a word it simply means "kill." We are aware of this, subconsciously at least, because we are all familiar with words like suicide, homicide, genocide, and fratricide. It is entirely appropriate, therefore, that all sorts of pesticides—herbicides, insecticides, avicides, termiticides, fungicides—are categorized as biocides, or simply killers of life. Pesticides, however, usually kill more than a single pest or a few specific pests for which they are intended. While herbicides, for instance, theoretically kill only certain types of vegetation, some are also lethal to fish fry when drainage eventually carries toxic compounds into streams. Fish, birds, mammals, even humans have been killed by some pesticides. Simplification among microflora and microfauna also occurs as pesticides enter soils. No one can even guess at eventual effects of pesticides on the decomposition system on which all plants are dependent for their nutrients.

Numbers of pesticides are known to cause cancer, to produce birth defects, and to cause mutations in cells. In addition, many pesticides are now known to depress immune systems. A statement in *National Geographic* in February, 1980, gives us an example of the unexpected consequences of pesticide use:

> According to Dr. Frank H. Duffy of the Harvard Medical School, exposure to even tiny quantities of certain insect killers similar to those found in the home can alter brain activity for more than a year and cause irritability, insomnia, loss of libido and reduced powers of recall and concentration.[31]

The Canadian Environmental Advisory Council, in 1981, clarified the situation by simply saying, "Pesticides by their very nature are environmental poisons."[32]

" . . . it is one of the miracles of science and hygiene that the germs that used to be in our food have been replaced by poisons."

Wendell Berry

What is more, pesticides are horribly widespread and truly present a serious global problem. They also make vast profits for the chemical industries, and this has led to much foot-shuffling and evasiveness at all attempts to do something to lessen the magnitude of their impact on life. Along with thousands upon thousands of other chemical compounds, they contribute to a chemical nightmare that is very much with us today. Even their real effectiveness is questionable, as may be discerned in testimony by a senior economist, Jan Newton, before a congressional subcommittee hearing in the U.S.A.: "There is no empirical basis for the increased timber yields that are claimed to result from herbicide use, (and) there does not appear to be a valid economic case for extensive herbicide use in forest management."[33]

A further question relative to herbicide use is postulated by J. Altman and C. L. Campbell in discussion of numerous cases of diseases of plants brought about as a *result* of herbicide use.[34]

Francis Chaboussou states in *The Ecologist* that all herbicides inhibit protein-synthesis and this is not only in the target species but in the main crop as well. He suggests the possibility that the cumulative effects of pesticides may lead to deficiencies in vital trace elements. Plants in this way may become sensitized to plant parasites. A number of tests have offered supporting evidence of this sensitization. Atrazine use apparently leads to increased sensitivity of corn to Dwarf mosaic virus. The seriousness of symptoms increases with the dosage. One hundred percent of the crop shows symptoms once soil concentrations of atrazine reach 20 ppm.

Other studies have shown that the herbicide 2,4-D predisposes corn to serious attack by cornborers, to an increase in parasitism by aphids, and to a susceptibility to nematodes. A number of herbicides have also been found to decrease the resistance of rice to various parasites. Chaboussou states as a conclusion that, "Pesticides are in fact poisons, not only for the pests they are designed to attack, but also for the host plant."[35]

Very much information exists about pesticides, both generally and specifically. Much of it is not reassuring. Much of it is, in fact, alarming; especially in view of the powerful political clout held by the chemical corporations. In the U.S., Dr. Robert van den Bosch and others have suggested an unhealthy influence by agribusiness on the U.S. Department of Agriculture. He also questions the merits of pesticides as used, pointing out that when synthetic insecticides were first attaining popularity the U.S. used about 50 million pounds (25,000 tons or 22,675 tonnes) of insecticides and lost about seven percent of crops from insect damage. At the time he published The Pesticide Conspiracy, in 1978, he stated that the U.S. was using 600 million pounds (300,000 tons or 272,000 tonnes) of insecticides annually and was losing 13 percent of the preharvest yield to insects. In short, although insecticide use increased more than eleven fold, insect damage doubled during the same period.[36]

So much evidence has been produced on the negative effects of pesticides that one wonders that their widespread use can either be recommended or condoned. In Canada, whereas the federal government licenses the use of certain pesticides and their use is recommended by Agriculture Canada, the Canadian Environmental Advisory Council has pointed out that, "If the 405 currently registered pesticides were subjected to proper environmental studies, most would likely have to be withdrawn. In addition, it is unlikely that any new chemical pesticide would be registered." The report also states that, "Pesticides are deliberate environmental poisons with profound effects on organisms other than the target, yet we lack a fundamental understanding of environmental impact."[37]

How is it, one might ask, that so little attention is paid to facts revealed by the ministry of environment? If one looks at a list of Canadian federal ministries according to precedence, one will find that far down the list, after the ministers of agriculture, finance, fisheries and oceans, even after the minister of state for fitness and amateur sport, and after the secretary of state of Canada and minister of state for multiculturalism and citizenship, in the lower one-fifth of the list "according to precedence" may be found minister of environment. Could it be that the ministry of environment is nothing more than a sop to conscience, or a cosmetic touch-up of sadly wrinkled government?

Since modern pesticides first arrived in World War II, one serious indictment after another has appeared. Eric Eckholm, of Worldwatch Institute, pointed out in 1976 that as much as one-fourth of all the DDT produced to that time had wound up in the oceans, recipients of continental runoff. Although DDT is banned in many nations including the United States and Canada, its use continues in other countries; India alone manufactured 19,400 tons (17,635 tonnes) of DDT in 1989/90. And, of course, the poison continues to contaminate the world's fish: so it continues to appear in imported food. Eight parts per million in the ovaries of sea trout prevents spawning, one part in 10 billion in water reduces growth rates of oysters, and two parts in 10 billion kill commercial species of shrimp and crabs.[38]

Valuable predatory insects are usually more sensitive to pesticides than target species. Target species, as a matter of fact, are often stimulated to higher reproductive rates and, in addition, infestations have also been triggered by use of some insecticides.

That predatory insects should succumb to pesticides more readily than herbivorous insects is not surprising. If you stop and think about it, many of the spices in your kitchen cupboard are substances which plants have developed to kill or repel insects. Herbivores thus have a long coevolutionary experience with various chemical substances and in many instances have become immune to them. The chemical adaptability of herbivorous insects leads to a situation in which stronger and stronger doses of poison are necessary. It is unfortunate that soil organisms, predatory insects, and birds share no such resistance or ability to adapt, and this accounts for frequent high mortality among such organisms.[39]

One of the results of the vulnerability of predatory insects is that their populations are frequently depressed to the extent that when the herbivore population resurges, the number of predators is inadequate to control the population—even to the extent that it did formerly.

Ehrlich, Ehrlich and Holdren mention that the prominence of mites as pests is "a creation of the pesticide industry." Overuse of DDT served to kill the insects that kept mites under control. They offer as an example the emergence of the European red mite as a major pest in apple orchards. The promotion of this pest to major status followed closely upon the use of DDT to control codling moths. The authors offer such occurrences as a strong argument in favor of biological control of insects rather than chemical control.[40]

Along with predatory insects, insectivorous birds have traditionally been a first line of defence in the protection of all sorts of crops. That they succumb regularly to pesticides, and in extreme numbers, has long been known. Kenneth Mellanby wrote of the many birds killed in England between 1956 and 1961 in one instance describing an area of 1,480 acres of woodland where 5,668 wood pigeons, 118 stock doves, 59 rooks and 89 pheasants were found dead along with a number of hawks and other predators. The use of dieldrin as seed dressing was involved in this bird kill. Mellanby said that the birds poisoned by dieldrin were also toxic to foxes that ate them. During the winter of 1959-60, some 1,300 foxes were found dead and sick ones were observed. This was the same area where dressed seed was used. The corpses of the foxes were analyzed and no infectious disease was found; but their intestines were found to contain high residues of insecticide.[41]

The destruction of birds has continued with regularity as pesticide use has increased. In New Brunswick during 1975, a minimum of three million birds were killed when insecticides were sprayed over about seven million acres of forest to control spruce budworm. Many species of birds including various warblers and woodpeckers are valuable insectivores. The destruction of such valuable agents of biological control seems particularly unwise in view of the fact that pesticides are rapidly proving to be more detrimental than beneficial.

The Province of New Brunswick has been using pesticides vigorously in its forests for nearly forty years. At best, the program has had limited effectiveness. Now, at last, Minister of Natural Resources Morris Green, contends that his government is committed to the reduction of chemical spraying.

His statement follows a 1989 season in which the insecticide fenitrothion was used to spray more than 600,000 hectares (1,500,000 acres) in an attempt to control the spruce budworm. Critics of the program claim that fenitrothion is a "health hazard to humans and animals."

New Brunswick has made some moves to reduce chemical spraying. In 1987, fenitrothion was used for 80 percent of the huge annual spray operation and following that season's use, studies by the Department of Natural Resources disclosed a threefold increase in budworm damage throughout the province. The most heavily sprayed area, Restigouche County, evidenced a likelihood of particularly heavy budworm infestations in 1988. In 1988, the program used fenitrothion on 50 percent of the area sprayed and on the other 50 percent used *Bacillus thuringiensis* (Bt), a biological pesticide. Some of the inert substances in Bt. have been questioned as to safety, but there is a general conviction that Bt. is less damaging to the environment. While it does kill some nontarget moths and butterflies, it offers less threat to birds and parasites that provide some natural control of the budworm.

After the 1988 season, government officials contended that areas sprayed with Bt. suffered twice as much defoliation as those sprayed with fenitrothion, with the result that the use of fenitrothion was 33 percent greater in 1989 than in 1988. Other areas that were sprayed with Bt. in 1989 are to be closely monitored with a view to using it more effectively during the 1990 season.

The conviction of the Conservation Council of New Brunswick that the entire spruce budworm problem is a result of overcutting and of poor forest management practices deserves serious consideration.[42]

Between 1973 and 1975, the insecticide carbofuran killed wild ducks in British Columbia's Fraser Delta on three separate occasions. This is another pesticide that has been found to have immunosuppressive effects in test animals.

The use of insecticides in southern Quebec in 1980 to control caterpillars in cornfields affected 50 percent of Quebec's honey producers. Millions of honeybees were killed and the financial loss to apiarists was at least $5 million.[43]

According to Dr. Paul R. Ehrlich, the huge petrochemical industry which profits from massive use of pesticides has applied constant political pressure and resorted to outright lies about the safety of pesticides in order to escape being more closely regulated. He states that the industry has steadily attacked responsible scientists, labeling them as cult members and as professional agitators, when these scientists—after painstaking research—have learned that various pesticides threaten the capacity of the earth to support life. Since the time of Rachel Carson, there has been a continual rain of chemical death upon the earth, but the pesticide industry has steadily bucked legislative control and has heaped scorn on public concern.[44]

A brief example of the technique that has been used by industry will suffice to indicate its questionable ethics. Tests of carcinogenicity on two closely related organochlorine pesticides, chlordane and heptachlor, and on heptachlor epoxide, were made under contract to the manufacturer, Velsicol Chemical Company, by two commercial laboratories: Kettering Laboratories of the University of Cincinnati, and the International Research Development Corporation, Mattawan, Michigan. Both concluded that the pesticides were noncarcinogenic, although they noted dose-related incidences of what they referred to as "liver nodules." Because the Mrak Commission in 1969 had concluded that heptachlor and its epoxide were carcinogenic on the basis of FDA mouse studies, and because there was doubt as to the validity of conclusions of the two commercial laboratories, the EPA had liver sections reexamined by independent pathologists headed by Melvin Reuber. "Reuber and his team found a high incidence of unequivocal liver cancers."

At hearings prior to banning chlordane/heptachlor, industry witnesses were in some instances aggressive and uncooperative and in the case of two consultants from Kettering Laboratories, they were forced to admit in court that they had no training or expertise in chemical carcinogenesis, although they had undertaken tests for Velsicol for the purpose of showing that chlordane/heptachlor were not carcinogenic. In December, 1977, the federal grand jury handed down an eleven-count felony indictment against six present or former Velsicol executives. The defendants were charged with conspiring to defraud the United States and hide facts from the EPA by failing to submit data which showed that the two chemicals induced tumors in laboratory animals and could pose a risk of cancer to humans.

Velsicol entered a series of motions to dismiss the indictments and various technical pleadings were made. The case was dismissed on procedural ground in 1979.[45]

The falsification of extensive test data on many pesticides by Industrial Biotest Laboratories is sufficiently well known to merit only mention here as another example of questionable ethics on the part of the pesticide industry.

We stand at some sort of crossroad. The adamant use of pesticides in spite of serious ramifications continues with unaltered zeal. It would be a strange form of hubris if "overweening pride" in technology should turn out to be the terminal disease of our species.

On the one hand, there is the single-minded, profit-seeking attitude of industry: "E. Blair of Dow Chemical Company defined a winning pesticide as one with a market lasting nine years, an annual sales level of $20 million (1970 dollars) and a return of investment of 40 percent before taxes."[46]

On the other hand, there is the insidious, ubiquitous nature of pesticides, appearing in places where they should not be, causing effects that threaten all life on earth. For example: "Despite the 1977 cancellations of the leptophos registration, a committee of the International Joint Commission reported in 1980 that leptophos was one of 33 chemicals found in the Great Lakes system that is known to cause chronic adverse effects in man."[47] In 1971, leptophos poisoned and killed a number of Egyptian peasants and killed about 1,200 water buffalo. Permanent nerve injury was done to some workers in the plant where it was produced.[48]

Temik is one of the most toxic pesticides purchasable. Howard Rhodes of Florida's Department of Environmental Regulation describes it by saying that if you picked up the product with wet hands on the way downstairs, "You wouldn't make it to the bottom of the stairs."[49] Four thousand wells on Long Island have been found contaminated with Temik, as well as 10 percent of wells in five Florida counties. Also, the poison has entered Florida ground water. In addition, it occurs in 25 percent of wells in Prince Edward Island, where Temik is used by 15 or 20 percent of potato farmers. Three hundred of 1,100 wells surveyed in Wisconsin also contain from one ppb to 101 ppb of the insecticide. What is important is that tests have shown that

Temik causes potentially damaging changes to human immune systems when people drink low levels in their water supply.[50] Immunosuppression is also caused by PCBs, dioxins, and some other insecticides, herbicides, and fungicides and is an insidious threat to human health, indeed to life itself.

Atrazine has been found in ground water samples in the Central Platte region of Nebraska and in all water samples taken in Iowa.[51] It was one of a large number of pesticides found in 159 of 237 wells analyzed in Ontario.[52] Primarily used on corn crops in the east, it is also used by the forest industry to control brush on logged-over land. It has been found in tissues and organs of deer in Oregon.[53] It has been found to have a negative effect on seedling growth and to act as a plant mutant (and most mutants are considered potentially carcinogenic). Along with 2,4-D, widely used in silviculture, it is suspected of having a role in the development of amyotrophic lateral sclerosis, a disease that affects the nervous system, causing degeneration of the spinal cord, muscular weakness and atrophy.[54]

If one lives in Saskatchewan, according to the Canadian Department of Environment, three forms of PCBs, seven herbicides including the Agent Orange combination, and 15 other pesticides are regularly found in surface water at testing sites throughout the province. Environment Canada officials admit that residents of Saskatchewan "regularly breathe pesticides from spring to fall."[55] Even fresh snow in the Rockies contains agricultural chemicals.

Detectable levels of pesticides have been found in the blood of 99 percent of United States residents examined in a recent study.[56] Yet it is known that among the 3,350 pesticides currently in use, information exists to make even a partial assessment of health hazards for only 34 percent of them.[57]

In Ontario, some sort of nadir of social concern on the part of politicians charged with the well-being of their constituents is evidenced in these words given in the House of Commons, on May 23, 1985, by Member of Parliament Bill Blaikie (Winnipeg, Bird's Hill):

> . . . I am sure that many Canadians will be saddened today upon hearing that the Ontario Government has had to decide to make free bottled water available to those whose drinking water is contaminated by the herbicide Alachlor, rather than ban its use. Who would have thought that the day would come in Canada when we would be reduced to handing out bottled

water? Is our fascination with herbicides and pesticides so great that we would rather give up our water than seek ecologically sound alternatives to the use of these dangerous substances?[58]

Soil

There are many misconceptions about soil. One is that soil is synonymous with dirt—that any conglomeration of earthy material is soil. The truth of the matter is that soil is not a mere cluster of mineral grains lying together. Real soil is characterized by the presence of untold numbers of living organisms. Peter Farb writes that a single teaspoonful of soil from temperate zones may contain some five billion bacteria, 20 million actinomycetes, a million protozoa, and 200,000 algae and fungi.[59] In addition there will be visible organisms such as millipedes, earthworms, mites, and insects which help break down organic debris and also help cultivate the soil.

It is to be expected that there would be human impact on soil, and this preceded the arrival of the white man inasmuch as North American Indians burned the prairies to increase the pasture areas for wild game. As E. S. Shaler writes, "these fires would extend to the forests to the east, killing the young trees that might have encroached on the open prairies." He claims that east as far as central Ohio and Kentucky, even into the Carolinas and south to the Tennessee River, the original forests had been stripped of their timber in this manner.[60]

With the advent of European settlers in North America, much additional land was cleared for farming; and with the destruction of the tight grass sods that protected the open plains from the winds that swept across their wide expanse, conditions were set for the blowing of the soil. The well-known Dust Bowl era of the 1930s caused massive

"Half of our misery and weakness derives from the fact that we have broken with the soil and that we have allowed the roots that bound us to the earth to rot. We have become detached from the earth, we have abandoned her. And a man who abandons nature has begun to abandon himself."

Pierre Van Passen

soil damage. By the end of that period, Hugh Bennett, one of the founders of the U.S. Soil Conservation Service, estimated that close to 50 million acres (20 million hectares) of cropland was in a state of near ruination in the continental U.S.A., and another 50 million acres reduced to marginal productivity. Some 3,000 soil conservation districts were organized and much reclamation was done, but as late as 1962 U.S. Department of Agriculture figures showed soil erosion to be a notable problem on 237 million acres (95 million hectares) of cropland, somewhat more than half of the total cropland in use.[61]

In 1983, it was estimated that fertile topsoil was being washed or blown off U.S. farmland at a rate of 5.3 million tons (4.8 million tonnes) per year, with some areas in Tennessee, Washington, Idaho, and Mississippi losing up to 100 tons (91 tonnes) per acre per year.[62] Whereas, on the average, nature produces an inch of topsoil in about 1,000 years, this amount was being lost in about four years in some parts of the United States.

In Canada, a federal report in 1984 called soil degradation a national problem requiring national attention. It pointed out that the erosion of a single inch (2.5 centimeters) of soil can reduce the yield of wheat by 1.5 to 3.4 bushels per acre (90 to 204 pounds per acre or 100 to 232 kilograms per hectare) and that in Southwestern Ontario erosion has reduced corn yields by 30 to 40 percent. Soil salination on some areas of the Prairies had reduced crop yield by 10 to 75 percent in spite of increased use of fertilizer by farmers. Using 1982 prices as a reference, it is also estimated that Prairie farmers would have to expend $239 million on fertilizer to fully recover the present loss of grain production from wind and water erosion.[63]

Another serious situation exists in the loss of farmland to urban use. Between 1961 and 1976, Canada lost 3.5 million acres (1.4 million hectares) of farmland in such a manner. This is extremely significant in a country where less than 9 percent of the land area is capable of cultivation. Half of this amount is actually cultivated with the other half being used for pasture, forests, transportation corridors, recreational lands, and urban or industrial land.

The deterioration of soils is not an issue without consequence. For years data has been accumulating which shows a strong relationship between the quality of soil and the health of organisms which are nurtured by the vegetation that grows on the soil.

One such relationship was described by Durward Allen and concerned the vast population of rabbits and other small animals which from soil by 485 bushels (15 tons)(13.6 tonnes) of wheat.

The late Dr. F. A. Wyatt, professor of soils at the University of Alberta, said that in the black soils belt of Alberta, the loss of an inch of topsoil would remove about twice that much nutrient: 1,500 pounds (681 kilograms) of nitrogen, 300 pounds (136 kilograms) of phosphorus and 15 tons (13.6 tonnes) of organic matter. The nitrogen loss alone is equivalent to the amount of nitrogen in 150 tons (136 tonnes) of farm manure.

Erosion by wind and by water is a serious problem throughout North America. By the end of the Dust Bowl era, about one-third of the precious topsoil of the North American prairies had been lost to erosion. The seriousness of erosion is intensified according to the slope of land. On experimental farmland in Ottawa, a rainfall of 15 inches (3.8 centimeters) in 4 months washed off 8 tons (7.3 tonnes) of soil from a field of corn on a 5 percent slope, and 22 tons (20 tonnes) from a field with an 11 percent slope. In 1946, a 3-inch (7.6 centimeters) rainfall removed 72 tons (65 tonnes) of soil from a summer-fallowed field on an 11 percent slope.

It was also known three decades ago that Prince Edward Island topsoil was eroding rapidly. Workmen at Charlottetown seeking a solid foundation for bridge piers had to go through 90 feet (27.4 meters) of mud which had once been fertile topsoil in order to find the stable footing they needed.

Would it seem logical that we need to reassess some of our priorities?

Source: "Conserving Canada's Resources," A Collection of Monthly Letters from The Royal Bank of Canada (Montreal: May 1960)

Erosion in Canada

While it is comforting to note that there has been a recent report on soil problems in Canada, it does not necessarily follow that the problems will be rectified. The Standing Senate Committee on Agriculture, Fisheries, and Forestry's report "Soil at Risk" is an attempt to focus national attention on a problem that has been growing steadily more serious since Canada was first settled.

More than thirty years ago we knew that the loss of one inch of topsoil (2.5 centimeters) from one acre (.4 hectare) was equivalent to losing 700 pounds (318 kilograms) of nitrogen, 155 pounds (70 kilograms) of phosphorus, and 5,380 pounds (2,243 kilograms) of potash. This amount of potash, according to the Canadian Department of Agriculture, is equivalent to the amount removed inhabit the region where the Ozark Mountains in Missouri are bordered by prairie. Much of the soil in this area has limestone beneath it and therefore has abundant calcium. Studies had taken place which involved taking the weight of 175,000 wild rabbits. The trapping, marking, and releasing was done in January, a month when food for the rabbits was less abundant than in most other months of the year. Dr. Allen compared these weights with the weights of rabbits taken in other nearby areas where soil conditions were less favorable. It was learned that where the good soil conditions existed, the large legbones of the rabbits were 12 percent larger than in areas where soil conditions were poorer. Further study disclosed that these large legbones were 37 percent stronger than the bones of the animals that lived on poorer soils. The same sort of stronger bone structure was found in raccoons in the area and it was determined that muskrats living in streams draining the better soil were larger and had thicker skins and better quality pelts than muskrats on streams draining inferior land.[64]

Similar studies have shown that larger fish are found in streams draining fertile land and that growth rates are faster in such streams. Lakes surrounded by fertile soil produce larger fish as well.

Louis Bromfield studied U.S. Selective Service records for World War II and found that nearly 75 percent of young men from a southern state with badly leached soil were rejected as physically unfit, whereas a comparatively new state with fertile soil (Colorado) produced young men whose acceptance was the reverse of the state with poor soil.[65]

It is not just some sort of freak of nature that in some areas where grass is knee deep, cattle will appear to be all ribs, hips and kneebones while in the west, where forage seems scanty, cattle will appear sleek and healthy. Slight deficiencies in the mineral concentrations of vegetation, it is known, may account for lowered health qualities, vitality, intelligence, and glandular function. Trace elements such as iodine, fluorine, manganese, copper, cobalt, boron, sulfur, and many other elements, are often missing from badly worn soils or may not have existed in soils when they were formed. We are all familiar with iodized salt, and are aware that goiter belts exist where iodine is not present in soil, thyroid malfunction being common in these areas.

An excess of selenium, Bromfield suggests, may have been responsible in some small way for the famous Custer massacre. When Custer was defeated at the Little Big Horn River, his horses were suffering from "alkali disease." They contracted this disease after feeding for days on vegetation in an area where soils are known to have an excess of selenium. Excessive amounts of selenium in vegetation have long been known to be the cause of "alkali disease" in cattle.

Much is known about soils and the minerals necessary to produce good food. It is fair to say, however, that much is yet to be learned.

As stewards of the land in North America, we have not been diligent. Whereas we expect to have some sort of ethical relationship toward one another, we often fail to see that the well-being of present and future generations does not depend solely upon our conduct toward others. It also has something to do with the ethical responsibility we take toward the land that nurtures all and must continue to nurture all until the last days of this planet have been reached. Careful guardianship of the land, air, and water are at all times essential and must be brought to the forefront of consciousness. A great task of reclamation lies ahead of us if we are to recognize our responsibility.

It is to be hoped that current redirection of attention to our now massive environmental problems will lead to substantial change in our attitude toward the earth. After a half century of massive use of chemical pesticides and fertilizers, we have become intensely aware that chemical runoff is polluting streams and lakes, and even more seriously, is entering ground water. At the same time, the deliberate focus on monoculture is exacerbating soil erosion problems. In September, 1989, a study by the U.S. National Academy of Sciences recommended that the U.S. government urge farmers to readopt crop rotation and mechanical weeding. The study cited these methods as being equally as productive as chemical methods.[66]

Knowledge that crop rotation is beneficial to productivity of farmland dates at least back to the Roman poet, Vergil, (70-19 B.C.), who in his Georgics advised husbandmen to "sow golden spelt (wheat), where before thou hadst reaped the pea with wealth of rattling pods, or the tiny vetch crop, or the brittle stalks and rustling underwood of the bitter lupin." (Peas, vetch, and lupin are all legumes, and have the ability to fix nitrogen for future crops).

If ever there was a time, it is now that we must stop what ecologist, Paul Sears, calls "The lustful march of the white race across the virgin continent, strewn with ruined forests, polluted streams, gullied fields," that "can no longer be disguised behind the camouflage which we call civilization."[67]

The Condition of Canadian Farmland

In 1986 Environment Canada identified the major problems affecting Canadian farmland, stating that excellent crops are still produced but that deteriorating soil quality is a matter of increasing importance.

Serious concern exists about the following:

- Loss of organic matter reduces the moisture holding capacity of soil. Fertility is also affected because humus is capable of holding valuable nutrient ions. In cultivated Prairie soils, organic matter has decreased by 40 percent since cultivation first took place. In the Mixed Wood Plain ecozone, some sites studied have lost more than half of the original organic content.

- Studies have indicated both a decline in nutrient content of soils and an increased demand for nutrient by new genetic strains of crops. Prior to 1960, crops obtained more nutrient from native soils than from artificial fertilizers. By 1980 the opposite was true in all provinces except Alberta and Saskatchewan. In Canada as a whole, chemical fertilizer sales increased by 9 percent annually between 1970 and 1977.

- Acidification of surface soils takes place naturally by crop removal and leaching. Increased acidification can occur as a result of acid rain and by the use of nitrogenous fertilizers. According to some researchers, the increases in soil acidity in much of eastern Canada are 40 percent due to acid precipitation and 60 percent the result of nitrogenous fertilizer use. Overacidity of soil reduces crop yields and releases toxic trace elements.

that may concentrate in plant tissues or in run-off.

- Soils may be naturally saline (salty) but salinity is increased by applying water to cultivated lands. As evaporation takes place, salt from subsurface layers is brought to the surface, altering nutrient balance and reducing crop growth. In some areas of the Prairies, the increase in salinity is estimated to be 10 percent yearly, with one hectare in 10 affected. One hundred thousand hectares (250,000 acres) in Alberta and Saskatchewan experience increasing salinity from excessive irrigation.

- Erosion of soil in Canada is estimated to cost $1.2 billion yearly. Many factors affect the rate of soil erosion. Soil type, slope, type of vegetative cover, organic content of soil, and general topography are among these factors. In the Prairies the elimination of wheat/summer fallow rotations, and replacement of these with a five-year rotation using wheat, oats, barley and hay has resulted in a 40-fold reduction of losses from erosion.

Identified among the major stresses on Canadian farmland are, cultivation practices (such as the wheat/fallow example above); ecosystem damage due to pesticide use, including destruction of natural enemies of pests and dispersal of pesticides into soil, water and vegetation where they may become a health hazard to animals and people; narrowing of the genetic base of seedstocks; and economic factors such as machinery cost, interest rates, increased land costs due to proximity to urban areas, and the pressure to maintain short-term profits.

"Canada's Environment, An Overview,"
Environment Canada, 1986, cat. no.
EN21-54/1986, p.4-5.

Water

The public is often lulled by tourist promotional literature that speaks of sparkling streams and lakes, of record fish, and of sailing and boating adventures on unsullied waterways. We nourish a fond hope that there are still such places although we know that they lie farther and farther from the beaten track and most of us know that we will never see them.

The truth is that we have extremely grave problems with North American water resources. Consider such a report on water as one given by J. R. Vallentyne, a senior scientist for Environment Canada. A single glass of drinking water from Lake Ontario, he reports, contains 10 million trillion chloride ions, 100 billion cyanide molecules resulting from industrial plating and mining operations, 10 billion molecules of industrial solvents, 4 billion molecules of freon from spray cans and refrigerator coolants, 500 million molecules of PCBs, 100 million molecules of chemicals released from the combustion of coal, 10 million molecules of insecticides, and 10,000 molecules of dioxin.[68] The numbers are so staggering that we cannot comprehend them; but the fact that we can easily grasp is that such water bears pollutants that obviously make it something other than a healthful, refreshing drink.

Someone might claim that such a situation must be exceptional, but a more thorough look at facts suggest that polluted drinking water is much more common than we would like to think. A 1982 survey by the Environmental Protection Agency (U.S.A.) found that 45 percent of large public water supply systems dependent on ground water were contaminated with organic chemicals. The EPA's survey of rural households throughout the U.S.A. found that two-thirds of the households were drinking water that violated at least one of its health standards. Every major aquifer or ground water formation in New Jersey is affected by chemical contaminants and a million Californians drink water tainted with pesticides.[69]

One wonders what water will be like in another fifty years if we continue on our present path of technological progress. One also wonders how far we might think we can proceed with such pollution of an essential resource before making an all-out effort to correct the problem. Is it not likely that we will either correct the situation or succumb to it?

A 1987 study paper prepared for the Law Reform Commission of Canada pointed out that Toronto drinking water taken from Lake

Ontario contains a number of pesticides which may be carcinogenic. These include lindane, heptachlor epoxide,[70] dieldrin, BHC and B-BHC. Studies disagree as to whether or not there is any diminishment of these pesticides in water which has passed through water treatment facilities. One study indicated no reduction of any of the aforementioned pesticides except dieldrin, and other data indicated the removal of some of the organochlorine pesticides. Even though the use of DDT was severely restricted over a decade ago, a persistent breakdown product, PP DDE, is still found in Lake Ontario and passes through Toronto's water treatment facility without being diminished.

Studies in 1980 found another pesticide, fenitrothion, an organophosphate compound, contaminating shellfish, including clams, mussels, and oysters, at trace level, over a large area of the Maritimes. Shellfish as far as fifty kilometers (thirty miles) from sprayed areas were found contaminated with concentration levels rising as the sprayed areas were neared.

Another chlorinated insecticide, endrin, has been found in concentrations in Prince Edward Island estuary sediments and fish kills on the island have resulted from improper handling of the chemical.

Municipal sewage constitutes a serious stress to many waterways. Although 85 percent of Canadians live in communities which have sewers, only about 70 percent live in communities that are served by sewage treatment plants. Many of the treatment plants provide only partial treatment of wastes. Still other communities, those without treatment plants, discharge wastes directly into rivers, lakes or oceans. Some major construction of new sewage treatment facilities is underway; the completion of Montreal's new treatment system, once operational, will have positive benefits to the St. Lawrence River.

Another serious impairment to water quality is the presence of toxic chemicals from industrial discharge, leaching landfill sites, mining and smelting activities, leaching pesticides, and the presence of toxic materials in municipal sewage. These wastes end up in sediments or directly enter aquatic food chains. Of the 30,000 or more compounds used in the Great Lakes basin, about 800 are known to be toxic. Many of these chemicals are persistent and the effect of long-term exposure to them is not understood. Both the St. Clair and Niagara rivers contribute many toxic chemicals to the Great Lakes, some of them from hazardous waste disposal sites. These contaminants may be detected in the water, fish, and sediments as far downstream as Quebec City.

Lakes and rivers cover nearly eight percent of the land surface area of Canada and eventually its rivers discharge nine percent of the world's fresh water into the Atlantic, Pacific, and Arctic oceans. Off the Pacific Coast, effluents from the mining and pulp and paper industries have buried the ocean bottom and caused a reduction of oxygen levels in the water. A number of rivers also discharge industrial wastes into the Atlantic, and some of these wastes travel downstream all the way from central Canada. Both the Pacific and Atlantic coasts have lost shellfish fisheries to municipal sewage and some coastal species are polluted by heavy metals. The Arctic Ocean is less threatened at present though the icy water is slow to break down or carry away contaminants which are present.[71]

Both the Atlantic and Pacific coasts experience the hazard of oil pollution. This is a worldwide problem. A study by the U.S. National Academy of Sciences a decade ago indicated that 6.6 million tons (6 million tonnes) of petroleum are the annual burden of the oceans. This amounts to nearly 770 tons (700 tonnes) an hour or 18,700 tons (17,000 tonnes) each day. All oceans are now mottled with floating lumps made up of the heavier fraction of petroleum.[72]

The impact of oceanic pollution is not new, of course, but is increasing each year. As far back as 1966, Sprague and Ruggles could report that the miles of apparently unspoiled seashore in the Atlantic region of Canada were a myth. They pointed out that 20 to 25 percent of shellfish beds along the shores were contaminated by sewage and that shellfish could not be considered safe for human consumption.[73]

In the same year, Monro and Solomon spoke of reliable observers in Newfoundland who reported fantastically high kills, probably in the hundreds of thousands, of seabirds from oil pollution.[74]

Incidents such as the grounding of the tanker Arrow, with 2.8 million gallons (10.5 million litres) of Bunker C Oil at Cerberus Rock in Chedabucto Bay, Nova Scotia, in February, 1970, receive treatment as sensational events, which indeed they are; but people tend to ignore the steady pollution of oceans that occurs on an everyday basis.[75]

The oil spill in 1969 near Woods Hole Oceanographic Institute in Massachusetts, though not a large spill, provided a good opportunity for close study of the effects of the spill. It was found that immediately after this spill, there was a 95 percent mortality of fish, shellfish, worms, and other sea animals in the immediate area. Shellfish which survived were unable to reproduce and some bottom organisms were still being killed eight months after the spill had taken place. Some of the shellfish that survived were transplanted some distance away to determine their ability to recover and they retained enough oil in their bodies to be inedible months after being moved. One marine biologist envisions the possibility that carcinogenic components of oil may eventually be incorporated into and contaminate entire food chains.[76]

Unfortunately we live our lives in another sort of ocean, namely an ocean of environmental indifference that has produced grave crises. In spite of reductionist assumptions that we could reshape natural systems according to our own whims without suffering significant adverse effects, we find that the holistic contention of ecologists is being borne out as whole food chains and webs are affected by certain human activities. Who would have expected that spraying DDT to control spruce budworm populations in New Brunswick would do more damage to salmon than was probably done to budworms? Who would have expected that the more than 60,000 chemical compounds produced by industry would almost unfailingly find their way into our drinking water?[77] Who would have suspected that the technological comfort quest, even though motivated by the hope for profit, would eventually become a blind, reckless, relentless profit race, arrogantly positive that its worldview is the only view to have, though it take us to the brink of extinction and hurtle us over its edge? Such priorities!

In the U.S., an aircraft carrier costs more than the entire annual budget allowed for occupational health and safety; and in 1977, an A-7E attack plane cost twice as much as the EPA was allowed to budget for safe drinking water programs.[78] John Muir is reputed to have said that ecology is pulling up a dandelion and finding that everything else is attached. We are finding out that he was right.

Forests

Throughout the world, half of the forests that were standing in 1950 have disappeared. Increasing world population has resulted in an ever-increasing demand for resources. Cultural Survival, an organization of social scientists, contends that by the year 2000 there will be only two giant forested areas remaining, one in Central Africa, the other in Western Brazil. Some biologists disagree; they feel that by the end of this century, there will be little, if any, undisturbed forest remaining.[79]

It seems to be true that in a world where we see forests as a resource, it is more difficult for us to see them as an integral part of the community of life. Franklin D. Roosevelt once described himself for *Who's Who* as a tree-grower, and he took particular delight in reforesting the eroded wastes of his acreage at Hyde Park, New York. He planted as many as 50,000 trees a year and was aware of their importance in the environment. He claimed that the forests are "the lungs of our land, purifying our air and giving fresh strength to our people."[81] We ignore such insight today.

Trees do add oxygen to the air, but that is just one of the important functions they serve. Interwoven roots of the forest community stabilize soil. Forest shade retards evaporation and the accumulated humus absorbs precipitation like a vast sponge. Communities of trees are the guardians of springs that gush from the earth and the monitors of year-round streams that are nourished by the ability of a forest to store large volumes of water and release it slowly. The forest's role in preventing floods is well known.

In addition, the forest serves to moderate temperature and to protect soil from frost penetration. Where snow comes early and blankets the ground before subzero temperatures arrive, the ground may stay unfrozen throughout the winter. Climate is modified by the forest's effect on wind, temperature, humidity, and rainfall. The recycling of oxygen, nitrogen, carbon dioxide, and water is carried on with regularity. Habitat is provided for many living organisms, dust and other pollutants are filtered from air, and, in the aesthetic and spiritual sense, forests are places of peace, majesty, and beauty.

To look upon forested areas as mere economic resources is a form of single vision of shocking, perhaps suicidal magnitude. Without being able to grasp this majestic scheme of things as an entirety, we are indeed shattering it to bits and remolding it nearer to our heart's desire. Unfortunately, and unlike the poet Omar Khayyam, we think we have the wisdom he knew he lacked, and we are proceeding full speed ahead with absolute zeal and with totally reckless abandon.

Apart from a tree's value for firewood, timber, or wood for pulp, G. Tyler Miller refers to a calculation of the sort not usually admissable to the world of economics. He speaks of an estimate made that a typical tree living for fifty years provides, without cost to anyone, ecological benefits that are worth $196,250 during its lifetime. Broken down, this amounts to $31,250 worth of oxygen production, $62,500 worth of air pollution control, $31,250 in control of erosion and maintenance of soil fertility, $37,500 in recycling water and controlling humidity, $31,250 in wildlife shelter, and $2,500 as manufactured protein.[80]

The assault on forests in North America did not really begin seriously until shortly after 1800. The circular saw and steam mill, combined with the discovery of the wood-pulp process for papermaking, led to increasing industrial demand for forest products that has continued unabated to this day. Cheap timber, often sold for as little as 10 or 15 cents an acre (25 to 37 cents per hectare), combined with cheap labor, led to a period of frantic harvesting that has sometimes been described as forest extermination. This has moved from east to west across North America and late in the twentieth century is in the final mop-up stages. Stewart Udall points to the fact that not all the devastation was caused by logging because "careless loggers caused fires that burned as much as 25 million acres (10 million hectares) per year."[82]

It is a usual thing to see annual reports of forest companies which depict acres of seedlings as testimony to the conscientious reforestation that is being carried out. The unfortunate truth is that such areas are exceptions rather than the rule. Many areas have been logged and left in the traditional "cut and run" fashion. This has been the hallmark of the logging industry in a fantastic timber heaven where optimists predicted that there was enough wood for a thousand years.

As early as 1862, John Langton addressed a Quebec audience and warned, "We go on practically treating our forests as inexhaustible, and in the face of the yearly increasing distances, to which lumberers have to go back from all our main streams, we have as yet taken no steps towards preserving what remains to us."[83]

Logging practices often do great damage to the land. In the United States, guidelines for clear-cutting were established in 1972. Like many guidelines or laws, they can be interpreted strictly or loosely, in the letter of the law or the spirit of the law. Under these guidelines, clear-cutting is not to be carried out on federal forest land areas where soil, slope, or other watershed conditions can receive major injury, where there is no expectation that the area will be adequately restocked within five years, where aesthetic values are more important than other considerations, and where clear-cutting is done simply because it will yield the greatest profit.

Actually clear-cutting is only supposed to be used as a technique where it is silviculturally essential to attain the desired forest manage-

Comments on present forest practices in Canada are no more favorable today than they were in John Langton's time (1862).

In testimony before the House of Commons Standing Committee on Environment, David Runnalls from The Institute for Research on Public Policy made the following comment in answer to a question on October 31, 1989.

"I think we have real problems in arguing against deforestation in international instances when our own forestry policy is so appalling. Our best forestry practices are lousy and our worst are really shameful. As a Canadian in international discussions, I have felt pretty naked when it comes to talking to developing countries about conserving their forest resources when you consider what we are doing with ours."

Source: House of Commons, Issue No. 19, October 31 1989 Minutes of Proceedings and Evidence of the Standing Committee on Environment, Supply and Services, Ottawa

ment goals and, according to the guidelines, the size of clear-cut blocks is to be kept to the minimum necessary to attain those objectives. In theory, the clear-cut blocks are to be shaped in such a manner as to blend with natural terrain. Protection is also to be given streambanks, streams, shorelines, lakes, wetlands, and other water bodies.[84]

In spite of these generalized precautions, practice followed is usually excessive and in violation of any great concern for the future of the land that is being subjected to harvesting.

Modern logging, with its dependence on heavy equipment, often bares excessive amounts of soil, buries topsoil beneath subsoil, leads to soil compaction by machinery, causes destabilizing changes in slope configuration, destroys the small trees that have achieved significant growth and could make another crop in a much shorter period than that required if total restocking is needed, causes major vegetation changes, and also creates conditions in which excessive runoff provides a serious threat of soil erosion.

Another serious concern is the depletion of soil fertility through the use of slash-fires, particularly on low fertility sites. These slash-fires, intended to burn waste wood, are unfortunately often used to burn good timber, inasmuch as the very profit-oriented logging industry habitually resorts to a practice referred to as "creaming" or "high-grading" (taking only the best). "Uneconomic" wood as well as legitimate waste wood is consumed by enormous slash-burns, ones in which hundreds of tons of wood are burned, often destroying most or all of the organic matter in the soil due to high temperatures. Hot burns may reach 800°–1,000°C. This causes loss of vitally needed soil elements such as phosphorus, potassium, sulfur, and particularly nitrogen. During such slash-burns, carcinogenic elements are also released into the air.

The smoke blankets wide areas, causing hazard to all and particular distress to victims of respiratory diseases. Such slash-burned sites often take years to recover before even seedlings can survive. Growth on these sites is also much slower than on nonburned sites. Additional damage by burning is also done to mycorrhizae, essential fungi that often have vital symbiotic relationships with various species of trees. Another concern is that the more desirable mycorrhizae are slow to reinhabit a slash-burned area whereas other species of mycorrhizae that enter the burn site more rapidly favor weeds, ferns, red alder, and maple.[85]

Of grave concern, although apparently not allowed to affect actual practice, is the fact that slash-burning encourages the development of the root parasite *Rhizina undulata* in soil. This fungus attack root tissue of conifers and eventually kills the trees. Forest pathologist Paul D. Morgan refers to the fact that in some places in the state of Washington, "the failure to obtain adequate regeneration is disturbingly common . . . Plantations are being annihilated; on some plantations there's not a tree left."[86]

Recent news reports indicate that *Rhizina undulata* is rapidly becoming a serious problem in British Columbia. Twenty-five percent of seedlings planted in the Nass Valley have succumbed to the fungus and in some locations the mortality is as high as 60 percent. The fungus has also become a problem in the Prince George area and in the Nelson forest district in southeastern British Columbia.

The problem of modern technological methods is reminiscent of a graphic example given by author William Vogt. He tells of new mental patients who were put in a room with concrete walls and floors and each handed a mop. An attendant would turn on a large water tap before leaving the room. As Vogt remarked: "The insane would go to work with the mops. The sane would turn off the tap."[87]

Our usual response to a technological problem is to replace it with an even more damaging one. We rarely think in terms of replacing the abuse with more benign methods that create less stress on ecosystems. In short, it is more likely that the search will be on for a powerful fungicide with unknown eventual effects than it is that we will cease clear-cutting and slash-burning and adopt logging methods that are less traumatic to the land community.

After clear-cutting of a heavily forested area occurs, there is an eruption of weeds and brush which some foresters believe smother and retard the growth of freshly planted seedlings. To solve this problem, the use of herbicides is encouraged. Selective cutting, as opposed to clear-cutting, leaves much of the smaller standing timber and eliminates the cost of expensive restocking. It also eliminates the need for herbicides that eventually drain off the watershed into lakes and streams, often poisoning aquatic life and entering the human food chain.

By eliminating clear-cutting, slash-burning could also be stopped, and very likely the use of herbicides would also be unnecessary. Roger Hart, a geo-chemist focusing on slash-burning, states the present problem succinctly:

> Slash-burning on a steep slope with shallow soil in dry conditions and heavy slash-loads can result in intolerable nutrient and soil loss. Partial cutting is the best alternative under these conditions . . .
> Slash-burning is an outmoded silvicultural technology and inflicts considerable damage on fish habitat, air quality, and forest productivity.[88]

To all the other impacts of logging on environment must be added the outright waste that stems from hasty logging methods which search for the most profitable timber, discarding other good logs that will not bring the highest profit. In the Queen Charlotte Islands of British Columbia, according to a 1987 *Globe and Mail* article by Toronto journalist Christie McLaren, Macmillan Bloedel left 27 percent of its cut lying on the ground to rot. As McLaren said: "Imagine 320,000 pickup trucks full of firewood stretched bumper-to-bumper on the Trans-Canada Highway from Vancouver through Calgary, into Saskatchewan . . ."[89] Bob Williams, MLA (Vancouver East) said bluntly, "That's the amount of waste MacMillan Bloedel is responsible for annually. That's a national scandal—not just provincial."[90]

Wildlife and
Old Growth Forest

Old growth forests are important to deer and it may be a merely well-advertised myth that the eradication of old growth is "good for wildlife." This was the theme of a paper presented to the 46th North American Wildlife and Natural Resources Conference in March, 1981, by Alaska wildlife biologists John Schoem and Matthew Kirchhoff, and Montana wildlife biologist Olof Wallmo.

Their studies presented evidence from historical records of high wildlife values in old growth forests. Deer were focused on only as one of the species in great abundance in primeval forests. Prior to and during early logging ventures, deer populations were high and market hunting was a lucrative business. Between 1755 and 1773, more than 600,000 deerskins were shipped to England from Savannah, Georgia, and similar quantities were shipped from North Carolina, Quebec, and other colonies. In the states around the Great Lakes, vast quantities of venison were shipped to Milwaukee and Chicago markets from 1860 onward. By 1880, 100,000 deer a year were shipped from a single state, Michigan.

By 1900, both timber and deer were gone from these states, at the very time when their populations should have been increasing—if advocates of improved hunting following logging were correct.

In West Virginia, as another example, deer were reported abundant in virgin forests whereas they nearly disappeared when heavy logging began to stimulate second growth with its supposed advantages of abundant food and escape cover. The biologists warn, though, that excessive market hunting preceded or was concurrent with timber removal and it is difficult to separate the two effects and assign a proper value to each.

Their research indicated high Columbian black-tailed deer populations per square mile on Vancouver Island, B.C., and on Admiralty Island, Alaska (25 to 60 deer per square mile, 10 to 23 per square kilometer).

The biologists' recent field studies in steady-state old growth Alaskan forests showed that black-tailed deer use old growth forest to a greater extent, both summer and winter, than any younger forest up to 150 years old. The reason for winter preference of old growth habitat is relatively shallow snow and greater availability of forage. By contrast, minimal understory forage is found in stands aged 30 to 150 years and recent clear-cuts, though providing abundant forage, have heavy snow accumulation.

In British Columbia, researchers studying Columbian black-tailed deer found that populations may decline 75 percent after logging.

The biologists stressed that old growth is an important habitat and is considered optimal or important seasonal habitat in some locations for many species, including black-tailed and white-tailed deer, mountain goats, moose, fisher, grizzly, and numerous smaller animal and bird species.

Their studies indicated that in Alaskan forests, the carrying capacity for deer is lower in a 100-year rotation than in a virgin, largely old growth forest.

Among the major stresses on forests identified by Environment Canada in 1986 are the following:

Wood harvest has increased in Canada by 50 percent since the 1950s. Careful study of the maximum allowable cut substantiate the conclusion that forests are being overharvested, particularly in British Columbia and the Maritime provinces.

Although efforts to reforest lands in Canada have increased substantially since 1986, only 20 percent of the area cut between 1975 and 1980 was replanted or seeded. Nearly 60 percent of the area harvested in Alberta was replanted, in British Columbia and Saskatchewan, about a third of the area harvested was replanted; and in Ontario about one-fourth was replanted. In other provinces, even less attention is paid to encouraging regrowth of forests.

Modern methods of whole-tree harvesting remove essential forest nutrients, and clear-cutting can result in slides and erosion, particularly on hillsides. Damage increases as clear-cuts increase in size. Haul roads create erosion channels, raise dust levels and compact soil. Siltation of streams may follow as a result. Intensive forest use exposes forests to attack by pests, reduces forage for wild animals and may reduce insect and bird populations when pesticide use occurs.

Substantial evidence exists that air-pollutants are having increasing effect on forests. Ozone causes damage to foliage and reduces growth rate. Acid rain is associated with the decline of maples in Ontario and Quebec. Forty-three percent of the two million lakes in Quebec and Ontario, as well as 40 percent of Canada's productive forest area are subjected to moderate to high levels of acid precipitation and are at least moderately susceptible to damage.[91]

More than a century ago, George Perkins Marsh, witnessing the assault on the forests of his time, recognized the necessity of thoughtful restrictions on human impact on land. In *Man and Nature,* he advocates the wisdom of restraint: "We have now felled forest enough everywhere, in many districts far too much. Let us restore this one element of material life to its normal proportions, and devise means for maintaining the permanence of its relations to the fields, the meadows, and the pastures, to the rain and the dews of heaven, to the springs and rivulets with which it waters the earth."[92]

There is now even less to preserve and no end to rapine in sight. It would certainly seem to be time to implement the kind of thought expressed by Marsh.

At the Edge of the Whirlpool

Coast-to-coast destruction of North American forests has taken little more than two hundred years. There is no evidence that the history of land use in the old world in any way curtailed the rapacity with which the resources of this continent have been savaged. With the assistance of technology we have accomplished a shocking degradation of forests, fisheries, grasslands, wetlands, wildlife, and even more shocking, of soil, water and air. There is little that is not poisoned today. From the food we eat, to the air we breathe and the water we drink, almost nothing is uncontaminated.

In truth we have shaken the foundations of the earth and of the intricate food webs that support life. Deep inside ourselves we know that things are very bad but if we really admitted that fact to our conscious selves, we would then be called upon to act. So we continue with the hackneyed belief that we live in the best of all possible worlds. We accelerate our mad dance a little. We laugh a little more frenetically. We assure ourselves with the pablum of the media. We comfort ourselves with the reassuring belief that technology will solve all the problems.

We fail however to ask ourselves two questions. Why should our species be immune from extinction? Considering the way we, as a species, act toward the land, toward each other, and toward other living things, why should any intelligent God want to pull our chestnuts out of the fire?

We have a habit of letting things go for about as long as we can. But we do tend to put air into a tire when it looks soft, rather than let it go flat. We usually don't wait until we run out of gas before we fill the tank. We try to prop up a shed before it falls over and we usually repair the roof before it is leaking into every room in the house.

In other words, we tend to respond, sooner or later, to warning signs. When it comes to the planet earth, we have been too remote from nature's signals for too long a while. The indications are everywhere, but we can no longer read the language. We have succumbed to too many of our own myths: that we are the most important beings in the universe; that we can dispose of toxic substances in the soil, air and water and they will be forever gone; that our plasticized, artificial world is the real world simply because many of us would like it to be that way; that every other living thing on earth, and the nonliving things as well, can simply be categorized as resources for our use; and that we can take and take from the natural world and give back nothing, neither love nor concern, neither time nor effort, not even a tiny bit of thought or a little conscientious restraint.

The twentieth century thus far has been a sustained epic of barbarism in which horrors of the great wars are over shadowed by the way in which potentially beneficent technology has been turned against not only humankind but against all life upon earth. Just as detached men in bombers remote in the night skies from their targets were able to rain explosive and incendiary death upon the warriors as well as the aged, the defenseless and the children below, so thousands of misapplications of technology continue to make a mockery of the boon that technology should be for present and future generations. Whilst nuclear war takes front and center stage among the bugaboos of our mortal fear, a whole host of less recognized threats to existence go almost unnoticed. We have launched cradle to grave threats to existence for generations to come. We have recklessly unbalanced hydrological, chemical, biological, atmospheric, even geological cycles, just to mention some of the accelerated changes we have introduced. Star wars, genetic manipulation, and annual crops of new mutagens, carcinogens, and teratogens are among the exotic harvest of our inventiveness. Shorn of any instinct that might protect us from ourselves we are recklessly committed to shooting craps with destiny. If we win we may be nothing more than a run-down species in a degraded environment, and if we lose — fairly soon and without too much more damage to the planet — earth may rehabilitate itself in time.

How much better off we would be in an ecologically sound society, one in which humans recognized their bond with the earth, one in which care of the earth was carried on with delight, even with a sense of devotion. Imagine an economy based on satisfying human need rather than on creating incessant, artificial desires. Imagine a world in which society was based on a higher order of values than material goods. Imagine a world in which people were truthfully taught to know that good health is contingent on good air, water and soil, plus exercise and philosophical acceptance of the beauty and meaningfulness of all life. Imagine living in a world of honest bookkeeping where the cost of pollution, the cost of carnage on the highways and the cost of rebuilding war-torn lands was not considered part of the Gross National Product.

Right now we are circling with increasing speed on the periphery of the whirlpool. Puzzled by the seeming meaninglessness of life we grasp the straw of the sycophant's promise that we are in the midst of some sort of progress and the rainbow will burst forth at any moment. Empty progress, the vortex of the whirlpool, calls us strongly but we are not quite sure. We can still break free if we swim strongly, and if we but do that, we can attain the shore.

Pondering on that shore we can see a meaningful world before us. There, "with firmness in the right" we must "bind up the nation's [world's] wounds."[93] The most worthwhile task we could undertake would be the rehabilitation of the earth, and in losing the sort of lives we now lead, we would find better lives by restoring our ancient compact with nature.

Moon of the Cracking Trees

January has traditionally been known as the Moon of the Cracking Trees, a name derived from the pistol-like sounds of trees cracking in intense cold. Tonight, though, I would vote for it being called the Moon of the Hooting Owl, or the Moon of the Singing Coyotes.

I went to the woodshed a while ago to get an armload of birch for the heater. It's a cold enough night so that the snow was squeaking underfoot and a bit of the aurora was dancing in the sky. Since the dog cavorted wildly at the idea of going outside, I put on a jacket and figured on taking a walk after getting the wood. While I was loading up the birch and the dog was rolling in the snow, a great horned owl started "hoo-ing" from down along the creek. A trail leads down that way, and though it is a fairly dark night, once outside for a while the white snow offers good contrast and it's easy to see where one is going.

Now we start off down the trail—I guess I could call it the "owl hoot trail" seeing that we are heading in the direction from which the owl was calling. The dog evidences great interest in a set of fresh rabbit tracks, and I think to myself that brother owl would probably be interested in them too.

A few more calls and the owl stops talking—possibly our intrusion is sufficient to send it away on silent wings. But, to replace the silence, punctuated only by the squeak of snow, a coyote begins a song down along the creek bottom, and pretty soon it is taken up from a knoll that the coyotes frequently use for a choir loft. Sometimes I have noted that coyote song is broken by a series of yaps and barks, but tonight the singers prefer clear melody, and their serenade seems to be a coyote attempt to perform an "Aria to the Wilderness."

Walking along and listening to what I think is a beautiful sound, I am hard put to understand why the sight of a coyote is enough to make an otherwise calm and reflective man drop what he is doing and run for a rifle. Time and again it has been proven that the slight harm the coyote does to hen house and sheepfold is a thousand times paid for in its control of ground squirrels and smaller rodents. As a carrion eater, it takes its place with other mammals and birds in keeping the woodland in spotless order. Sometimes I wonder whether we have not become so sedentary (a better word than civilized in this instance)— that the sight of a wild, free thing is enough to arouse the killer instinct in us. Since our creation of the dollar bill as an object of worship, anything causing even a momentary spot of red ink in the loss column must be removed from the face of the earth—and thus it has been with the coyote.

Since much has been recorded about the coyote that makes it seem like a malicious, savage and cowardly beast, it might be in order to say a few good things about these animals. They display many attributes that we consider virtues. There is much evidence that they mate for life and, providing that life is not interrupted by a bullet or steel trap, this may be for as long as a decade or more. Studies have indicated a rather high rate of loyalty, showing that coyotes have less use for divorce courts than do humans. They are also known to be cooperative, frequently using teamwork or relay systems while hunting their food. They are known to be playful and it has even been recorded that they have formed friendships with other animals, such as badgers and cougars. Enos Mills reported seeing a cougar following happily in the tracks of a coyote, and saw enough later evidence of the travels of the two to indicate that they had formed an association. Mills comments that though one might expect to see a coyote following a cougar to clean up remnants of its kill, it is more unusual to come upon a partnership in which the coyote is the leader. He comments that it is another of the many unexplained attachments that have been recorded among different species of animals.

In *Lives of the Game Animals,* the great Canadian naturalist Ernest Thompson Seton indicates his high regard for the coyote in the following passage:

> Every plainsman in the West has heard and learned to love your song, and every dweller in the West that is to be, will know it well, for still it abounds from the level buttes in the early dark.
>
> Sheep-men may rage and governments set a blood-price on your head—but wise are you as you are swift and brave.
>
> How complete was the Red-man's understanding when he called you the "Wonder-Dog" and made you the incarnation of the Deity, the one who brought the divine fire to earth in the beginning, the one who will live to see it die when all the world is dead.
>
> If ever the day should come when one may camp in the West, and hear not a note of the Coyote's joyous stirring evening song, I hope that I shall long before have passed away, gone over the Great Divide, where there are neither barbwire fences, nor tin cans, nor hooch-houses, nor improvement companies, nor sheep-herds, nor flies, but where there is peace, and the Coyote sings and is unafraid.[1]

I do not think that any civilization can be
called complete until it has progressed from
sophistication to unsophistication, and made a
conscious return to simplicity of living and
thinking.

Lin Yutang

3

Insights and Inklings

At some time during the Chou dynasty, in the millennium before Christ and prior to Confucius (551-479 B.C.), the writers of the 81 poems (chapters) of the Tao Te Ching (The Book of the Way and Its Virtue) made highly significant statements about the meaning of life and the joy of living in harmony with nature. Authorship of the Tao is attributed either to a group of writers or more particularly to Lao-Tzu, whose birth is assigned as taking place between 604 and 575 B.C.[1]

Chinese legend has it that Lao-Tzu, aged and infirm, riding on an ox, heading into oblivion in the remote peaks of the Himalayas beyond civilization, was stopped by the keeper of Hankow Pass and implored to write down his teachings for the keeper of the pass. He obliged by writing a book in two parts which consisted of some 5,000 words. Then he disappeared into the peace he sought.

Provocative and profound throughout, two stanzas seem particularly pertinent to those who would convert nature solely to human use and who might better be employed in attempting to repair society's destructive impact on natural systems.

> As for those who would take the whole world
> To tinker it as they see fit,
> I observe that they never succeed;
> For the world is a sacred vessel
> Not made to be altered by man.
> The tinker will spoil it;
> Usurpers will lose it.

and

> So the Wise man wants the unwanted; he sets no
> high value on anything because it is hard
> to get. He studies what others neglect
> and restores to the world what multitudes
> have passed by. His object is to restore
> everything to its natural course, but he
> dares take no steps to that end.[2]

Perhaps the essence of the thought of Lao-Tzu is the belief that the way of Nature is taught by every tree, by every stream, rock, star, and cloud. A life of wisdom is a life lived in accordance with the laws of the universe. Beauty is seen in rough clothing, delight taken in simple food, and gratitude is felt for simple accommodation. Happiness can be found wherever one happens to be and one does not have to roam the world to be fulfilled. Though transportation exists, people have no need to use it nor are weapons used, because there is no desire to subdue others. To Lao-Tzu, the life of moral innocence and love of peace is compromised by inventions and the beginning of the craving for things. The Stoic acceptance of nature that Lao-Tzu encouraged would obviously pose difficulties in today's world of 5.25 billion people although there is little that would so benefit the earth as much as the moderation of our industrial pace and the election of lives of voluntary simplicity by large numbers of people in the overdeveloped nations of the world. Who knows but that a less frantic pace might stimulate sore-needed reflection upon what the worthwhile goals of life should be.[3]

While it is interesting to speculate how different the world of today might be if the view of the Taoists had prevailed, it is obvious that civilization has proceeded to develop without recognizing the integrity of the sacred vessel referred to in stanza one above. There have been other people in our past who have had similar insights and the history of their reflections on nature and on the necessity of treating the earth as a sacred vessel offers us a different view of history. The reflections which follow are well worth examining if we are ever to acquire the insight we so desperately need.

Since humans are a part of the natural world, that which is conservative of (good for) the natural world is, in the long run, good for humanity. This is a basic principle which many thoughtful people have been aware of for a long time. Deterioration of the planet's life-support systems and daily reports of environmental problems are therefore a cause for concern on the part of an increasing number of individuals.

One of the oldest historical documents, the Holy Bible, indicates the importance of man's role as steward of the earth. In Chapter two

Although it was not until the eighteenth century that industrial societies flourished in western Europe, the silk-weaving industry throve in China more than a thousand years before Christ. Industrial guilds, which date from 300 B.C., passed laws and arbitrated the disputes of employers and employees with mediation boards representing each side equally. The guilds represented not only manufacturers and their workers but even the less prestigious trades such as barbers, coolies, and beggars.

In a western society dominated by mercantile interests, it is sobering to become aware that the ancient Chinese society arranged its priorities differently and did not display high regard for those who indulged in trade. Chinese custom assigned top rank to scholars, teachers, and officials, while placing farmers in the next class, artisans in the next, and merchants in the lowest, for it held that merchants made profits simply by trading the products of other peoples' labor.

Source: Will Durant, The Story of Civilization,
Our Oriental Heritage: Part I
(New York: Simon and Schuster, 1954), pp. 776-780.

of the Book of Genesis, Verse 15, we read: "And the Lord God took the man and put him in the Garden of Eden to dress it and keep it." In spite of the importance assigned humanity, people are assured that they are not exempt from the laws of nature. One example of this is found in Ecclesiastes 3:19: "For that which befalleth the sons of men befalleth the beasts; even one thing befalleth them; as the one dieth, so dieth the other; yea, they have all one breath; so that a man hath no preeminence above a beast; for all is vanity."

In earlier pages, we have seen that Plato was disturbed by the erosion and general decline of the environment in Attica. Actually he was one of a number of ancient writers who observed environmental effects and who pondered on the relationship of places and the organisms that lived in them.

Hippocrates, the legendary Father of Medicine, was a member of a guild that traced its lineage to the God of Healing. Born in 460 B.C., he lived to a great age, dying somewhere between 375 and 351 B.C. In an essay attributed to him, "On Airs, Waters and Places," he wrote about the relationship between locations of cities and the effects these locations had on the people who lived in them. He advised, "... when one comes into a city to which he is a stranger, he ought to consider its situation, how it lies as to the winds, and the rising of the sun; for its influence is not the same whether it lies to the north or the south, to the rising or to the setting sun." He also felt it important to consider the water source of the city, whether the water was soft or hard, whether it came from high, rocky places or from a marsh. He contended that the climate, the general topography, the prevailing winds, elevation, and prevailing temperatures all affected both the physical vigor and mental attitudes of the inhabitants. These factors, he determined, also affected the plants and animals of the region. In terms of following general scientific procedures, he was a keen observer of the general environment and attempted to derive conclusions from his observations.[4]

The Greek philosopher, Aristotle (384-322 B.C.), during the time he studied at the academy begun by Plato, earned distinction as "the intellect of the school." In his *Metaphysics,* Aristotle argued that wisdom is knowledge of principles and causes and that "things are causes of one another, as, for example, hard work is a cause of a sound body, and a sound body of hard work." Pondering the nature of the universe, he comprehended the interrelationship of all things: "And all things are ordered together somehow, but not all alike . . . both fishes and fowls and plants; and the world is not such that one thing has nothing to do with another, but they are connected. For all are ordered together to one end."[5]

Aristotle's lengthy *History of Animals* has earned him the title "Father of Ecology." The marvel of his work lies not in the errors that have been found in his studies but in the pathfinding set of observations he made, which have guided others in their studies.

> In winged creatures, the tail serves, like a ship's rudder, to keep the flying thing in its course. . . . Further, birds that are not made for flight have a tail that is of no use; for instance the purple coot and the heron and all water-fowl. These fly stretching out their feet as a substitute for a tail, and use their legs instead of a tail to direct their flight. . . .
>
> Of all insects, one may also say of all living creatures, the most industrious are the ant, the bee, the hornet, the wasp, and in point of fact all creatures akin to these; of spiders some are more skilful and more resourceful than others.[6]

Aristotle discussed a variety of ecological phenomena, such as territoriality among animals, population explosion, competition, migration, and parasitism. However, he apparently did not comprehend, as John Muir later expressed it, that animals and plants exist primarily for their own sake. Aristotle was more inclined toward an hierarchical view, that plants exist for animals and that everything ultimately exists for the sake of man.

Aristotle's pupil Theophrastus extended the work of his teacher, specializing in what is now known as plant ecology. He recognized the enrichment provided to soil by legumes and fallen leaves, understood that some environmental conditions favored growth more than others, and observed that various plants were adapted to growth in locations where they were directly exposed to sunlight whereas other plants thrived in shady places and that some were capable of living in saline soils. His approach to study was systematic and took into cognizance the effect of climate, slope, and elevation.

In 30 B.C., the Roman poet Vergil, (Publius Vergilius Maro) published the *Georgics,* intended as a farmer's guide. The *Georgics* consisted of four books which concerned crops and the weather, and the raising of bees. The entire work is a sincere praise of agriculture and demonstrates Vergil's personal conviction that the life of a farmer is a worthwhile endeavor. He portrays the happiness of the farmer's life:

> Happy the man, who, studying nature's laws,
> Through known effects can trace the secret cause.
> His mind possessing in a quiet state,
> Fearless of Fortune, and resigned to Fate!

and

> Nor envies he the rich their happy store,
> He feeds on fruits, which of their own accord,
> The willing ground and laden trees afford.[7]

Columella, the Spanish-born Roman writer of the first century A.D., wrote faithfully of agriculture in *De Rustica*. At the time he wrote, crop yields were declining and blame had been variously attributed to poor and exhausted soil and to poor climate. Columella denied that these were the causes of poor crops and blamed poor husbandry of the land as the main reason. He charged that farmers were shirking responsibility and had, in effect, turned care of the land over to uninterested slaves. Contending it better to "admire large farms, but yet a small one till," he discoursed on the fact that a large farm subjected to improper husbandry would not produce as well as a small one that was properly tilled. Aware that newly cleared land produced well, but only until it was deprived of residual nourishment left from the forest that had grown upon it, he advocated that the earth could be "quickened" again by addition of "frequent, timely, and moderate manuring." He cautioned that plowing should take place when the land was damp but not when it was "immoderately wet," and reminded farmers that on slopes the furrows should be run across, rather than up and down the slope. He advocated that manuring should take place shortly before plowing, "for on such food . . . the land grows fat." He advised that every form of manure, including human, should be used.[8]

Lucretius (94-55 B.C.) was a Roman poet-philosopher, known to this day for his didactic poem "De Rerum Natura," (Of the Nature of Things). His poem was an obvious attempt to popularize the conclusions of the Greek philosopher Epicurus. Although faithful to Epicurean materialism in his outlook, Lucretius exhibited a devotion to Nature as creatress and life-giver. He went beyond Epicurus's gratitude toward Nature as a giver of good things and teacher of wisdom and justice. Lucretius personified Nature to a certain extent, trying to indicate what might be said about life and death if Nature had a voice. Recognizing both the transience and permanence of life, he reminds us of the living earth that constantly brings forth new life, only to reclaim it again by death. The interaction of living things, the blossoming of life from death, is made graphic in his verse, "Hence too it comes that Nature all dissolves/Into their primal bodies again, and naught/Perishes ever to annihilation./... since Nature ever/Upbuilds one thing from other suffering naught/To come to birth but through some other's death."[9]

Pliny (23-79 A.D.), a Roman naturalist and scholar, was among the first who recorded dismay at the way men of his time were abusing the earth in their search for wealth. In *Natural History, Book II,* he wrote:

> For what luxuries and for what outrageous uses does Mother Earth not subserve mankind: She is flung into the sea, or dug away to allow us to let in the channels. Water, iron, wood, fire, stone, growing crops, are employed to torture her at all hours, and much more to make her minister to our luxuries than our sustenance. Yet in order to make the sufferings inflicted on her surface and mere outer skin seem endurable, we probe her entrails, digging into her veins of gold and silver and mines of copper and lead; we actually drive shafts down into the depth to search for gems and certain tiny stones ... we seek a jewel merely to be worn upon a finger.[10]

Obviously Pliny looked upon the earth as a living being, but he remained aware of the difference between necessities and luxuries. His writing describes the mining, quarrying, and clearing of land with fire, and other practices employed by the Romans. Even today, his opinion of the mining of gems "merely to be worn upon a finger" is a valid comment on human vanity, and on other rather useless purposes for which land may be exploited. Admitting that even some small fraction of our economic aspirations are foolish is not yet a part of our general awareness.

As early as Roman times, humanity had begun to act as "geological forces" changing the basic structure of the world. Pliny's comments are of further interest in this matter:

> Headlands are laid open to the sea, and nature is flattened. We remove the barriers created to serve as the boundaries of

nations, and ships are built especially for marble. And so, over the waves of the sea, Nature's wildest element, mountain ranges are transported to and fro . . . When we see the masses of marble that are being conveyed or hauled, we should each reflect, and at the same time think how much more happily many people live without them.

Pensively, he wrote: "When I ponder and weigh these things in my mind, I must needs think great shame and impute a great fault to our forefathers that lived long since . . ."[11]

In reflecting upon Pliny's writing, we must note that his attitude was probably considered as "un-modern" in his own time as it would be today. Very likely his horror at bulldozers and blasting technique would know no bounds. His viewpoint was simply that natural structures were useful in their own right. He states that nature formed mountains to strengthen earth, to tame the violence of great rivers, and to break the force of the sea. His opinion that humankind would be happier without so many material objects is one that has been expressed by thoughtful people in many nations. Thoreau stated it as simply as anyone when he commented: "A man is rich in proportion to the number of things which he can afford to let alone."[12]

In addition to Pliny's opinions, his descriptions are vivid, displaying both the extent of the ravages against nature and the randomness involved in the search for precious metals. He describes a method used to mine gold which involved the destruction of substantial portions of mountainsides. Tunnels were dug into the mountains and then,

> . . . beginning at the last they cut away the wooden pillars at the point where they support the roof . . . The mountain, rent to pieces, is cleft asunder, hurling its debris to a distance with a crash which it is impossible for the human imagination to conceive; and from the midst of a cloud of dust of a density quite incredible the victorious miners gaze upon this downfall of Nature. Nor even yet are they sure of gold nor indeed were they by any means certain that there was any to be found when they first began to excavate.

Pliny explains that the debris left after the collapse of the mountain had to be washed to obtain any gold that might be present, and for this purpose the Romans sometimes diverted rivers from a distance of as much as a hundred miles. The sediments upon reaching the ocean greatly extended the shores.

Both Lucretius and Pliny, it may be noted, were aware of the wholeness of earth and of the continuity of life. These two concepts are basic to the development of an earth ethic which we must establish to guarantee the integrity of the planet.

A studied, philosophical comprehension of the magnificence of earth was first eloquently expressed by Marcus Aurelius Antoninus (A.D. 121-180), considered by many to have been the greatest of the Roman emperors. In his *Meditations* he wrote:

> I travel the roads of nature until the hour when I shall lie down and be at rest; yielding back my last breath into the air from which I have drawn it daily, and sinking down upon the earth from which my father derived the seed, my mother the blood, and my nurse the milk of my being—the earth which for so many years has furnished my daily meat and drink, and though so grievously abused, still suffers me to tread its surface.[13]

> Always think of the universe, as one living organism, with a single substance and a single soul; and observe how all things are submitted to the single perceptivity of this one whole, all are moved by a single impulse, and all play their part in the causation of every event that happens. Remark the intricacy of the skein, the complexity of the web.[14]

Clearly Marcus Aurelius would not be uncomfortable in a modern biology class discussing holism and the web of life; nor would he be surprised that quantum physics and systems biology find "relationship" at the basis of all definitions. Elsewhere he writes:

> All things are interwoven with one another; a sacred bond unites them; there is scarcely one thing that is isolated from another. Everything is coordinated, everything works together in giving form to the one universe. The world-order is a unity made up of multiplicity; God is one, pervading all things; all being is one, all law is one (namely the common reason which all thinking creatures possess) and all truth is one—if as we believe, there can be but one path to perfection for beings that are alike in kind and reason.[15]

Those Amazing Dolphins

In an incident in the Sea of Okhotska, a Russian doctor aboard a fishing vessel gave first aid to a dolphin that had been attacked by a blue shark. The bleeding dolphin swam to a small boat from the Russian trawler *Ardmatovo* and tried to leap aboard. Crewmen helped the dolphin into the boat and Dr. Lariso Lazarenko stitched its wounds and gave it an injection. Crewmen poured water over the dolphin while first aid was performed. (Question: How did the dolphin know a doctor was aboard? Or did it?)

On the other side of the ledger, four South African fishermen reported that their lives were saved by four dolphins. As one stated:

It was the most frightening experience I have ever had. We were lost, the mist was very thick. We were steering toward the rocks when the dolphins arrived.

When the men began to panic, one went to the bow, endeavouring to peer through the mist. He felt a bump on the right side, and looking over, saw two dolphins. The dolphins forced the boat to the left, where two more were swimming. The two mammals on the right kept pushing the boat toward the left, more than once it narrowly missed the rocks on the right side. After a while, all four dolphins stopped pushing the boat and began swimming around it in circles.

We saw that we were now in calm water, and dropped anchor. When the mist cleared we realized that we were safely in port.

Strange world, isn't it? While it doesn't seem likely the lion will lay down with the lamb, such incidents as those above give strength to Marcus Aurelius's conviction that, "All being is one . . . a sacred bond unites them."

Source: Greenpeace Chronicles, April, 1979
B.C.S.P.C.A. News, June, 1979

The profound implication of such thought still eludes us. Although science texts are filled with acknowledgments of the interwoven relationships of things, technology rends asunder the fabric of nature with single-purpose goals. Fortunately, we know enough to abhor such clichés as, "What is good for General Motors is good for the U.S.A.," or "What is good for the forest industry is good for the people of

Canada." However, the quest for immediate gain ignores the simple fact that our industrial economy rests tenuously on the tightly integrated natural world. It remains for us, as we seek an ethical relationship toward the earth, to become as wholly aware as Marcus Aurelius of the sacredness of the tie that binds us to other living things on this planet.

To awareness of the interrelatedness of living things and knowledge of human dependence on the bountifulness of earth, Marcus Aurelius added the realization that happiness depends on something other than the mere acquisition of possessions. To the extent that we still hesitate to admit the validity of such thoughts to ourselves, we jeopardize our ability to adjust to the very real parameters of earth's tolerance of our multifaceted abuses. Through some self-inflicted form of blindness, we have instituted material possessions as the prominent indicator of success in life.

In spite of the fact that no previous civilizations have been as burdened with possessions as present-day North America, we seem to view even moderate curtailment of the production of endless, and often meaningless goods, as some form of shocking deprivation.

Thales of Miletus, (640-546 B.C.), often placed first among the Seven Wise Men of Greece, intuited that every particle of the world has life and that life and matter are inseparable. He held that an immortal soul was present in animals, men, plants, and metals and that the essential vital spirit that inhabits all things may change form but never perishes.[16]

Perusing ancient ideas—one becomes aware that modern civilization with its anthropocentric focus has imposed severe limitations upon thought. One suspects that we are indeed encapsulated people. Content to know in our heads only what we can quantify and observe in isolation, we have narrowed our view of the entirety of the cosmos. Rhapsodic fantasy in which the stars and planets of the universe are the storehouse of resources for our exploitation indicates that we have limited our vision to material things.

To an observation attributed to Socrates by the Greek writer, Diogenes Laertius, about 200 A.D., "Those who want fewest things are nearest to the gods," we can only respond with cynicism and disbelief. Though impressed with our own moderate intelligence, we scoff at the possibility that the universe may contain an intelligence greater than our own. Although Plato might conjecture that we are midway in a Great Chain of Being which involves intelligences far beyond our own, we prefer to be like the legendary worm who lived in the midst of a hickory nut, certain that, "I live in the heart of the whole round world and it all belongs to me."

Interestingly enough, when it is convenient, our society sometimes purports to be Christian. Yet it apparently pays little attention to the words of the Saviour it exhorts in times of stress, war and bereavement: "Lay not up your treasures on earth, where moth and rust doth corrupt, and where thieves break through and steal." Humankind is instead counseled to cultivate treasures of the spirit.

From the standpoint of the health of the planet and our own health, we might consider how much purer air, water and soil would be if we North Americans were more conscious that natural things left in their natural state provide an environment of which we are a dependent part.

We would benefit by placing more value in enduring intangibles ranging from relationships with our fellow man to protection of the magnificent order in which we, as transients, have been invited to live and have our being. That this life is a way station in an eternal progression is something that was once given a credibility and which should be reflected upon anew.

We might well draw lessons from the practical Benedictine monks who made realistic application of good land practices throughout Europe during the sixth century A.D. In the process they earned a reputation for themselves as the civilizers of Europe.

St. Benedict, (480–543 A.D.), founder of the Benedictine order, was born in Nursia, Italy, of a relatively well-to-do family. He was sent to school in Rome but was distressed by the way of life he experienced and saw there, and decided to become a monk.

He moved to Subiaco, about forty miles from Nursia, and lived there as a solitary monk for many years. His steadfastness, after numerous trials, led to the successful establishment of the monastic Order of Benedict. Part of the rule he established was that, "At fixed times the brothers should be occupied in manual work, and again at fixed times in holy reading." This part of his Rule stemmed from his conviction that the active and contemplative life are both necessary for the perfection of the complete person. The lifestyle ordained for the Benedictines was markedly diligent but unobtrusive.

Author D. C. Butler quoted this comment made on St. Benedict by John Henry Cardinal Newman:

St. Benedict found the world, physical and social in ruins, and his mission was to restore it in the way, not of science, but of nature, not as if setting about to do it . . . but so quietly, patiently, gradually, till the work was done, it was not known to be doing. It was a restoration . . . Silent men were observed about the country, or discovered in the forest, digging, clearing, and building . . . by degrees the woody swamp became a hermitage, a religious house, a farm . . . [17]

So great was their concern for the land that a high level of compatibility with environmental quality was maintained. The impact of Benedictine monasteries on Europe was great inasmuch as the success of the order led to the formation of thousands of these monastic communities. Between 500 and 1100 A.D., the Benedictine monasteries were among the largest developers and holders of arable land in Europe.

To assume that the relationship of the Benedictines to the land was nothing more than a way of making a living would be incorrect. It was a conviction of the Order that "to labor is to pray." Benedictines were fully aware that as they improved the land and associated closely with nature, they gained wisdom from the relationship thus established.

Centuries later, the famous Benedictine monk St. Bernard (1091–1153) told those he invited into his Order, "Believe me upon my own experience, you will find more in the woods than in books; the forests and rocks will teach you what you cannot learn of the greatest masters." He used to say that he had no other teacher in his studies of Holy Scriptures than "the oaks and beeches of the forests."[18]

For obvious reasons, Dr. René Dubos, a microbiologist and experimental pathologist, suggested that Benedict of Nursia deserves recognition as a patron saint of those who recognize "that true conservation means not only protecting nature against human misbehavior but also developing human activities that favor a creative, harmonious relationship between man and nature."[19]

It is part of the experience of this century that we are widely separated from nature. The congregation of life in urban centers is only in part a conscious choice. Much of it has resulted from mechanization of agriculture, from concentration of industry, and from the marvelously efficient system of transportation that has been developed. Although we may frown in doubt at the intimate relationship with nature spoken of by St. Bernard, we also suspect in our hearts that it may be possible. The social problems caused by crowding

The Price of Progress

The pace of modern society weighs heavily on individuals. Dr. Milton Greenblatt of the University of California contends that the number of Americans suffering from serious emotional and mental disorders almost constitutes a national emergency. He indicated that more than 20 percent of Americans are seriously ill due to such disorders. According to Dr. Peter Matthews of the University of Saskatchewan psychiatry department, the problem is similar in Canada, although he did not refer to it as a national emergency. Dr. Matthews feels that 25 percent of Canadians will likely suffer from psychiatric problems at some time during life.

Editor Henry Geiger, writing in *Manas*, pondered the question of how individuals may regain their mental health, and suggested that the problem is not taken seriously enough because we have no idea how sick humanity has become. He comments that, according to doctors, a population suffering from such disorders, which finally constitute a wasting illness, simply live at a lower level, not realizing that a deep-seated affliction has grasped their lives. He also referred to Thoreau's observation that when people become obsessed with acquiring the "ostentatious necessities of a civil life, they lose the opportunity to profit by civilization itself.

How to Be Sensible, Manas,
Los Angeles, CA, January 22 1986

and the statistical evidence that urbanized humanity suffers from a variety of tensions and neuroses suggests that complex life in a technological society weighs heavily on the human spirit.

However, increasing demand for outdoor recreation in woods, fields, and on waterways suggests that the burdened human spirit still feels a strong bond to nature and seeks its solace for reasons that are not always understood. A troubled North America looks upon diminishing natural areas with increasing concern. The return flow of peace and understanding, indicated by St. Bernard, has in this generation made us ripe for comprehending that our roots penetrate beneath these turbulent times into a greater reality. We are ripe for a reaffirmation of the absolute value of healthy land to the quality of life and to human survival.

An observation of Dr. Dubos's helps us to more fully appreciate the impact of the Benedictines: "They have brought about profound transformation of soil, water, fauna and flora, but in such a wise manner that their management of nature has proved compatible in most cases with the maintenance of environmental quality."[20] It is worth reflecting upon the point that diligent men working with hand tools are very likely able to treat land modifications more carefully than men using earth-moving machinery, especially when one takes into account the modern desire to measure success in terms of yardage moved.

Concern for nature was again brought to the forefront during the thirteenth century by St. Francis of Assisi (1182-1226 A.D.), who preached a doctrine of total identification with nature. The Franciscans renounced worldly possessions, saying, "This world is this kind of field; he who has a larger part of it has the worst part." St. Francis looked upon all living creatures as brothers and sisters. He also spoke of "Sir Brother Sun" and "Sister Mother Earth." Because his concern for fellow living creatures was so great, he once stated that if presented to the emperor he would ask for an "edict prohibiting anyone from catching or imprisoning my sisters the larks, and ordering all those who have oxen or asses should at Christmas feed them particularly well."[21]

In the spring of 1224, he composed the last of many poems he wrote during his life. Evidence of his profound respect for nature and his recognition of it as a manifestation of God is apparent in the lines of "The Canticle of Brother Sun."

The Canticle of Brother Sun

Most high, all-powerful, all good, Lord!
   All praise is yours, all glory, all honor
   And all blessing.

To you alone, Most high, do they belong.
   No mortal lips are worthy
   To pronounce your name.

All praise be yours, my Lord, through all that you have made,
   And first my Lord Brother Sun,
   Who brings the day; and light you give to us through him.

How beautiful is he, how radiant in all his splendor!
Of you, Most High, he bears the likeness.

All praise be yours, my Lord, through Sister Moon and Stars;
In the heavens you have made them, bright
And precious and fair.

All praise be yours, my Lord, through Brothers Wind and Air,
And fair and stormy, all the weather's moods,
By which you cherish all that you have made.

All praise be yours, my Lord, through Sister Water,
So useful, lowly, precious and pure.

All praise be yours, my Lord, through Brother Fire,
Through whom you brighten up the night.
How beautiful he is, how gay! Full of power and
strength.

All praise be yours, my Lord, through Sister Earth, our
mother.
Who feeds us in her sovereignty and produces
Various fruits and colored flowers and herbs.

All praise be yours, my Lord, through those who grant pardon.
For love of you; through those who endure
Sickness and trial.

Happy those who endure in peace,
By you, Most High, they will be crowned.

All praise be yours, my Lord, through Sister Death,
From whose embrace no mortal can escape.

Woe to those who die in mortal sin!
Happy those She finds doing your will!
The second death can do no harm to them.

Praise and bless my Lord, and give him thanks,
And serve him with great humility.

It would be a mistake to think of St. Francis as typical of his faith. Historian Lynn White calls him the "greatest radical in Christian history since Christ," and suggests that one of the great miracles about the life of St. Francis of Assisi "is the fact that he did not end at the stake, as many of his left-wing followers did." Lynn White suggests that St. Francis's efforts to establish the brotherhood and sisterhood of all things on earth may indicate a direction our own thoughts should take. White proposed St. Francis, as a patron saint for all ecologists.[22]

Father Murray Bodo, O.F.M., who has written extensively about St. Francis describes the life of Francis as the tale of how one man found God and how in finding God everything else thereby became more meaningful and more holy. In his words, "The whole creature world is enhanced instead of being neglected and de-emphasized for some spirit world, as often happens in pseudospirituality." To Francis, every living creature was a creature of God and anything that "demeans and devalues the creature demeans the Creator." The love of Francis for all the creatures of the earth was a natural outcome of his love for God.[23]

Such a view as Francis held, if applied today, would revolutionize our attitude toward the environment and all life on earth. Such an attitude, with a moderate compromise between his extreme frugality and our incessant want of material things, would together probably suffice to reduce our demands on earth and bring them to a truly sustainable level.

In 1691, John Ray, a devout English thinker and student of natural history, wrote a book that was read closely for a century thereafter. He entitled it *The Wisdom of God Manifest in the Works of His Creation*. The book stands as a sturdy defense of nature and recommends the attentive study of nature as well as the study of books. Two important thoughts lie at the heart of his writing. The first of them is that nature created other animals not solely for the sake of mankind but for their own sake as well: "Surely a good God takes pleasure that all His creatures enjoy themselves that have life and sense and are capable of enjoying it." His second point remonstrates man for failing to "consider the works of God and observe the operations of His hands. Let us take note of and admire His infinite goodness and wisdom in the formation of them. No creature in the sublunary world is capable of doing this except man, and yet we have been deficient therein."[24]

In France, Jean Jacques Rousseau (1712-1778) argued effectively that human education should be closely linked to the natural world.

He distinguished between the natural needs of all humans and the artificial wants imposed by civilization. He charged that artificial pursuits had alienated man from his own inner nature and taken away his humanity. On a positive note, he recommended that experience in primitive nature could help offset the artificialities of civilized life.

In England at the time of the Enclosure Acts, an anonymous saying went the rounds: "The law locks up the thief who steals the goose from off the common, but leaves at large the larger thief who steals the common from the goose."

A troubled Oliver Goldsmith (1728-1774) saw husbandry decline as farms became larger and as people moved to towns. In his famous poem, "The Deserted Village," Goldsmith describes the fate of Auburn, a fictitious name for an Irish village, probably similar to Lissoy where he spent his youth. His suspicion that care of the land would disappear as farms grew larger is a problem that is apparent today as agriculture becomes more and more an industry and land becomes more and more a commodity.

The value Goldsmith felt was inherent in rural life is markedly evident in these lines from "The Deserted Village," in which he shows deep comprehension of the rural population as the strength of the nation, the foundation upon which all else rests:

> Ill fares the land, to hastening ills a prey
> Where wealth accumulates, and men decay.
> Princes and lords may flourish, or may fade;
> A Breath can make them, as a breath has made;
> But a bold peasantry, their country's pride,
> When once destroyed, can never be supplied.
>
> A time there was, ere England's griefs began,
> When every rood of ground maintained its man;
> For him light labor spread her wholesome store,
> Just gave what life required, but gave no more;
> His best companions, innocence and health;
> And his best riches, ignorance of wealth.[25]

Among the English poets, Alexander Pope (1688-1744) ranks as one who has given our language many deeply thoughtful lines and phrases. In his *Essay on Criticism,* he spoke strongly of the central role of nature in life:

First follow Nature, and your judgment frame
By her just standard, which is still the same:
Unerring NATURE, still divinely bright,
One clear, unchang'd, and universal light,
Life, force, and beauty, must to all impart,
At once the source, and end, and test of Art.[26]

Again, in his *Essay on Man,* he returns to the theme of Nature as the visible manifestation of the Great Mind that lies behind all things.

All are but parts of one stupendous whole,
Whose body Nature is, and God the soul;[27]

Of course William Wordsworth (1770-1850) is often considered the greatest among the English nature poets. His love of nature was developed during his boyhood among the Cumberland Hills and matured in an outlook which intuited a divine spirit resident in all natural settings and living things. It was a logical thing to him that:

One impulse from a vernal wood
May teach you more of man,
Of moral evil and of good,
Than all the sages can.

Sweet is the lore that Nature brings;
Our meddling intellect
Misshapes the beauteous forms of things—
We murder to dissect.

Enough of Science and of Art;
Close up those barren leaves;
Come forth, and bring with you a heart
That watches and receives.[28]

And in his famous ode, "Intimations of Immortality," which has been called the high-water mark of poetry in the nineteenth century, he addresses the enigma of life in this sturdy fashion:

Our birth is but a sleep and a forgetting;
The soul that rises with us, our life's star,

Hath had elsewhere its setting,
And cometh from afar;
Not in entire forgetfulness,
And not in utter nakedness,
But trailing clouds of glory do we come
From God, who is our home.[29]

It is surprising, even today, though we may reject the "nature mysticism" of such writers as Wordsworth on an intellectual level, that his words reach deeply into our souls and stir an emotional response which we are often at a loss to explain.

To an immeasurable, but probably large extent, the focus of the nature poets and writers on wild, mysterious Nature, in which one wandered in God's presence, had enormous impact on North American thought.

Prior to this vision of God in nature, the seventeenth century was characterized by a militant attitude toward nature. Theologian Michael Wigglesworth spoke of the newly settled continent of North America as a devil-infested, howling wilderness and, in 1662, spoke of the unsettled lands as a place inhabited by none "but hellish fiends and brutal men,"[30] thus identifying undeveloped lands as a devil's stronghold, fit only to be conquered. Much of the energetic pioneering effort to conquer the wilderness, can, in retrospect, be seen as a crusade against infidels and evil spirits of all sorts.

Cotton Mather, a New England minister, author, and amateur scientist, wrote of ghosts and witchcraft in his *Wonders of the Invisible World* (1693). He identified the native American people as "not merely heathens but as active disciples of the devil." His best known work, *Magnalia Christi Americana* (1702), describes New England history before 1690 as a struggle to emancipate the country from the Devil and the Devil's disciples, the Indians.

The general attitude, in agreement with these men, prevented a more rational approach to settlement of the new lands, and to establishing harmony with its native inhabitants and rightful owners.

With the ideas expressed by poets and other writers of the late seventeenth and eighteenth centuries, a new attitude developed: that God was present in His creation, and that one walked in God's temple in the wilderness. This, coupled with John Ray's idea that the mountains were the handiwork of God, possibly even his image, was a stunning new way of thinking of the wild and pristine lands of North America.

Seeds of appreciation for the majesty of the land were germinating, and are perhaps only now, at this late stage, rising above the surface of a ravaged land.

One of the most unequivocal statements regarding the central importance of Nature in our lives was made by the British scientist Thomas Henry Huxley in an address given at the South London Working Men's College in 1868. In this address, Huxley, a strong advocate of compulsory education, stated what he believed to be the purpose and scope of a liberal education.

He posed an analogy: suppose we all knew that at some time or another our lives and fortunes would depend on winning or losing a game of chess. We certainly would all want to know the names of the pieces that made up the game, and the rules and moves of the game.

He then went on to make a comparison between each individual's life and a game of chess.

> The chessboard is the world, the pieces are the phenomena of the universe, the rules of the game are what we call the laws of Nature. The player on the other side is hidden from us. We know that his play is always fair, just, and patient. But also we know, to our cost, that he never overlooks a mistake, or makes the smallest allowance for ignorance. To the man who plays well, the highest stakes are paid, with the sort of overflowing generosity with which the strong shows delight in strength. And one who plays ill is checkmated—without haste, but without remorse.[31]

When we see the staggering effect of pollution upon our overtaxed environment, the truth of Huxley's analogy becomes apparent. There is also an answer to the disclaimer often ventured that the

"The man I meet with is not often so instructive as the silence he breaks. This stillness, solitude, wildness of nature is a kind of thoroughwort, or boneset, to my intellect. This is what I go out to seek. It is as if I always met in those places some grand, serene, immortal, infinitely encouraging, though invisible, companion, and walked with him."

Henry David Thoreau

problems of our society are to be blamed solely on industry and government. The answer is simply this. Each individual must know the rules of the game and must ever be on guard, contributing effort every day to assure that society functions in such a manner as to avoid being checkmated.

North America, in the years in which Goldsmith, Pope, Wordsworth, and Huxley were thinking and writing, was being subjected to its taming. Immigrants viewing the abundant resources of the New World were not thinking of adapting themselves to the beauty and splendor of the verdant continent, but were focusing on the age-old gambit of acquiring wealth in the fastest, most convenient manner.

Before examining more recent observations which take into account mankind's impact on this continent as well as on the entire world ecosystem, we might ponder the fact that in the last few hundred years we have created a full-blown environmental crisis. Addressing that crisis, the World Commission on Environment and Development, in the published report, *Our Common Future,* has said that its "hope for the future is conditional on decisive political action now to begin managing environmental resources to ensure both sustainable human progress and human survival."[32] It stresses the fact that the time to begin making significant changes is *now.*

Some of the thoughts expressed in this chapter may have considerable value in promoting these changes. They may help us develop a real philosophy about many basic things that have been ignored in recent years. What is the nature of life? What sort of attitude should we have toward other living things that share this planet with us? Does mass extermination of another species bode well for our own future? If we consider it an obligation to protect the world for our children, it is obvious that we are leaving the opposite of a healthy, thrifty world of high potential for future generations. Should we not begin immediately to take serious, determined action to restore the health of soil, water, and air? Have we not already proven that we are acting irresponsibly toward the planet? These and other questions should not be ignored a moment longer.

In the next chapter, we look at additional thoughts and reflections of the past two centuries which will broaden the base for consideration of the problem.

Stealth

One early November day, I got a sudden yen for a meal of trout, and consequently went a-fishing. In due course I found myself beside a fallen log over a small stream, with one trout on the log and another showing curiosity about a wet fly that I was using as temptation. When my best efforts failed to lure the second fish, I reached back to collect the first one, prior to moving downstream, and almost grabbed a weasel.

From the first it was a stalemate. The weasel wanted the trout, and being a weasel, it wasn't about to accept no for an answer, even though I outweighed it by a matter of at least 500 to one. With ears flattened, tail tip twitching, and a not-quite-comical ferocious growl—for it meant it—the weasel threatened me with all sorts of dire consequences as I picked up the fish.

Now if weasels were the size of collie dogs, or possibly even the size of housecats, I think I might move to Calgary and take an indoor job because, pound for pound, they have a disposition that would make a saber-toothed tiger seem meek as a grain-fed lamb.

But weasels are not as large as the animals mentioned and, as I said, I had a yen for a meal of trout; so I settled the issue by cleaning the fish and thereupon leaving the entrails and head for the weasel. During the proceeding, the weasel alternately advanced and retreated a few inches at a time, possibly sensing that it had at least threatened me into a compromise.

It was the second experience I had had with a weasel attempting to sabotage a fishing trip. Once, while fishing a stream up north, I had left some fish behind me on the bank. It was a cool day and they were under the shade of a small bush. When I glanced at them I was surprised because I saw four, whereas I thought I had caught five. A bit downcast at my mathematical error, I continued fishing, then decided to move along and went to collect my fish—but there were only three!

I looked around for the villain, but not a twig was moving, nor a branch stirring. The woods were open for a long distance, with only a fallen log here and there. I sat down on a big rock and watched my three fish, and finally saw a weasel slip out from a crevice under a log and make for the strange manna that had fallen from heaven. Well, I chased that weasel off, and figured that he had taken sufficient tax on my efforts . . . not that the weasel didn't growl and carry on like a six-ounce demon.

In both cases, the weasels I encountered while fishing were short-tailed weasels. Their adult length, including the four-inch tail, is about twelve inches. There are larger weasels in North America, but short-tailed weasels seem to fill a greater variety of habitat than most of the other species. Like all weasels, short-tailed weasels are extremely slender, and would probably serve well as a mascot to be emulated in the fashionable reducing salons.

As predators, they are highly successful; and their temperament is such that they will tackle animals many times their size. They have been known to kill birds as large as turkeys and have no hesitation in attacking a rabbit. Their reputation for blood-thirstiness is well-justified, as more than one farmer who has had a weasel in his henhouse can testify.

Nonetheless, as a guest on a farm, they can be extremely valuable. If mice are raising havoc around grain supplies, and a weasel happens to be passing through the neighborhood, the high population of mice will prove an irresistible attraction. Mice will be pursued into the farthest corners, and soon the population of mice will diminish and eventually disappear. Lest we unjustly accuse weasels of depredations in the henhouse, it has been noted many times that a weasel will live on premises with high mouse populations, quickly reduce those populations, and move on without interfering with the orderly life of the hens in any way.

When hunting, weasels are virtually tireless, and myriad tracks after a fresh snowstorm will testify to the endless turning, twisting, bounding, and leaping carried on by a single weasel. In spite of their tiny size, a study of their anatomical structure will disclose a formidable array of teeth, worked by a truly massive amount of muscle for so small an animal. Remarkably versatile, the weasel is capable of climbing most trees, is an agile swimmer, and has an almost magical ability to disappear from sight.

In spite of what seems to be an attitude of complete savagery, weasels are known to be admirable parents; and though they are fierce hunters, the talons of hawk and owl frequently seek them out and put an end to their career. It is part of this strange, interwoven fabric of nature that all things have their particular skill and adeptness, but when they become careless for a moment, something equally skillful and adept in some other way is waiting to not so gently remind them that the sin of forgetfulness is not easily forgiven in the world of reality.

A citizen of an advanced industrialized nation consumes in six months the energy and raw materials that have to last the citizen of a developing country his entire lifetime.

Maurice F. Strong
Canadian Member of the World Commission on
Environment and Development

The Arrival of Conservation

In his book, *An Inquiry Into The Human Prospect,* professor of economics Robert Heilbroner raised a provocative question for anyone who pauses to reflect on human ability to control the power it possesses. "There is a question in the air, more sensed than seen, like the invisible approach of a distant storm, a question that I would hesitate to ask aloud did I not believe it existed unvoiced in the minds of many: 'Is there hope for man?' "[1] Bureaucratic circumlocution that talks sustainability while endeavoring to maintain the status quo simply guarantees the doom of civilization. The status quo is what has brought us to the brink.

Even the most untutored mind cannot avoid seeing the rapid degradation of the planet. Fouled and unusable beaches greet the would-be swimmer, smog irritates the respiratory passages of urban dwellers, leaden skies produced by slash-burning block autumn sunshine and blanket valleys in the forested parts of the nation. Fortunately, more and more groups oppose the rape of resources, the rain of pesticides, the contamination of food, and a host of other conditions imposed by a relentless pursuit of wealth.

If we are so fortunate as to survive our efforts to master nature, it will only be because the rising concern for what we are doing to the planet, finally reaches the consciousness of those who have enjoyed the dance without realizing that the piper must be paid. A changing attitude toward the earth is developing in spite of the attitude of the business world which urges people to measure progress by the excessive availability and consumption of goods and the lavish use of energy.

It is appropriate to observe that if we should change our outlook and advance in the direction of ethical responsibility toward earth, we may move quite close to the sort of thinking that was held by the native people of North America. That North America's Indian nations had deep reverence for, and understanding of the life-giving earth is less commonly known than it should be. An interesting example of this attitude may be taken from the words of Ohiyesa, a Santee Dakota physician and author:

> In the life of the Indian there was only one inevitable duty—the duty of prayer—the daily recognition of the Unseen and Eternal. His daily devotions were more necessary to him than daily food. He wakes at daybreak, puts on his moccasins and steps down to the water's edge. Here he throws handfuls of clear, cold water into his face, or plunges in bodily. After the bath, he stands erect before the advancing dawn, facing the sun as it dances upon the horizon, and offers his unspoken orison. His mate may precede or follow him in his devotions, but never accompanies him. Each soul must meet the morning sun, the new sweet earth and the Great Silence alone!
>
> Whenever, in the course of the daily hunt the red hunter comes upon a scene that is strikingly beautiful or sublime—a black thundercloud with the rainbow's glowing arch above the mountain, a white waterfall in the heart of a green gorge; a vast prairie tinged with the blood-red of sunset—he pauses for an instant in the attitude of worship. He sees no need for setting apart one day in seven as a holy day, since to him all days are God's.[2]

Lest we think of the native American's land wisdom as entirely mystical and without practical application, we might consider that the Algonquian Indians, who lived at the mouth of the Ottawa River, practiced game conservation for centuries before the white man appeared. Tribal hunting grounds were divided into family-sized areas in which only a single family might hunt. When species declined, closed seasons were observed and killing of game was kept within the limits of annual increase.[3]

The Indian's sense of brotherhood existing amongst all living things, and his recognition of the vitality of rain, sun, wind, and clouds is an *awareness* that we need to regain. We need to extend our consciousness to other vital components of life not merely to better manage the world but also to make our own lives more complete, to make ourselves know that we are one kind of living thing among many others. While we may have much specialized knowledge, it has been easy to forget our roots. Some idea of this was given by Tatanga Mani (Walking Buffalo) a Stoney Indian who spent his early years in Morley, Alberta. In 1959, when Walking Buffalo was in his eighties, he was asked by the government to make a world tour to represent the Indian people. Addressing an audience in London, England, he pointed out,

> Hills are always more beautiful than stone buildings. Living in a city is an artificial existence. Lots of people hardly ever feel real soil under their feet, see plants grow except in flower pots, or get far enough beyond the street lights to catch the enchantment of a night sky studded with stars. When people live far from scenes of the Great Spirit's making, it's easy for them to forget his laws.[4]

Scoff at the thought though we may, one of the factors that makes it so difficult for people to recognize the environmental crisis we face today is that vast numbers of people, because of how and where they live, have been deprived of any experience of living in close contact with nature. Excursions to the countryside, often under quite artificial conditions, have given many people only the most superficial contact with reality.

Since the Indians stood above the idea of individual land ownership, a vast gap of understanding existed between them and the land-hungry Europeans who came to this continent. From coast to coast, the native peoples' concept was, "The land is our mother." Tribal

117

Excerpts from a Speech Delivered by Chief Seattle in 1854

"The Great Chief in Washington sends word that he wishes to buy our land . . . How can you buy or sell the sky, the warmth of the land? The Idea is strange to us.

"Every part of this earth is sacred to my people. Every shining pine needle, every sandy shore, every mist in the dark woods, every clearing, and humming insect is holy in the memory and experience of my people. The sap which courses through the trees carries the memories of the red man. . . .

"We are part of the earth and it is part of us. The perfumed flowers are our sisters; the deer, the horse, the great eagle, these are our brothers. The rocky crests, the juices in the meadows, the body heat of the pony, and man . . . all belong to the same family. . . .

"If we sell you land, you must remember that it is sacred, and you must teach your children that it is sacred. . . .

"We know that the white man does not understand our ways. One portion of land is the same to him as the next, for he is a stranger who comes in the night and takes from the land whatever he needs. The earth is not his brother, but his enemy, and when he has conquered it, he moves on. . . . His appetite will devour the earth and leave behind only a desert. . . . I do not know. Our ways are different from your ways. The sight of your cities pains the eyes of the red man. But perhaps it is because the red man is a savage and does not understand. . . .

"The white man does not seem to notice the air he breathes. Like a man dying for many days, he is numb to the stench. But if we sell you our land, you must remember that the air is precious to us, that the air shares its spirit with all the life it supports. . . .

"So we will consider your offer to buy our land. If we decide to accept, I will make one condition: The white man must treat the beasts of this land as his brothers . . . . Where is the thicket? Gone. Where is the eagle? Gone. And what is it to say good-bye to the swift pony and the hunt? The end of living and the beginning of survival. . . .

"So we will consider your offer to buy our land. If we agree, it will be to secure the reservation you have promised. There, perhaps we may live out our brief days as we wish. When the last red man has vanished from this earth, and his memory is only the shadow of a cloud moving across the prairie, these shores and forests will still hold the spirits of my people. For they love this earth as the new-born loves its mother's heartbeat. So if we sell you our land, love it as we've loved it. Care for it as we've cared for it. Hold in your mind the memory of the land as it is when you take it. And with all your strength, with all your mind, with all your heart, preserve it for your children, and love it . . . as God loves us all. One thing we know Our God is the same God. This earth is precious to Him. Even the white man cannot be exempt from the common destiny. We may be brothers after all. We shall see."

lands were held in common, used by the living, and passed on to the coming generations. The tyranny of possession was not part of their philosophy and, indeed, the ceremony of Potlatch—the ceremonial giving away, or sometimes destruction of possessions—was a tradition of many tribes. To a certain extent they lived the dictum later expressed by Henry Thoreau that wealth "cannot buy a single necessity of the soul." Tecumseh, a Shawnee chief, expressed the Indian philosophy: "Sell the country? . . . Why not sell the air, the clouds, the great sea?"[5]

One who displayed empathy with what might be learned from nature and would have been unsurprised at the profoundness of native American thought was the German poet-philosopher-naturalist, Johann Wolfgang von Goëthe. It was Goëthe's own conviction that by adhering closely to nature's teachings an individual will come to possess knowledge that is true, even though it may seem modest when compared to the formalized knowledge of technical society. Knowledge gleaned from nature, however incomplete it may seem, is adequate for guidance throughout life. Furthermore, the insights instilled by nature will lead the student to a pure and undiluted comprehension

---

The Wisdom of Chief Seattle

Goëthe's reflections about insights given by nature leading to a comprehension of all meaningful ethical and religious convictions, seem to be borne out in the following observation made by Chief Seattle in a letter to President Franklin Pierce of the United States, in 1855. (Chief Seattle was chief of the Dwanish tribe (Salishan) which occupied Puget Sound region. The present city of Seattle is located on land that he surrendered in the Port Elliott Treaty.) In Chief Seattle's words:

And what is there to life if a man cannot hear a lovely cry of a whippoorwill or the arguments of the frogs around a pond at night? For all things share the same breath—the beasts, the trees, the man. The white man must treat the beasts of the land as his brothers. What is man without the beasts? If all beasts were gone, man would die from a great loneliness of spirit, for whatever happens to the beast also happens to the man. All things are connected. Whatever befalls the earth befalls the sons of the earth.

(Compare also to Ecclesiastes 3:19.)

of all the meaningful ethical and religious convictions that have appeared during the spiritual history of our race. Since Goëthe held that "Truth is Wisdom" he would have found native American insight to be of high quality.

Johann Eckermann, Goëthe's private secretary, confidant, and author of *Conversations With Goëthe,* recorded a remark made by Goëthe during the last years of his life: "Nature is always true, always serious, always severe; it is always right and mistakes and errors are always the work of men. It disdains the incapable, it gives itself up and reveals its secrets only to that person who is honest and pure and capable."

To Goëthe, no creature exists for the sake of another, for "every creature is an end in itself." The design of nature rests simply in each organism fully living its own life. And the essence of the matter, as Goethe states, is his conclusion, "I am firmly convinced that the spirit is an indestructible being."[6]

What he feels is the greatest mistake a person can make lies as the focus of his famous work *Faust.* This mistake is self-alienation of an individual from nature. Discontented with what he could learn of the world, Faust indulges repeatedly in magic, demanding of the world spirit that he could know all there was to know about the world. After each unsatisfactory experience, he returns to a new life in nature, then turns again to magic until at last he craves, at whatever cost, a natural relationship with the natural world. In the end, Faust finds himself content to spend his life reclaiming land from the sea, that it may produce fruit for people. Accepting the challenge of real life as one that must be continually faced, Faust, in his dying speech, reflects:

> Yes, to this thought I hold unswerving,
> To wisdom's final fruit, profoundly true:
> Of freedom and of life he only is deserving
> Who each day must conquer them anew.[7]

Just as Faust made his bargain with Mephistopheles, it is sometimes argued that modern man has made a Faustian bargain for technological knowledge which now turns upon mankind in the form of nearly endless threats to human existence from products of our own devising. Nature has been ignored, subdued, virtually throttled; and human aspiration still seems focused upon an artificial world of human design.

As Goëthe's Faust learned, and as we must yet realize, it is only in reforging our own bonds with nature, and in renewing our individuality and spirituality, that we can escape the rapidly tightening bonds of our own Faustian bargain.

When the first trees were felled at Quebec City and Jamestown in the early years of the seventeenth century, the great specter of change spread its wings over North America. The concept of a land abundant in timber, game, minerals, and wealth in many forms and shapes has been with North American people since that time, and lingers to this day. We have accumulated enough statistics to know better but we treat those statistics as though they were a separate entity without relationship to the world in which we live and move and have our being. Whether we detach the information from our consciousness or not, we know that inestimable amounts of valuable topsoil have already been washed away and timber and mineral resources wasted at a staggering pace. Likewise some species of birds and mammals have already been rendered extinct and others brought close to the threshold of extinction.

The growth of North America was rapid, and the pursuit of wealth in many instances ravaged areas of the country that had not yet even been mapped. At the same time, other perceptive men were taking time to try to comprehend the total meaning of life and the times in which they lived. Walt Whitman (1819-1892) saw the "Seasons pursuing each other, the plougher ploughs, the mower mows, and the winter grain falls in the ground." Looking at the world of nature, he marveled and wrote:

> I believe a blade of grass is no less than the journeywork of the stars,
> And the pismire is equally perfect, and a grain of sand, and the egg of the wren,
> And the tree-toad is a chef-d'oeuvre for the highest,
> And the running blackberry would adorn the parlors of heaven,
> And the narrowest hinge in my hand puts to scorn all machinery,
> And the cow crunching with depress'd head surpasses any statue,
> And a mouse is miracle enough to stagger sextillions of infidels.[8]

Fortunately, Whitman was not alone in keeping alive the tenuous bond that has served to remind us of the awe-inspiring natural world in which we live. Though few in number, other powerful voices have striven to remind us that there is something vitally important that we ignore in our pursuit of wealth and glory.

By the spring of 1845, Henry David Thoreau moved into his cabin at Walden Pond near Concord, Massachusetts, and wrote of the relationship between man and the world in which he lived. He described himself as a self-appointed inspector of snowstorms and rainstorms, of forest paths and across-lot routes. He studied the terrain in which he lived, was abroad at all hours of day and night, befriended the Irish shantymen who worked on the railroads and the Frenchmen who came from Canada and made their living in the woods. He decided that "With respect to luxuries and comforts, the wisest have ever lived a more simple life than the poor." Pondering the relationship of man to his environment, he wrote:

> While almost all men feel an attraction drawing them to society, few are attracted strongly to Nature. In their reaction to Nature, men appear to me for the most part, notwithstanding their arts, lower than the animals. . . . How little appreciation of the beauty of the landscape there is among us! . . . Nature is a personality so vast and universal that we have never seen one of her features.[9]

In keeping with his deep love of the natural landscape, Thoreau suggested in 1858, before Yellowstone became the first U.S. national park, that there be "national preserves, in which the bear and the panther, and some even of the hunter race may still exist, and not be civilized off the face of the earth." It was his thought that wild things should be left for true inspiration and re-creation of the human spirit. He would not hold with the view that wild things should be left for idle sport and he reminded his readers that "the squirrel you kill in jest dies in earnest." It was his conviction that no intelligent person past the

---

"He is richest who is content with the least, for content is the wealth of nature."

Socrates

Squirrels may have a more valuable role in nature than is commonly recognized. They can be very valuable agents of reforestation. Squirrels have been known to collect and store as much as 600 quarts (634 liters) of seed and other foods for winter. By spring they have used only about one-tenth of their hoard. Much of the remainder is available for propagating future forests. In the east, squirrels have been referred to as "uphill planters of oak trees." Since acorns are round and normally roll downhill, squirrels collecting them and hiding them serve to spread the acorns (and the oaks) uphill!

Source: Common Sense, no. 5, 1979, p. 10.

thoughtless age of boyhood would wantonly kill any animal that held its life "by the same thin thread we hold our own."

He anticipated that the time would come when people would need wild places to recreate themselves from the pressures and tensions of life lived far from the healing balm of their ancestral world. This is quite valid today. Increasing population and congestion, and more leisure time have all contributed to make the topic of recreation a paramount concern. Unfortunately, the business aspect of modern recreation has obscured its central value as an escape into reality from the technological world that "is too much with us." The thousands of gadgets developed from the industrialization of recreation raise the perturbing question of whether or not we are entirely losing the path back to simple experiences that might restore our wholeness.

While visionaries have persisted since the time of Whitman and Thoreau, the North American continent did not escape the impact of a growing technology or even the age-old scorched earth policies attendant upon warfare. In the American Civil War, General William T. Sherman's army wreaked vengeance and land destruction upon South Carolina. One of Sherman's officers commented, "On every side . . . our column might be traced by the columns of smoke by day, and the glare of fires by night . . . over a region of 40 miles in width . . . agriculture and commerce cannot be fully revived in our day."[10]

If the history of the development of this continent has been that of ruthless subjugation of a virgin land, the cause is that short-sighted humans have thought principally of short-term gain, with no concern for anything farther away than the immediate future. Stewart L. Udall refs to the outlook of early settlers as a Myth of Superabundance, observing: "According to the myth, our resources were inexhaustible. It was an assumption that made wise management of the land and provident husbandry superfluous."[11]

In 1864, a prodigious book, of which we shall say more later, appeared on the market and rapidly gained worldwide attention. Its author, George Perkins Marsh, has been referred to as the first "land philosopher" in North America. Appearing on the title page of his book were the words of H. Bushnell from his *Sermon on the Power of an Endless Life:* "Not all the winds, and storms, and earthquakes, and seas, and seasons of the world, have done so much to revolutionize the earth as MAN, the power of an endless life, has done since the day he came forth upon it, and received dominion over it."[12]

Our brief look at what has happened to salmon and bison and other resources refreshed our awareness of what impact man has had on nature. Marsh accurately noted how the enormous squandering of resources has been a characteristic of human behavior. He pointed out that wild cattle in South America had been slaughtered by the millions for their hides and horns; that bison were killed for their tongues and skins, and the carcasses left to rot; that elephants, walruses, and narwhals were killed for their tusks; whales for oil and whalebone; and many bird species for their plumage.

Such habits persist today. The Grzimeks, in *Serengeti Shall Not Die,* record poaching activities carried on simply for the benefit of the tourist trade. Zebras, they report, were killed in hundreds so their tails could be cut off and sold as flyswatters; elephants were killed so their feet could be cut off and made into wastebaskets; and other animals were similarly destroyed for some small portion of their body.[13] A current case in point is the practice of killing black bears for their claws and gall bladders, the latter of which are exported to the Orient for medicinal purposes. As Marsh had written in reference to bison and other animals: "In nearly all these cases, the part which constitutes the motive for this wholesale destruction, and is alone saved, is essentially of insignificant value as compared with what is thrown away."[14]

The pace of technology has been furious in North America and if it be considered a race between destruction and preservation, the race is being won by destroyers. In truth, it is less simple because human greed has triggered the rapid pace of events and, thus far, voices of restraint have been an inaudible whisper, lost in the shout for unceasing accumulation of possessions. That man has been an undoer less from deliberate intent than from easily magnified cupidity matters not at all in the precarious condition of toxicity and instability in which the planet now exists.

At the time Marsh was writing, in the early 1860s, realization was also dawning in Quebec and Ontario that the forests could no longer be looked upon as inexhaustible. The most accessible sites had already been logged and each year loggers had to go farther back from the main streams to find available timber.

In 1877, Carl Schurz, steeped in forest practices in Germany, his native land, became Secretary of the Interior in the U.S.A. In spite of charges that he was employing Prussian methods, Schurz fought corruption in the industry and advocated forest reserves to protect the timber base. He pointed out that lumbering activity was already so severe as to destroy the self-renewing capacity of forests.

In the following year, Major John Wesley Powell, American geologist who first explored the Colorado River and Grand Canyon, recognizing the grim reality of agriculture in western arid lands, was proposing that irrigation districts be formed and that the division of lands be based on drainage basins and watersheds, rather than on arbitrary geometrical arrangements suitable for easy survey techniques. Economic considerations were first and foremost in political and commercial minds, however, and little heed was paid to his ideas.

Still, the impact of both Schurz and Powell was significant, although it was not until the decade of the 1890s in the U.S. that legislation was passed to set aside public reserves, timbered or otherwise; and it was in 1893 that drought-decimated livestock herds in the southwest proved Powell's contention that "water is king in the arid west."[15]

In 1872, Canadian Prime Minister John A. Macdonald was moved to write the Ontario premier concerning the passage downstream of log rafts by his home: "The sight of the immense masses of timber passing my window every morning constantly suggests to my mind the absolute necessity there is for looking into the future of this trade. We are recklessly destroying the timber of Canada and there is scarcely a possibility of replacing it."[16]

His concern was echoed in a letter to *Canadian Monthly,* in June, 1872, by a man associated with a Halifax shipping firm, Captain N. W. Beckwith. "We are wasting our forests, habitually, wickedly, insanely, and at a rate which must soon bankrupt us all in that element of wealth . . . Destroying a forest because we want timber is like smothering a hive of bees because we want honey."[17]

Another who noted the decline of Canadian forests was Bernhard Fernow, founder of the first university forestry programs at Cornell University, in Ithaca, New York, and at the University of Toronto, Ontario. Fernow calculated that between 1867 and 1913, Ontario had cut 25 billion board feet of white pine. After traveling across Canada, Fernow concluded that the timber wealth of Canada was exaggerated, that the country, though extensively wooded, had a relatively small total area suitable for commercial harvesting.[18]

In 1907, the word "conservation" was borrowed from the name "conservancies" which had been given to government forests in India. The battle to save something for the future, and to make wise use of resources, finally had a name. In his book, *The Fight for Conservation*, published in 1910, Gifford Pinchot sought to identify the vital role of conservation in national stability: "When the natural resources of any nation become exhausted, disaster and decay in every department of national life follow as a matter of course. Therefore the conservation of natural resources is the basis, and the only permanent basis, of national success."[19]

Speaking of the interests of the public, Pinchot wrote:

> Conservation is the most democratic movement this country has known for a generation. It holds that the people have not only the right, but the duty to control the use of natural resources, which are the great sources of prosperity. And it regards the absorption of these resources by the special interests, unless their operators are under effective public control, as a moral wrong . . . [20]

Here, in Pinchot's thoughts, was a truth so apparently sublime that we are only beginning to approach an understanding of it. It is that there is a definite moral relationship between the environment and humankind. Since the ultimate welfare of the human race depends on the health of the land, man—for the sake of future generations, as well as his own—is morally responsible for wise stewardship in his relationship to earth. Since the idea of stewardship implies *service,* we can readily recognize that devastation of the land for a quick profit is high on the list of immoral acts. To Pinchot this was the most vital problem that confronts the human race.

It is sobering to realize that injuries to the land have been steady and unremitting. Already North America has lost such quantities of fertile soil that it will take centuries of geologic soil-forming processes to repair the damage. In 1910, Pinchot could state,

> We have allowed erosion, that great enemy of agriculture, to impoverish, and over thousands of square miles, to destroy our farms. The Mississippi alone carries yearly to the sea more than 400,000,000 tons (364,000,000 tonnes) of the richest soil within its drainage basin. Our streams ... are less navigable than they were fifty years ago, and the soil lost by erosion from the farms and the deforested mountainsides, is the chief reason.[21]

In spite of Pinchot's call to attention regarding soil erosion, the problem has been with us right up to the present. In 1942, Professor A. F. Coventry's study of Ontario's Humber River in flood revealed that 2,400 tons (2,180 tonnes) of sediment were being carried downstream each hour. When Coventry addressed the Toronto Field Naturalists' Club, he warned them soberly, "We have for a long time been breaking the little laws, and the big laws are beginning to catch up with us." More recently, *Soil at Risk* (1984) warned that the erosion problem in southwestern Ontario had caused corn yields to be reduced by 30 percent to 40 percent.

In 1908, U.S. President Theodore Roosevelt, in his annual message to Congress, stated:

> The lesson of deforestation in China is a lesson which mankind should have learned many times already from what has occurred in other places. Denudation leaves naked soil, then gullying cuts down to bare rock; and meanwhile the rock waste buries the bottom lands. When the soil is gone, men must go, and the process does not take long.[22]

In 1913, Roosevelt returned to thoughts of man's disregard of the earth in his review of a book written by W. T. Hornaday. His optimism was understandable even though, as Aldo Leopold later suggested, conservation continues to be "letterhead piety" and pre-election oratory. Roosevelt's hopeful comment was: "Here in the United States we turn our rivers and streams into sewers and dumping grounds, we pollute the air, we destroy forests, and exterminate fishes, birds, and mammals—not to speak of vulgarizing charming landscapes with hideous advertisements. But at last it looks as if our people are awakening. Many leading men, Americans and Canadians, are doing all they can for the Conservation Movement."[23]

An eloquent statement concerning the earth and human relationship toward it, was made by Liberty Hyde Bailey, upon his retirement as Dean of the New York State College of Agriculture at Cornell University, Ithaca, New York. A prolific writer, Bailey chaired the President's Country Life Commission established by Theodore Roosevelt, the findings of the commission leading to substantial improvement in the lives of country people. Born in 1858 and raised among pioneers and Indians, Bailey expressed the conviction in all his writings that the majestic earth is a Divine Creation.

In *The Holy Earth,* (recently reprinted by Cornell University), he expressed a fundamental conclusion of life that the earth is hallowed and "We must deal with it devotedly and with care that we do not despoil it." He claimed that the focus of our lives, which is in trade, should instead be in morals. "This will be very personal morals, but it will also be national and racial morals. More iniquity follows the improper and greedy division of the resources and privileges of the earth than any other form of sinfulness."[24]

Contrary to what some might expect from a deeply religious viewpoint, Bailey stated flatly that, "We are parts in a living, sensitive creation. . . . The living creation is not man-centered: it is biocentric. . . . We can claim no gross superiority and no isolated self importance. The creation and not man is the norm."[25]

In many ways, *The Holy Earth* offers the silent suggestion that a theology embracing the earth and humanity is a necessity. Offering the view that a good farmer is a religious man, Bailey states that the conquest of man of himself is of more value than the taking of a city and also "the final conquest of society is itself." He also argues the moral wisdom of plain and simple food and drink, of frugality and control of pleasures. Self-indulgence he equates with weakness. He suggests that it is folly to detach our insights from the earth and its rhythms and to live mechanically and irreverently "from the box and the bottle and the tin can."[26]

Written simply and with conviction, *The Holy Earth* stirs consciousness and meditation in such a manner that it could be stimulating text and discussion material in many North American classrooms.

A rising tide of consciousness about ill health of the land followed the stock-market crash of 1929 and the subsequent slowdown of the economic machine. In effect, much of the salvation of the people was worked out on the land, and had it not been for the unfortunate onset of World War II, a very serious program of reforestation and other conservation measures might well have resulted in an enduring attitude of beneficence toward renewal of the badly scarred continent of North America.

In the United States, the president was Franklin Roosevelt, an avowed conservationist. Early in his career, Roosevelt objected to the policy of allowing business interests to go into wooded areas and cut the trees "root and branch for the benefit of their own pocket." He contended it a "destroyer of liberty" to let land lie uncared for and in a condition of waste.[27] In groping for a way to solve employment problems, the U.S. formed a Civilian Conservation Corps. By 1935, a half-million young men were living under semimilitary conditions in CCC camps. Corpsmen planted more than two billion trees on logged-over land, built small dams for erosion control, thinned four million acres of trees, built trails, stocked millions of fish, and built more than 30,000 wildlife shelters. Of all the forest planting done in the history of the United States to the mid-1960s, the CCC did more than half. Yet, in reality, this was but a small amount of the work that needed to be done, and when more prosperous times returned, the work was dropped.

"I find television very educating. Every time somebody turns on the set I go into the other room and read a book."

Groucho Marx

Here and there a lonely voice or two counseled that a new relationship was necessary between men and their machines. The English writer, Havelock Ellis, seeing people everywhere succumbing to the dictates of technology, reflected that "the greatest task before civilization at present is to make machines what they ought to be, the slaves instead of the masters of men."[28]

By the mid 1940s, an expanding technology produced machines such as the bulldozer, which greatly increased man's ability to alter the landscape. Land clearing became easier, and removal of trees on hillsides increased runoff, sometimes causing lowland flooding. Growing scientific knowledge also led to greater understanding of consequences. Two alternatives were thus presented to our attention: the knowledge of how we might best conserve, and the technical ability to undo the organization of nature with great rapidity and devastating thoroughness. Judging by the environmental crises that keep popping up in spite of pretensions that they do not exist, the ability to disorganize far exceeds the ability to repair, maintain, or improve.

Experience often shows, for instance, that long-standing agricultural practices should be abandoned in favor of more conservative methods. An example can be found in Ralph Bird's *Ecology of the Aspen Parkland of Western Canada*. Bird points out that the practices of burning straw and stubble and of summerfallowing, damage the soil.

> A direct effect of intensified agriculture has been a marked increase in wind and water erosion. Plant fiber and soil structure have been broken down. . . . Many farmers still have the destructive habit of burning off the straw and stubble with little thought to the future condition of the soil. It is a general practice to summer-fallow every third year. . . . This destroys all trash cover and so pulverizes the soil that it is easily eroded. . . . It is estimated that soils that have been under cultivation for 22 years have lost a large percentage of organic matter, 20 percent for prairie soils and 30 percent for gray wooded soil.[29]

Before erosion became a monumental problem of international concern, stubble burning and summerfallowing were seen as the best ways to control weeds and conserve moisture. In recent years they have been proven to be more detrimental than beneficial in all but a few areas of the Prairies. However as the Canadian report *Soil at Risk* points out, bad habits are hard to change: "The long-hallowed and treasured practice of summerfallowing in a monocultural cropping system is perhaps the most singular mismanagement practice that has been in vogue since this country opened up."[30]

If the years since World War II have shown a rapid growth of technology and a somewhat slower growth of the realization of the severity of environmental problems, events now in the making are rapidly creating a new focus on the environment. Detectable climate change is now raising the specter of reduced agricultural yields and possible widespread famine. The quest for luxury conveniences may pale quite rapidly in a situation where life's most basic needs, food and drink, can no longer be taken for granted. The weight of consumer advertising has tried to convince people for years that the ownership of new things is sufficient reason for being. However, knowledge has been building, and is now being repeatedly expressed, that each exorbitant demand contributes to declining environmental quality. We are beginning to realize that the Madison Avenue approach to life has been a fantasy that we can no longer afford to entertain.

Fortunately, some scientists have been taking note of what has been happening and have been passing on information to a public that is starting to show signs of increased concern. That we may have been ill-served by a technology intent on selling us its latest achievements is unfortunate but it is what we have desired. At least now we have factual data to consider and can see that the direction we must take is that of reducing our own impact on a planet overburdened with toxic wastes.

Barry Commoner has pointed out the tremendous increase of toxic substances in our atmosphere, our land and seas. In *The Closing Circle,* he states that smog-forming nitrogen oxides from automobiles have increased 630 percent since 1946; tetraethyl lead from gasoline, 415 percent; mercury from chloralkali plants, 2,100 percent (much of the rise in mercury having to do with the rise in production of plastics); inorganic nitrogen fertilizer, 789 percent; and nonreturnable beer bottles, 595 percent.[31] All of these are substances that either have to be detoxified in the environment or remain as permanent pollutants in air, water, and soil. Mercury, for instance, can wind up entering lakes, where action by bacteria can form methyl mercury—which leads to poisoning of fish and eventually people. As the Science Council of Canada points out, "Fish in the James Bay region contain higher levels of mercury than fish anywhere else in the world."[32]

The problem of high nitrate levels in water has been related to the heavy use of nitrogen fertilizers, particularly to the excessive use that is sometimes involved to make a crop profitable rather than merely marginal in return. As a result of runoff from farmland, nitrate in domestic water supplies can reach levels that are particularly dangerous to infants. Certain intestinal bacteria, more active in infants than in adults, can convert nitrate to nitrite, which combines with hemoglobin in blood to interfere with the ability of the blood to carry oxygen. An infant affected by resulting methemoglobinemia will turn blue and may die from oxygen deficiency. Dr. Barry Commoner identifies methemoglobinemia as a worldwide problem.[33]

Actually, we have so many well-defined problems that it is amazing so few environmentally effective actions have yet been taken. It is possible that technological innovations have appeared so rapidly their consequences could not be determined. Evidence indicates, though, that the consequences of such innovations often are understood well before any attempt is made to remedy them. The knowledge of the link between chlorinated fluorocarbons, (CFCs), and destruction of the ozone layer is but a single case in point. The discovery by researchers Mario Mollina and F. S. Rowland that CFCs could easily be broken down by ultraviolet radiation in the high stratosphere took place in 1974. Following the disclosure of these long-lasting effects, prominent scientists at Harvard University, at the University of Michigan, at Lawrence Livermore Laboratory, and other groups at other institutions calculated the effects of increases of chlorine on ozone. Stephen Schneider quotes F. S. Rowland upon realizing the CFC-ozone interaction: "There was no moment of 'Eureka!' really. I just came home one night and told my wife, 'the work is going very well, but it looks like the end of the world.' "[34] Study of the matter indicates that once again, economic considerations outweighed common sense.

Combined with the double-edged sword of population growth and hasty technology, there has been an increasing demand for an ever-higher standard of living. It appears that the finite nature of resources and the limited carrying capacity of Spaceship Earth have been recognized but not accepted as truth. It has even been suggested that although humanity has the knowledge to solve its problems, it has confined its efforts to the acquisition of facts and techniques, but steadfastly refrained from developing sufficient wisdom to put this knowledge into proper perspective. One can ask, for example, if the knowledge involved in building thermonuclear weapons capable of destroying all life on earth, should ever have been put to use, because even the most rudimentary use of wisdom would dictate against the use of weapons that might render vast areas of the planet, or the entire planet, uninhabitable. Clearly there are basic problems that must be faced: curbing our numbers, curbing our wants, and developing a truly civilized attitude toward the earth and other people. We only compound these problems by our hostility toward one another and by the devotion we display for lethal engines of war. There is more to being civilized than proper table manners and standards of dress.

By now, it should be obvious that we have a staggering environmental crisis. We have heard of it formally from the UN Conference on the Human Environment, in 1972, and again in 1987 in the readily available report, *Our Common Future,* the result of a multinational study conducted by the World Commission on Environment and Development. We have heard specific aspects of the problem from concerned scientists. We have been warned by philosophers that we are desperately in need of renewal.

Only by ceasing to be mechanical puppets of an economic machine devoted to acquisition can we find a path toward regeneration that will enable us to save our species and our planet. That the ruling class must exert self-denial sufficient to permit the renewal of society is essential. The World Commission on Environment and Development has stressed the need to reorient attitudes and emphasis. It also has rejected the idea of "quick-fix" solutions and pointed out the fact that little time remains to correct the problems we have created.[35]

Lecturing at Westminster College in Fulton, Missouri, in November, 1968, C. P. Snow informed his audience, "One hears young people asking for a cause. . . . Peace! Food! No more people than the earth can take. That is the cause."

To that we can add respect for all living things, wise and restrained use of natural resources, and a realization of duty to restore the planet continuously, even as we are utilizing its resources.

Philosopher Lewis Mumford nicely summed up the nature of the changes which are needed, in a conversation with author Anne Chisholm:

> Most of the really important, really decisive changes will have to be human changes, not technological changes. We have to change our habits of life. . . . These are fundamentally moral changes.[36]

The Greatest Show on Earth

Down on the lake, there is a rock point that slopes gently into deep water. Among its stony convolutions may be found a comfortable seat, carved by erosion. It has a mossy cushion and a—needless to say—firm backrest. The view from the seat faces west, making it an excellent place from which to study sunsets.

My son Nelson and I sat in the armchair provided by nature and watched a small blue stretch of sky, in which floated five golden clouds. The sun had already set behind the mountains, and a thin, golden line etched itself along the mountaintops—but only to the extent that was allowed by the blue patch of sky as, to either side of the clear air, there were ominous thunderclouds massing above the hills.

Before retiring to our 'chair' to watch the building storm, we had taken a swim off the point. The late afternoon sun had been pleasantly warm, so that we emerged from cool water into an atmosphere of warmth that seemed "just right" for basking and drying off. We had eaten supper there on the rocks as the sky clouded rapidly and thunderheads began to tower above the mountains. After visiting some huckleberry bushes down the shore, we rested to watch the storm approach.

For a while we sat quietly. I had suggested to Nelson that we remain silent and use our senses as acutely as possible. We "heard" profound silence, broken at times by the momentary excited chatter of some geese across the lake. The rhythm of the incoming wavelets rippling and gurgling over a few miniature promontories below where we were sitting seemed only to enhance the silence. For a few moments there was the tinkling, whispering sound of kinglets working in the trees. We noticed a brief, raucous chatter of a pair of pileated woodpeckers, and were aware when a light breeze began to rustle steadily in the conifers behind us. Once, by gestures, Nelson called my attention to an intricate spider's web strung between two clumps of bushes, and we left our seat to study it, crawling beneath some of the strands to view it better at its points of attachment to the shrubs.

When the first flickers of lightning came, we noted the number of seconds before the rumble of thunder became audible. Since sound travels about 1,100 feet a second, it takes about five seconds for it to travel a mile; and by counting elapsed time between flashes and thunder, we were able to determine how many miles the storm was, from where we sat. When the flashes and thunder were just a few seconds apart, we moved from our exposed location to a more sheltered and safer spot.

A stronger wind arrived, seemingly out of a magician's hat, and in short moments, larger waves were rolling on the lake. A small flock of crows beat by overhead, retreating to some sanctuary where wind and rain would not be a discomfort. The golden clouds had long ago turned sullen pink and then been obliterated in a sweeping mass of dark, turbulent clouds.

Although it was not normal time for darkness, grayish nightfall descended, and we headed home, pausing for a moment at the irresistible summons of a red huckleberry bush, holding its somewhat sour berries dimly, but tantalizingly, in our path.

We got just a little wet on the way home. If one uses the expression "it was raining cats and dogs" to signify a heavy rain, then this time it rained "walruses and elephants." We did find shelter in the heaviest downpour, under the shake roof of an old settler's shed. Finally, though, we decided we might as well walk on—which we did—and the only thing we didn't have to "wring out" when we got home, was ourselves.

But, somehow, it was worth it. The complex pleasures of modern life are undoubtedly delightful, but the Greatest Show on Earth is still put on by the elemental forces of the Universe. I, for one, dearly enjoy being a spectator and participant under the Big Top of the Master Showman.

*It is a welcome symptom in an age which is
commonly denounced as materialistic, that it
makes heroes of men whose goals lie wholly in
the intellectual and moral sphere. This proves
that knowledge and justice are ranked above
wealth and power by a large section of the
human race . . .*

Albert Einstein

Pathfinders of the Future

The useful idea derived from the Chinese language, that *crisis* involves both *danger* and *opportunity* is pertinent in considering the full-blown environmental crisis that now confronts us. The concept that we must strive for a sustainable society is a good one. But it is optimistic to think that we can attain sustainability as long as we cling to values that are essentially materialistic. Economic aspirations that persist in fragmenting the planet's life-support systems put all life in jeopardy.

One of the most difficult changes we must make is in our fundamental outlook on life. Nothing less will suffice. It will demand our highest level of attainment if we are to modify the strange combination of belligerence toward the planet and avidity in possessions that now seems a hallmark of our species. The long-suppressed spiritual aspect of human nature must necessarily be welcomed by the leaders of society if we are to turn the corner and begin mending the health of the planet and of its occupants.

Paul and Anne Ehrlich approached the core of our problems in saying, "It must be one of the greatest ironies of the history of *Homo sapiens* that the only salvation for the practical men now lies in what they think of as the dreams of idealists. The question now is: can the 'realists' be persuaded to face reality in time."[1]

The conclusions of Henry David Thoreau, George Perkins Marsh, and Dr. Albert Schweitzer bear more than a cursory examination once it is accepted that the "dreams of idealists" may indeed have some bearing on life today. That our "practical age" is entrenched in its own form of single vision is rarely considered plausible. Yet it is bringing the planet to ruin. As exponents of a more harmonious, less rigidly anthropocentric view of the natural world, the three individuals mentioned above offer a composite vision that could serve as a starting point for a new worldview and provide a true basis for sustainability. Certainly the relentlessness of our present pursuit of material acquisition might suffer a setback. On the other hand, aspects of the human personality that have been subdued to the point of endless neuroses might be given the opportunity to expand into a full flowering of human potential.

With this in mind, it is worth examining some of the penetrating thoughts these men have offered.

Henry David Thoreau

"He died as he had lived, with complete faith in the wisdom of nature."[2] So wrote Brooks Atkinson about the death of Henry David Thoreau, on May 6, 1862. Thoreau's own sister commented that he was the most upright man she had ever known.

A quite remarkable story is told about Thoreau's last days. As the tale goes, a minister was accosted downtown in Concord, Massachusetts, and was asked if he knew that Henry was dying. The minister responded by calling on Thoreau, who was lying in bed looking through the window at an apple orchard in bloom. "Henry," he said, "I've come to see if you have made your peace with God." Thoreau turned toward the window for a moment, gazing at the landscape before replying, "God and I have never quarreled."

Thoreau was the genius of Concord and his doctrine of unyielding individuality speaks to us today as it has never spoken before. In an age when technological complexity has rendered life bewildering and at a time when government everywhere trespasses on human freedom, it is eye-opening to ponder Thoreau's thoughts. He was so intent on what was right that he sometimes showed an almost ruthless disdain for what was accepted as fact. Yet, as he pointed out, "A grain of gold will gild a great surface but not so much as a grain of wisdom." The grain of wisdom will often tell us that what is accepted as fact may not necessarily be fact, or may be fact only if viewed in the short term. Decades of acceptance of half-truths have enabled innovations to be rendered "acceptable" even if they are threats to health, peace, environment, or the stability of society—as long as they are not uneconomic. We have thus simplified the matter of good and bad. That which is economic (makes a profit) is good; that which is uneconomic (fails to make a profit) is bad.

The essential point of Thoreau's writing is that we should never mistake the means for the end. We should never assume that commerce, professions, agriculture, or any way of making a living, is the meaning of life itself. He felt that the greatest blunder we might make would be to spend the greater part of our life earning our wherewithal, leaving no time for the more essential pursuit of developing qualities of character. When he read Howitt's account of the Australian gold-diggings, he reflected that we should all sink a shaft within ourselves and mine the essential gold of our own inner beings.

Few people would argue the point that we are caught up in superficiality. As Thoreau expressed it:

> Our life is frittered away by detail. . . . Simplicity, simplicity, simplicity! I say, let your affairs be as two or three, and not as a hundred or a thousand; instead of a million count half a dozen,

"It is essential that the student acquire an understanding of and a lively feeling for values. He must acquire a vivid sense of the beautiful and the morally good. Otherwise he, with his specialized knowledge, more closely resembles a well-trained dog than a harmoniously developed person."

Albert Einstein

and keep your accounts on your thumbnail. . . . Most of the luxuries, and many of the so-called comforts of life are not only not indispensable, but positive hindrances to the elevation of mankind.[3]

Although Thoreau is sometimes considered a radical, it must be recognized that he was radical principally in the sense that he believed in adherence to the highest laws of the universe. He voluntarily seceded from the State of Massachusetts because that state supported slavery, a condition to which he was vehemently opposed. He believed it was possible for a man to be beyond the laws of his own country if the principles to which he adhered were of a higher order. Thoreau felt the soil a person needed to till was that of his own innermost nature. The household to be put in order was that of his own thoughts and motives. Once order had been brought to his own being, he would not be apt to find himself opposed to a just government "if he should chance to meet with such."

His doctrine was the doctrine of the individual. His was a "do your own thing" philosophy insofar as that thing was the most elevated expression of which an individual's nature was possible. To Thoreau it was not an adequate form of citizenship to vote in occasional elections or put all one's eggs in the basket of a popular political party. As he saw it, true civic responsibility depended on daily behavior and on constant attention and involvement in the affairs of society. Conscience was not a garment to be changed for different occasions but a spiritual suit of mail that was a perpetual shield for personal integrity.

It was his own characteristic of standing foursquare with the world that offers much interesting insight for us today. He recognized the "inexhaustible vigor" of nature as the elemental force of the world. He saw mankind, preoccupied with its pursuits, all unaware of the vital world of which it was a part. As a surveyor, he noted a miser looking for a posthole in the midst of "Paradise," all unaware of the angels coming to and fro.

Some of his observations are particularly well worth considering in light of our current way of life.

It is doubtful that Thoreau could have been interested in a round-the-world cruise, or a vacation in the Bahamas. "It is not worth the while to go round the world to count the cats in Zanzibar." He estimated that it was all a person could do to see and understand the countryside within a ten-mile radius of where he lived. Yet he was able to claim that he had traveled all over the world around Concord. The difference is that of seeing superficially or seeing in depth. He noted that men had built railroads and could now travel thirty miles an hour but he doubted that they would get to heaven any sooner. "I would rather sit on a pumpkin and have it all to myself than be crowded on a velvet cushion. I would rather ride on earth in an ox cart, with a free circulation, than go to heaven in the fancy car of an excursion train and breathe a malaria all the way."[4]

He observed that men had become machines, "tools of their tools," and that by working at the pace demanded by machinery, they could no longer sustain their true individuality, or their concern and compassion for one another. Life for many consisted of succumbing blindly to the market-call for production. Most men dutifully followed a bandwagon, and just assumed that somebody knew where it was going.

Modern materialism would be as insufferable to Thoreau as was the burden of the farmer he envisioned dragging his house, barn, and sixty-acre woodlot down through life.

Thoreau understood that an individual could not arrive at a judicious comprehension of life as long as material cravings were his dominant concern. When he recommended voluntary poverty as the best vantage ground from which to observe life, he was being extreme only in the necessary sense that such a statement might cause a society dedicated to materialism to recognize the monolith it pursued. Thoreau saw clearly the paradox of fine feathers and doubted that they made fine birds. People laughed at old styles of dress and devotedly followed new ones. He quipped that the head monkey in Paris had only to wear a purple shawl and all those who followed styles in North America would don one as well. He emphasized his point by advising

"Agur said, 'Give me neither poverty nor riches, and this will ever be the prayer of the wise. Our incomes should be like our shoes: if too small, they will gall and pinch us, but if too large they will cause us to stumble and to trip. But wealth, after all, is a relative thing, since he that has little, and wants less, is richer than he that has much, but wants more. True contentment depends not upon what we have; a tub was large enough for Diogenes, but a world was too little for Alexander.'"
Caleb C. Colton, 1780-1832

people that it was more important to renew themselves than to become mere wearers of new clothes. "Every generation," he claimed, "laughs at the old fashions, but follows religiously the new."

Graphically he drew an analogy to illustrate the manner in which we burden ourselves with objects. "I had three pieces of limestone on my desk, but I was terrified to find that they required to be dusted daily, when the furniture of my mind was all undusted still, and I threw them out the window in disgust."[5]

At the core of Thoreau's life was his own relationship to nature. At a time when men were busy, as they are now, conquering nature, his own comprehension was much more subtle. He understood then, what we are still groping to understand, that man is but an inhabitant on earth, part and parcel of nature. He realized that there are hordes of champions of civilization and too few champions of the natural world. Seeing New England's forests falling before ax and saw, he was moved to comment that men would cut down the clouds if they could.

He puzzled over a society which considered a man as a loafer if he walked in the woods for love of them, while it looked favorably upon a speculator who entered the same woods only to assess their commercial value. He lamented that towns had no interest in their native woodlands other than to see them as a source of revenue. It is remarkable that there has been little change in viewpoint to this day, even though we now know that the overcutting of forests everywhere is a major contributing factor to world climate change.

Deep insight warned Thoreau that the vitality of nature is the source of our own physical, mental, and spiritual well-being. That which is yet unsubdued is the most alive and the greatest source of inspiration. Human roots are in the wild and untamed, and a creature shorn from its roots will eventually wither and die. "In Wildness is the preservation of the world," he stoutly maintained.[6]

Everywhere today we see organizations striving to create wilderness areas for the aesthetic and spiritual satisfaction of mankind. At the same time, extractive industries fight tooth and nail against the creation of such areas. On their side, they cite economics and employment. It is as though we have advanced in a single direction wherein we can only measure with economic yardsticks ruled off in dollars and cents. Nowhere yet has there been created a measure of spiritual or aesthetic income which will offset our passion for deforming the landscape for immediate gain.

To Thoreau the future was clear. "Hope and the future for me are not in lawns and cultivated fields, not in towns and cities, but in the impervious and quaking swamps." He saw in them the strength and marrow of nature and sensed them as the strong meats on which human health would feed.

A town is saved, not more by the righteous men in it than by the woods and swamp that surround it. A township where one primitive forest waves above while another primitive forest rots below—such a town is fitted to raise not only corn and potatoes, but poets and philosophers for the coming ages.[7]

Thoreau would probably agree that people rarely live their lives fully. Pushed by circumstance, addled by every mosquito wing that drifts across our paths, we wander willy-nilly through this great gift of life. His thunderous comment on life was, "Pause! Avast! Why so seeming fast and deadly slow?"[8]

His own reason for living in relative isolation at Walden pond for two years was that he wished to live deliberately, to "confront only the essential facts of life," and not come to the end of life realizing he had not lived at all.

The problem of his own time is still the problem of today. He contended that we are more concerned with the quality of the foundations upon which we build our houses than we are with the quality of the ideas upon which we build our lives. Content that we have granite as the underpinning of our homes, we permit the sills of our personal lives to be built on insubstantial ideas. What is the value of a man, he lamented, whose basic tenets do not convince us that they rest upon the bedrock of truth?

As a writer and a thinker, Thoreau wounds. When we read his convictions we find that he is not toying with the superficial areas of our intelligence, but is jabbing with rapier thrusts at the fetters which bind our individuality. He is saying, look here, I will not let you be complacent. You must face yourself where you have been ignoring yourself for a lifetime. When he lambastes what we think of as democratic society, we may mumble platitudes about standards of living, greatest good for the greatest numbers, just societies, and bask in our technological bliss; but we know that he is striking at the indifference that is the root of our daily lives.

Thoreau's pondering convinced him that life is a startlingly moral experience in which one must continually choose between being part of the problem or part of the answer. That he saw life as clearly black or white, and never for an instant gray, is evidenced in his own conclusion that there is not even momentarily a truce between vice and virtue. He expressed the view that in terms of universal law, "Goodness is the only investment that never fails."

As spartan in his intellectual discipline as he was in his personal habits, Thoreau would have looked askance at the steady media onslaught that deafens thought today. He viewed ordinary social functions as situations in which exterior surfaces of people met with one another and little depth of thought was shared. It was his belief that the mind can be "permanently profaned" by continual attendance on trivial things, but he also held that inspiration from the "courts of heaven" could come to the attentive mind that held itself in readiness.

In spite of his conviction that the majority of people lead lives of quiet desperation, uncommitted to anything meaningful, Thoreau still felt that each individual had a seed of inspiration within himself. That, he would say, is the star we should follow.

> If one advances confidently in the direction of his dreams, and endeavors to live the life which he has imagined, he will meet with a success unexpected in common hours. . . . If you have built castles in the air, your work need not be lost; that is where they should be. Now put the foundations under them.[9]

Thoreau did not live out his forty-fifth year, and his penetrating thoughts received few accolades during his own life. However, the fame and respect he earned as a man of principle has since become worldwide and his views on conservation been recognized as exceptionally far-sighted. One of his essays, originally entitled, "Resistance to Civil Government" (1849) and later retitled "Civil Disobedience," has been ranked with the major statements of Tolstoy and Ghandi on the value of passive resistance in opposition to violent authoritarianism.

Ralph Waldo Emerson concluded the address given at Thoreau's funeral service by reflecting: "The scale on which his studies proceeded was so large as to require longevity, and we were the less prepared for his sudden disappearance. The country knows not yet, or in the least part, how great a son it has lost. . . . His soul was made for the noblest society; he had in a short life exhausted the capabilities of this world; wherever there is knowledge, wherever there is virtue, wherever there is beauty, he will find a home."[10]

Thoreau himself had expressed his own belief in the eternity of nature in the concluding lines of *Walden.* "The light which puts out our eyes is darkness to us. Only that day dawns to which we are awake. There is more day to dawn. The sun is but a morning star."[11]

George Perkins Marsh

Whatever the means of accounting, George Perkins Marsh was an unusual and remarkable person. Born in Woodstock, Vermont, in 1802, his diversified career at law, scholarship, and diplomacy led him to many of the impoverished nations of the world. He noticed that in those countries, stupendous resource degradation had already enslaved whole populations to denuded landscapes where subsistence had become the grim reality of life. Seeing what had happened to other nations of the world, he attempted to prevent a repeat of these abuses in the new world. Marsh was a visionary, a man whose principal writing has been referred to as *the beginning of land wisdom* in North America.

Before he died in 1882, Marsh turned out a resource masterpiece entitled *Man and Nature—or Physical Geography as Modified by Human Action.* The book was an immediate success in both Europe and America. Since its first appearance in 1864, it has been consistently recognized as a landmark work, the importance of which has already begun to permeate human thought. Unfortunately, its acceptance in theory has not yet resulted in its acceptance in practice. Much of the reason for this is that business interests which are tied to short-term goals have dominated society since the industrial revolution began.

"At present, there can be little doubt that the whole of mankind is in mortal danger, not because we are short of scientific and technological know-how, but because we tend to use it destructively, without wisdom. More education can help us only if it produces more wisdom."
E. F. Schumacher
Small is Beautiful, p. 82.

Marsh's own experience with the Vermont Central Railroad Company and in later service as state railroad commissioner had caused him to comment about the practices of corporations in their unending search for wealth, "Joint stock companies have no souls; their managers, in general, no conscience."

His travels in Europe, Africa, and America convinced him that, "Even now, we are breaking up the floor and wainscoting and doors and window frames of our dwelling, for fuel to seethe our pottage."[12] Everywhere he saw humans undermining the foundations of a balanced natural world and teetering its new imbalance to their own greater peril. Deforestation and overgrazing he comprehended as enormous evils leading to both the devastation of the landscape and the decline of civilization in nations where these conditions prevailed. He foresaw accurately that continuous ravaging of the earth for profit would reduce its fertility through destruction of the harmonious relationship of its parts. He warned that climatic change could be produced by seemingly minor events. As a single example, he explained that due to the demand for charcoal, there was widespread destruction of the forests around Piazzatorre, Italy. This was followed by increased severity of climate which prevented maize from ripening. Dismay at this fact resulted in formation of an association to restore the forests. Following their renewal, maize once again flourished on the farms at Piazzatorre. This convinced him that, within limits, man might restore his undoing of nature.

So succinctly did he record his observations, his research and conclusions, that it is no wonder Lewis Mumford, the popular philosopher and writer, recognized *Man and Nature* as the "fountainhead of the conservation movement." It remains unfortunate that technological schools and universities rarely, if ever, include such classical observations in the training of foresters, agriculturists, and technical support people who work in these areas.

Marsh's observations of land degradation in southern Europe convinced him that men, by altering nature without forethought, unleashed consequences beyond expectation upon themselves. He recorded the history of floods which had threatened the total destruction of upper Provence in France and commented on the floods of the Po in Italy which annually, by deposition, carried the coastline into the Adriatic by more than 200 feet (60 meters) in one year. He described how removal of the woods permitted heavy rains to lubricate subsoil clay and cause avalanches such as the one that destroyed Goldau,

Switzerland, and 450 of its people in 1806. Through his studies, he reminded his readers that " . . . she (Nature) has left it within the power of man irreparably to derange the combinations of inorganic matter and of organic life, which through the night of eons she has been proportioning and balancing."

Marsh admitted the necessity of alterations to lands newly subjected to human settlement. He recognized that the processes of nature had been exceedingly slow and that a balance existed between the proportions of land and water, the climate, and the distribution of vegetable and animal life. Human development, he knew, would cause alterations to the amount of land left in forest cover and to other aspects of the natural arrangement.

The attitude he developed toward change stemmed from his own conviction that in nature's vocabulary there are no effects that are mere trifles. Arrangements we may think of as small or insignificant are still parts of the whole fabric of nature, and intervention in seemingly insignificant ways can produce large effects. He felt that Nature's laws "are as inflexible in dealing with an atom as with a continent or planet." He noted, for example, that the leaves and small branches of trees supplied the greatest amount of ashes upon combustion—four times as much ash from a cubic foot (.028 cubic meters) of leaves, and

The annual leaf fall of forests exercises a considerable effect upon the temperature of the earth and upon the atmosphere. If you study the surface of the earth in a natural woodland there will be a deposit of undecayed leaves, twigs and small branches loosely heaped upon the earth, then more compact masses of the same as you dig deeper, and progressively decaying layers at yet deeper levels. Black mould with hardly detectable traces of organic material will be observed beneath clearly discernible organic deposits. Beneath this will appear mineral soil with an admixture of organic flecks. The ability to absorb, radiate and conduct heat is greatly affected by the organic surface layers. Organic material is an effective retainer of soil heat; and ground in protected woodland, even when not protected by a blanket of snow, will not freeze as deeply as will the soil in an open field. The clearing of dead matter from the forest floor will render it, within a short period of years, to an artificial character.

twigs as from a cubic foot of stem wood—and that twigs and ash thus supplied a great amount of nutrition for seedlings. He understood that the mosses, leaves, and twigs acted not only as a substitute for manure but, by keeping the ground soft and friable, as a substitute for plowing. He also realized that the carbonic acid given off by rotting leaves was taken up by water and aided in decomposing the mineral matter of the soil and underlying rock, thus releasing more nutrient for plant growth. He stated without hesitation that the leaves and twigs "belonged" to the soil and without their active role the trees would languish.

From extensive study and observation, Marsh advocated that man-made alterations to natural landscape should be undertaken with caution and respect. Wherever possible, he felt, it is wiser to fit human activities into natural landscapes than to produce great changes that would be beyond human power to rectify or restore in the future.

Justifying his view that man should proceed with caution, Marsh gave many examples of the reckless destruction of forests and of unforeseen consequences which resulted from this hasty action. Calling attention to the manner in which the fibrous roots of forest trees bound soil to the rocky slopes of mountains and at the same time regulated the flow of springs and mountain streams, he reminded readers that the same controlled flow of water was necessary for the refreshment of cattle and the fertility of fields. He referred to the forests as the natural protection of the soil and suggested that many of the problems we created for ourselves would be nonexistent if here and there a belt of woodland were left to spontaneously propagate itself. In other areas, hasty actions on the part of farmers had torn the thin soil of vast plains, without providing protection from wind, and thereby established conditions for soil-blowing. As well, destruction of the semiaquatic plants along coasts had allowed sand dunes to spread inland and threaten cultivated land. He also thought it unwise that protection had not been afforded birds which prey upon insects which were destructive to agricultural harvests.[13]

That his warning has not been heeded is obvious. We have developed complex, powerful machinery which we unleash against the earth without sufficient study. Drainage patterns that took millennia to form have been wiped out for the ostensible purposes of power generation and flood control. It has been more "economically desirable" to encourage lavish use of energy than to strive for energy conservation that would protect the vital land base. Paradoxically, the headwaters of flood-control dams are often deforested with the result that snowmelt and consequent runoff are more rapid. This nullifies, in whole or in part, the flood-control functions of the dam. At the same time, the erosion which occurs because of the increased runoff causes heavy siltation of the reservoir, thus shortening its life.

In Marsh's time, as in our own, there were authoritative voices which argued that man's impact upon nature differed from that of wild animals only in *degree,* and not in *kind.* Marsh took issue with this viewpoint. Wild animals, he contended, act instinctively with a single, direct purpose in mind. Humans, on the other hand, are guided by an intelligent willpower, which also has secondary and remote goals in mind. As he saw it, wild animals could make slight changes to an environment, changes which were compensated for by natural checks and balances. The changes wrought by humans, quite to the contrary, are often of such enormous magnitude that geological ages, and even new processes of evolution, will be required to repair their effects.

Well aware of damage caused by human action in older civilizations, Marsh pointed out that parts of Asia Minor, northern Africa, Greece, and Alpine Europe had been rendered almost as desolate as the surface of the moon. Yet, within human memory, these areas had been luxuriant, verdant, and fertile. He cautioned that continued action of the same sort could easily lead to the "depravation, barbarism, and perhaps even extinction" of our species.[14]

While modern science might scoff at Marsh because of his holistic approach, in which he included the moral as well as the objective, he comes very close to meeting the qualifications of the "informed generalist." When anthropologist Margaret Mead was president of the Scientists' Institute for Public Information (SIPI), she pointed to the great need we have for generalists to compensate for the increasing numbers of specialists being turned out by universities. She felt that we have a plethora of individuals whose specialties involved taking things apart but a paucity of generalists who might comprehend any means of restoring wholeness. Marsh was a generalist with a varied background which enabled him to call attention to the impact of deforestation on all aspects of the environment.

He also pointed to the value of reforestation in the drying of waterlogged soils which had resulted from erosion and blocked drainage following logging. He gave as an example the formation of swamps and marshes after deforestation in Sologne, France. With the subsequent planting of maritime pines, the taproots penetrated the underlying hardpan, allowing water to follow the roots through the hardpan. The result was that bogs and sheets of water dried and the land was restored to productive forest use.

The collection of research data that Marsh interwove in *Man and Nature* is formidable and is worth pursuing because it provides some insight into the tremendous pressure that has continually been put on resources. Marsh pointed out, for example, that in the first two years of the Civil War in the United States, twenty-eight thousand walnut trees were cut down to provide wood for a single European manufacturer of gunstocks for the American market.

Commenting on how resource use affects history, he suggested that Spain lost her political power during the years following Phillip II. At the time, destruction of Spain's forests had caused the price of timber to rise above the resources of the state, and the empty exchequer could not afford the funds necessary to build new fleets.[15]

Trees as Casualties of War

On October 7th, 1571, a great naval battle took place near Lepanto, Greece. The adversaries were a combined Christian fleet supplied by Genoa, Venice, Spain, and Malta versus the fleet of the Ottoman Empire. The Turkish fleet of 300 ships was almost wiped out by the smaller Christian fleet of 250 ships. Only 40 of the Turkish vessels escaped destruction.

There were 20,000 Turks killed or captured, 8,000 Christians killed and 16,000 seriously wounded in this battle.

One might say however, that forests suffered a worse fate. The fleets which fought at the Battle of Lepanto required the falling of some 250,000 trees. The Christian flagship *El Real,* has been replicated. Hull timbers for the replica required more than 300 mature oaks, planks and spars utilized 300 pines and firs, and the huge galley consumed fifty beech trees for its oars.

The Ottoman fleet was rebuilt by Grand Vizier Sokolli and regained supremacy within a few years. As a result of this type of resource extraction, Mediterranean forests were so shorn of timber that shipbuilding moved northward.

Reference: David Attenborough,
The First Eden, The Mediterranean World and Man
(Toronto: Little, Brown, & Company, 1987), pp. 166-173.

Before the time of Marsh, the French philosopher Denis Diderot expressed his concern in his *Encyclopedie* (completed in 1772) over the vast quantities of wood required for the heating of buildings in Paris. The forests around Paris had already been severely depleted and wood was floated down the Seine in huge rafts from hundreds of miles away. Diderot had indicated the necessity of using coal to replace wood for space heating and coal began to be used increasingly from that time on. Marsh indicated that even in 1815, about 1.5 million cubic yards (1.2 million cubic meters) of firewood were required annually by Parisians but that this amount had dropped to about 650,000 cubic yards (501,805 cubic meters) by 1859. The consumption of coal had risen more than proportionately.

Returning to the negative effect of war on the chance for human survival, Marsh spoke of the heavy drain placed on resources to supply the "navies of Christendom." He observed that if it had not been for the development of new techniques in metallurgy, which enabled metal to be used in place of wood, the twenty-five years that preceded his writing of *Man and Nature* would have stripped Europe of the last remaining trees suitable for shipbuilding and other military use. He pondered upon the fact that the improvement of military techniques since the time of Napoleon had been such that attack and defense now began at distances to which military reconnaissances, not many years before, had hardly extended. In this sophistication of military capability, he saw the possibility that the human race could "become its own executioner," on the one hand stripping earth of resources and on the other devising ever more effective methods for "extermination of the consumer." The fact that we are at present able to destroy virtually all life on earth could hardly have been foreseen by Marsh, but certainly gives credence to the grave concern he expressed about the direction of man's warlike efforts.[16]

"Every gun that is made, every warship launched, every rocket fired, signifies, in the final sense, a theft from those who hunger and are not fed, and those who are cold and are not clothed. This world in arms is not spending money alone. It is spending the sweat of its laborers, the genius of its scientists, the hopes of its children."

Former U.S. President Dwight D. Eisenhower

More striking in our own time than in the time of G. P. Marsh, is the habitual transience of population. In his far-ranging manner, he scrutinized the fact that mobility had already become a characteristic of the population and warned that "the life of incessant flitting" is inimical to the establishment of permanent improvements of all kinds. He saw that this was particularly so in the renewal of forests, inasmuch as a single generation cannot hope to plant and harvest a forest within its own lifetime. He recognized that the tendency to live in "hired housing" meant that there was no permanent attachment to a piece of land and offered no incentive to cherish and maintain some small acreage. With even more rapid and exaggerated transience an in-grained habit today, there is even less attachment to native rocks and rills. The only real solution to diminished interest in the well-being of land seems to lie in rethinking our whole value system and recognizing as a first principle that the health of the entire human family is utterly dependent on worldwide integrity of the land base.

Although Marsh was a strong adherent of Christian doctrine and believed that the earth is "the Lord's and the fullness thereof," his view of man's responsibility toward the earth was almost mystical. He envisioned all things as moving beyond the moment we call the present and displayed a fondness for the English mathematician Charles Babbage's view that every movement of every atom in the universe left an indelible record of the thoughts, actions, and emotions of each individual who lived; and that there was thus constituted an ineffaceable, imperishable record of human behavior from the dawn of time to the extinction of our race—and that the physical record thus affected was part of that eternity of which divinity alone takes cognizance.[17]

It was his general conclusion that human intervention throughout history was such as to assure the exhaustion and desolation of every aspect of nature which man had "reduced to his dominion."[18]

It is not surprising then that he became the first advocate of a modification of human behavior in order to develop what we might today call an *earth ethic.*[19]

First of all actions to be undertaken, in his estimation, was the restoration of the forests. Fully recognizing the fact that the individual who buries an acorn will not live long enough to see the result in the form of a majestic oak, he begged that we consider the tremendous advantages that are derived from the existence of forests and the terrible evils that result from their destruction. He called the restoration of forests "the most obvious of duties which this age owes to those

> "If it is something to make two blades of grass grow where only one was growing, it is much more to have been the occasion of the planting of an oak which shall defy twenty scores of winters, or of an elm which shall canopy with its green cloud of foliage half as many generations of mortal immortalities.
>
> "I have written many verses, but the best poems I have produced are the trees I planted on the hillside that overlooks the broad meadows. Nature finds rhymes for them in the recurring measures of the seasons. Winter strips them of their ornaments and gives them, as it were, in prose translation; and Summer clothes them in all the splendor of their leafy language."
>
> *Oliver Wendell Holmes*

that are to come after it." His own comprehension of the role of forests being vast, he was not simply referring to the establishment of resources for future human use; but was speaking of all the beneficial roles of forests, from ameliorating soil erosion and flooding, to stabilization of climate in all parts of the world.

In discussing the consequences of the destruction of forests, Marsh signified that once the forest has disappeared, everything else changes. Land radiates its heat away in winter and bakes under unobstructed rays of the sun in summer. Winds sweep over it, removing its scanty moisture at all seasons, and drift the winter snow that protects it from frost. Melting snow is no longer soaked up by highly absorbent vegetable matter but rushes seaward over the baked or frozen ground. Perennial springs become dry because of lack of seepage into the earth. The fibrous rootlets that held soil together dry or decay and soil erodes freely. The earth, instead of acting like a sponge is in effect a dust heap. Heavy rainfalls run swiftly over soils, carrying away particles of earth, which increase the erosive power of streams, eventually filling stream beds and obstructing outlets. Rivulets, no longer fed by ground water absorbed beneath forest cover, and no longer shaded by vegetation, are heated and evaporated in summer and become raging torrents during fall and spring rains. Constant degradation of uplands results as does the siltation of watercourses, of lakes, and eventually of estuaries and harbors. Stripped of its vegetable mantle, the earth becomes less and less productive and ultimately barren, and is "no longer fit for the habitation of man."

And, while we hypothesize that it cannot happen here, with our favorable climate, we must remember that we know that climate is now changing, and we also know that the things Marsh describes as consequences have already taken place in other lands. Think again of the admonition that to ignore history is to be forced to repeat it.

Marsh called for an approximately fixed relationship between the amounts of plowed land and woodland and held the view that much of the land already cleared had proved unfit for agriculture and could be profitably restored to forest cover, in every nation.

Focusing on the restlessness of his countrymen, "not in form only, but even in spirit," he suggested that the time had come to forego the love of change which caused the people to be nomadic in their habits. He believed that landowners would be far more apt to plant a wood or make other permanent improvements in their properties if they knew they would pass these paternal acres on to their own descendants. It was his belief that stability in maintaining the relationships between kinds of land and also stability of the generations living on the land were both desirable qualities to be established in society. He recognized that there must be some flexibility to accommodate change but that this flexibility must be attached to a core of stability.

Speaking of the stability of nature's landscapes that had developed through centuries of grading by action of wind and water, by frost and deposits of vegetable matter, Marsh saw mankind as co-workers with nature, redeveloping an equilibrium which would sustain life in modest abundance. "Man has too long forgotten," he contended, "that the earth was given to him for usufruct alone," (this being the right to enjoy property belonging to another) "not for consumption, still less for profligate waste." The changes we need to begin the great task of restoration before us, he saw as dependent upon conquest of ourselves and as "great political and moral revolutions in governments and peoples" that would fit us to rehabilitate the lands that have suffered from uncaring occupation and exploitation.[20]

Albert Schweitzer

Albert Schweitzer was a most unusual man in many respects. It had been claimed that it was not possible to tame a wild African boar. Yet every Sunday when Dr. Albert Schweitzer preached in the chapel at Lambaréné a formidable wild boar, with the unlikely name, Josephine, stood beside him. What subtle message of being loved had filtered into the perceptive brute brain of this formidable animal? What thoughts passed through its mind as it stood beside him at the pulpit? Was it affirming a reverence for life? Did it deliberately stand side by side with this man in affirmation of his view on the relationship of all living things?

Dr. Schweitzer (1875–1965) was brought up in Gunsbach, in Alsace, where his father was the local Protestant pastor. He received his doctorate at Strasbourg and studied organ music under Charles Marie Widor. With a music career in view, he still contemplated his duty to the world. At twenty-one, he decided he would dedicate his life to art and science until he was thirty and after that time he would devote himself to the service of humankind. He retrained and became a doctor of medicine and went to western equatorial Africa where he founded Lambaréné Hospital. Internationally honored for his humanitarian efforts, he was awarded the Nobel Peace Prize in 1952. With the money from the prize, he added a leper village to the Lambaréné complex, where the unfortunate victims of that ravaging disease could receive treatment. Norman Cousins commented on the frugality that Schweitzer imposed on himself so that every possible penny could be saved for hospital expenses. He observed that Schweitzer shaved without soap or lather because he considered it a luxury, and that he wrote the entire manuscript for his book, *The Kingdom of God,* on the back of old envelopes and other scrap paper. Schweitzer told Cousins that he traveled third class only because there was no fourth class.[21] His writings and his concept of "reverence for life" as a starting point for a comprehensive philosophy that would renew the world, remain as a legacy to a world beset with environmental problems that cannot be solved in the context of the most widely held contemporary worldview.

Also possessing a doctorate in theology (as well as in philosophy and later in medicine) Schweitzer's basis for his view of reverence for life stemmed directly from the scripture that reads, "Thou shalt love thy neighbor as thyself." He extended that scripture to embrace a love of all living things.

In his time, as in ours, it was the general view that the inclusion of lower animals in our ethical system was both philosophically meaningless and functionally impossible. Schweitzer disagreed. He comprehended all life as feeling, experiencing, and suffering, and he held that all life should be embraced by a single system of ethics. The bee sipping nectar from a flower before your view is a living creature just as you are. It struggles for existence, enjoys its moment in the sun, and experiences fear, joy, and pain as you do. If you crush it beneath your foot, it becomes decaying material, as all living things become sooner or later.

Wherever we see life, we see ourselves. The oneness of all things is reflected in myriad ways before our eyes. The fact of our mortality constantly beckons us to contemplate that which transcends the fleeting moment of this life. Schweitzer comments on a snowflake. The snowflake, one of untold trillions, falls upon your hand and attracts your attention. You look upon its sparkling fragility and intricacy. The warmth of your skin provokes a quiver, the rays of the snowflake contract and it melts to a drop of water and is gone. As he says, "The snowflake which fluttered down from infinite space upon your hand, where it sparkled and quivered and died—that is yourself. And in the same manner, wherever you see life, you have merely to project your sensitivity and know it is yourself."

It is commonly pointed out that today we suffer from extreme forms of reductionism. As philosopher Lewis Mumford has explained, our lives are increasingly governed by specialists who know little about what lies outside their expertise. As he says, these are, "unbalanced men who have made a madness out of their method."[22] It is obvious that many human undertakings are broadly anti-life, that many are focused on unnatural control of nature or on manipulation of systems in a destructive sense. To destroy a single insect pest or weed, we rain death from pesticides upon "the just and the unjust." We endlessly sacrifice life in an unrelenting effort toward domination of a world we could neither hope to create nor understand.

The reductionist intellect, illustrated by today's scientific single vision, has been characterized by the great educator Dr. Abraham Maslow as a "cognitive pathology" usually born of fear, and popular with those who are afraid to look at the possibility of a greater world of truth standing beyond this world of experience.

Chief Luther Standing Bear, of the Oglala Sioux, may have been nearer an essential truth than we are when he said:

> We did not think of the great open plains, the beautiful rolling hills, and winding streams with tangled growth as "wild." Only to the white man was nature a "wilderness" and only to him was the land "infested" with "wild" animals and "savage"

people. To us it was tame. Earth was bountiful and we were surrounded with the blessings of the Great Mystery. Not until the hairy man from the east came and with brutal frenzy heaped injustices upon us and the families we loved was it "wild" for us. When the very animals of the forest began fleeing from his approach, then it was that for us the "wild west" began.[23]

Schweitzer pondered the Great Mystery as well, and from the first commandment, "Thou shalt love thy God with all thy heart and with all thy mind and with all thy strength," and from the principle of love of our fellow man, he arrived at the principle of reverence for all life.

In one of his famous sermons at St. Nicolai's Church, Strasbourg, (February 16, 1919) he explored the matter of loving God. He suggested that the use of the word love in relationship to God was meant figuratively, in an ethical sense, and that absolute understanding of this magnificent, incomprehensible Being was beyond our capability. He asked whether loving God meant that we should love him as we might love some creature we encountered in daily life, reflecting that God has no need of us. As we think of love among one another it means sharing empathy with one another, indulging in common experiences, and giving assistance where it is needed. But our love of God is more akin to reverence, to profound respect mingled with love and awe. "God is infinite life." Therefore, he concluded, knowing that God encompasses all life, we demonstrate our reverence, respect, and awe toward this infinite, omniscient Being by considering ourselves and all other living things as a part of His wholeness and compassion. Our love of Him is actively expressed when our lives display behavior that shows awareness of the oneness of all life.

In his writing, a few years later, is a clear statement of both the fulfillment of our own needs and of reverence for things other than human. Answering his own question about what a concept of reverence for life would mean in terms of the relationship between men and other living creatures, he suggested that we might have to think in terms of a principle of necessity.

This principle advises that we should never injure life of any sort unless we are certain that it is necessary and should not go beyond the point of necessity in even the most insignificant way. He points out that the farmer who cuts hay to provide his livestock with food in winter is entitled to do so by reason of necessity. But, the same farmer, returning home after his day's work, must not strike off the head of a single flower along the roadside in a casual manner. To destroy life wantonly or idly is to commit a wrong against life.

It was Schweitzer's claim that those who experiment with other animals for the ultimate welfare of mankind must never excuse their actions with vague assumptions that the experimentation is directed toward a valuable result. He contended that in each individual case the experimenters should invoke the principle of necessity and inquire whether there is an absolute necessity to impose upon an animal the sacrifice of its life for human well-being. In reflecting upon the pain and indignity imposed upon animals, he urged that we take every opportunity to show succor to animals of every kind. Even by helping an insect in difficulty we can help repay some minuscule portion of mankind's ever-increasing debt to the animal world.

When his book *The Decay and the Restoration of Civilization* appeared in 1923, it opened with the statement, "We are living today under the sign of the collapse of civilization."[24] He contended that the decline proceeded from the submergence of ethical and spiritual ideals beneath the rampant juggernaut of a mechanical, materialistic worldview focused on no goal other than sating the demands of what has more recently been called unprincipled consumerism.

He saw this reflected in the attitudes of standoffishness and lack of sympathy which are shown by strangers toward one another. Such behavior is no longer regarded as signs of rudeness but as natural attributes displayed by the "man of the world."[25]

The dilemma of the modern world, in Schweitzer's view, is the lack of any philosophical agreement about the nature and purpose of the universe. These are hefty considerations by any stretch of the imagination, but all the more difficult in a world where people are primarily focused on economic goals that leave little time for reflection or spiritual development. In his conviction that life close to nature serves as food for the spirit, he echoed Marsh in saying that there is only too much truth in the contention that life entered a state of disarray once people gave up their own fields and rural dwelling places.

In his thoughts, Schweitzer shares the view of Renaissance man and the Illuminati who believed that the world was in great need of renewal. The imperative factor, he would agree, is the spiritual awakening of mankind. No progress which is material and technological in its essence can really be a step toward civilization. The essence must be spiritual so that growth can have direction. Otherwise nothing but chaos, such as we are now seeing, can be the outcome. After all, "What profiteth it a man if he gain the whole world" in exchange for his soul?

In his *Civilization and Ethics,* Schweitzer remarked that the world had been without a worldview since the middle of the nineteenth century, and that it was falling more into the error of having no sense of purpose at all. From this condition our lack of civilization proceeded. Not until we develop the conviction that civilization can only be renewed when we renew our personal outlooks upon life, thus harboring an ethical and constructive worldview, will it be possible to set our feet upon a path that will lead to a stable and enduring way of life.[26] One constantly senses a note of optimism in his thoughts, a sense that the human spirit will continue to demand those ideals which must emerge from humanity for its purpose to be fulfilled.

Knowing, as we all know, that we do forge the chains that shackle us, we must find within ourselves the strength of spirit to break these fetters. Even in our overorganized societies which in a hundred ways have us in their power, each person must somehow develop an independent personality.

We have to differentiate between the truth that is really true and a contemporary world where, as Schweitzer contended, we are overwhelmed by propaganda posing as truth. We live within a fallacy in which national civilizations are an idol. The ideal of humanity working toward a common, shared civilization has been demolished by military fervor and by the focus upon differences between nations, rather than on similarities.

As Schweitzer saw it, we can do nothing but go round and round in ever enlarging circles until a meaningful worldview exists within humanity. What is the meaning of our society? What is the meaning of our lives in this world? What will we gain from this world? What is our duty to it and to one another? Which are the truths that are true?

... We have now a generation which is squandering the precious heritage it has received from the past; and is living in a world of ruins, because it cannot complete the building with which that past began.

... For individuals as for the community, life without a view of things is a pathological disturbance of the higher capacity for self-direction.[27]

Finding meanings to life, developing a worldview; these are not insuperable tasks. The wellsprings of truth clamor for our attention. But we do not choose to heed them. As fast as the water of life can burst forth we throw rubbish in to check the flow. At no time in history has there been such constant distraction. The spiritual drought in which society now languishes results from unreflective lives dedicated to incessant activity. Always too busy; always on the run; now behind the wheel; now before the television; denying thought by not taking time to face it . . . we accept change in the world but never think that there is the necessity of fundamental change in ourselves.

Schweitzer suggests that our modern, industrial age is distinguished by a lack of reason that is unparalleled in history. If we continue to draw our spirit from the artificial world we have created, we will destroy the real world and go down with it to ruin.

The alternative, he contended, is that we once again draw upon the human spirit and develop the strength of character to create the conditions that will put our world on the path to a truly ethical civilization.

As Schweitzer pointed out, each year there is a perfection of the techniques by which opinions with no thought behind them, can be spread. He wrote this thought before the invention of television but probably would have agreed that its advent marked the existence of one of the most efficient tools ever devised for the stupefaction of society—regardless of the fact that it might be used otherwise. Schweitzer pointed out that it was already possible in his time to popularize and make public opinion out of silly ideas that had no foundation in truth.

To Albert Schweitzer the turmoil of World War II completed the trend that had had its beginning in the nineteenth century. He felt that by the end of the war, the psychological manipulations of minds by the barrage of propaganda had achieved the result that propaganda had replaced truth. People had lost their capacity for judgment and with it their ability to discriminate between fact and fiction. Through succumbing to external pressures advising them what to think and believe, people had gradually surrendered the ability to guide themselves by independent thought and as a result had suffered massive spiritual disorganization.

In a serious way, spiritual sight had suffered the fate Milton alluded to in reference to his own blindness: " . . . And that one talent which is death to hide/Lodged with me useless."[28]

Schweitzer calls for what amounts to philosophical renewal in a world so committed to bustle that it decries the concept of reflective thought. We are committed to action whether or not it is meaningful. He suggests that the cleansing action of purposeful reflection would remove much of the mental clutter of a world preoccupied with marketplace idolatry. Certainly some healthy skepticism toward what we look upon as unquestionable progress would be of great value.

"The beginning of all spiritual life of any real value is courag. faith in truth and open confession of same."

What might serious reflection tell us about the world in which we now live? What might it say about the adequacy of the values we now hold to be important? What might it suggest about an ever-increasing population making incessant demands on a deteriorating planet? What might it advise us about the integrity of the media? What might it indicate about the quality of education that conveys the message that more of what we are doing is better? What might it suggest about an alternative view of life that might be more meaningful to us, and more caring and respectful to the other living things that share the planet with us?

Deliberating upon the problems facing mankind, Schweitzer was moved to say that the man of today, "with his diminished need of thought is a *pathological phenomenon.*" He expressed doubt whether or not people conditioned by years of propaganda substituting for truth could stir themselves enough to indulge in sober reflection about themselves and the world, which process must precede development of a reflective worldview. He saw the path that must be followed as extremely difficult because it had to contend with powerful institutions, already entrenched, which would be a hindrance rather than a help.

Yet, he did not see the task as impossible; he comprehended that renewal undertaken against such formidable odds could indeed lead to a true civilization, earned out of the common effort toward a more noble form of life.

Schweitzer suggests that if we succeed in renewal it will be in very much the same manner as a pasture that turns green in spring, for the cause of that greening is the millions of new green shoots that arise from the roots that have survived the winter. Similarly, renewal of society will take place by millions of individual decisions.

At such a time, "the ideals, born of folly and passion, of those who make public opinion and direct public events" will be seen as form without substance, chaff without kernel or germ.

Thoreau, Marsh, Schweitzer:
Contributors to a New Worldview

Society is hurtling along the Techno-Industrial Highway, proud of the speed it is making. At the beginning of a marked S-bend in the road, a sign appears, "Bridge Out." The artist driving the car begins to apply the brakes, saying "I'd better slow down." His three passengers are annoyed. The industrialist looks at his watch and says, "I can't afford to be late." The objective scientist admonishes sharply, "You're just reacting emotionally, we haven't seen any bridge out yet." The politician rasps, "This is an outrage and I'm going to find out who's responsible!" The words are hardly out of his mouth as the car starts into the other side of the bend, hurtles out into space, and tumbles end over end into the canyon below.

Just as St. Benedict found the world of his times in disarray, so the world is now. We are in the grips of an arms race with the specter of nuclear war hanging imminently over the world. We have acid rain problems, a deteriorating climate and disappearing ozone layer. The famine problem is grave, the oceans are succumbing to toxins, and chemical residues exist in food, drinking water, and air.

Thoreau, Marsh, and Schweitzer have real importance for us today. They viewed human activity, critically, as we all should and in their collective wisdom they wrote highly readable thoughts which offer us a path out of the dilemma that confronts us today.

Thoreau was the doughty defender of Nature, the austere monk, who focused on man's essential ties with nature. He began one of his famous lectures with the words,

> I wish to speak a word for Nature, for absolute freedom and wildness, as contrasted with a freedom and culture merely civil,—to regard man as an inhabitant, or a part and parcel of Nature, rather than a member of society. I wish to make an extreme statement, if so I may make an emphatic one, for there are enough champions of civilization: the minister and the school-committee and every one of you will take care of that.[29]

Yet, withal, he was an admirably civilized man, one capable of obeying a higher law than most people are aware exists.

Marsh was the well-traveled observer who saw firsthand the impact that hasty and ill-advised actions could have on the natural world.

He realized that the excessive felling of trees was the primary cause of the derangements that man had unintentionally caused. From over-cutting stemmed excessive erosion, erratic runoff of streams, drying of soil, and interruption of the flow of springs. He was also aware that trees moderated temperature extremes, slowed the rate of snow melt, and abetted the storage of moisture in the ground. He knew that men must modify nature in the development of civilization but knew too that this must be done in a careful, well-planned, responsible manner. He also knew that "Our victories over the external world" would simply afford "a vantage-ground to the conquest of the yet more formidable and not less hostile world that lies within."[30]

Schweitzer's philosophy of reverence for life is striking in view of the nearly total irreverence for life, (other than human) that exists today. He recognized clearly that in focusing on self-centeredness and in assigning nil worth to other living things, we could do nothing but debase ourselves. He also recognized the fundamental sickness of a society that grew so passive it refused to think, lest in thinking it found itself forced to change and reevaluate its behavior.

All three of these men would heartily agree with Socrates's view that "the unexamined life is not worth living."

These recent wise men could serve us well today. They were pathfinders whose trailblazing thoughts may truly act as beacons to guide us toward a more sustainable worldview than the one we currently hold.

Schweitzer spoke of the necessity for renewal of society. For renewal to occur there must be ideas with which our minds can react. While Thoreau, Marsh, and Schweitzer have no monopoly on ideas, their analyses hit closely at the root of our present, day problems.

In Thoreau's words: "There are a thousand hacking at the branches of evil to one who is striking at the root . . . "[31]

We may not have time, individually, to work our way from the branches to the root, but we cannot delay in making the effort.

Is **Anybody There?**

When the moon is filling and is riding high in the sky, the snowclad woodland trails are silvered lines wandering through a frosty fairyland. I enjoy an hour of walking at such times. Roaming amid stately trees, I can admire the glittering snow crystals lighting the trail ahead, or I can look upward and see sparkling stars marking another trail to an out-yonder that is light years away. Occasionally I hear a deer bound away, or see one standing like a statue as I walk by. Sometimes a coyote will yap a few times or an owlhoot will come like a mournful question from the treetops. For the most part, though, the walks are quiet and uneventful.

I find that as I walk, thoughts come unbidden, stay a while, and move on. Perhaps, like a placid cow with a cud, my mind ruminates and in so doing makes life's experiences more digestible. Walking, I like to think, is one of the finest synthesizers of experience. Knowing how little we really know, I can find myself fancying that the very stars may be naught but individual ideas in the mind of God; and as they wheel, dip, and cross in their orbits, they too are being synthesized toward some future perfection, a Paradise, I believe it would be called.

At any rate, as I sauntered the other night, there came to mind two men I have known. One, a university professor, once told me, more than half-seriously, that he had never married because he had not met anyone he liked better than himself. The other, an administrator, told me he was an atheist because it is not rational to believe in a Higher Power. In the way that ideas shuffle themselves and line up with one another, as the apples, oranges, or lemons do in a slot machine, I found these men side by side in my mind with a third individual about whom I had read—the Earl of Orrery.

So the story goes, Charles Boyle, fourth Earl of Orrery (1676-1731), lived in the north country of England in the eighteenth century. Because he had an interest in Kepler's laws of planetary motion, he caused a model solar system to be constructed in his castle, mainly for the education of his children. Intricate apparatus was assembled. The center of the model solar system was a brass sun, about which the planets revolved. The complex model included a moon orbiting the earth, and four moons orbiting Jupiter.

It happened that the Earl of Orrery had an atheistic guest who visited the castle mainly to see the model solar system. When the atheist asked who constructed the model, Orrery said: "Nobody!" He explained to the atheist that the model solar system "just happened," and had no builder. The atheist, of course, could not accept that it "just happened." He pointed out the necessity of precise design, and the various gears and wheels controlling the apparatus. Obviously, and indignantly, he insisted that intelligence had been required to construct the system.

As Orrery continued to insist that the whole thing "just happened," his guest became nearly totally frustrated and enraged. He vehemently demanded that any such product of thought and precise mathematical arrangement could not exist without creative skill. Yet Orrery remained implacable.

We will have to admit that Orrery must have been a master actor; but finally he saw fit to make his point. Orrery said this: "I will offer you a bargain. I will promise to tell you truly who made my little sun and planets down here, as soon as you tell me truly Who made the infinitely bigger, more wonderful and more beautiful real sun and planets up there in the heavens."

To say any more about this subject, should not be necessary. Whether it is "not rational to believe in a Higher Power," or impossible to get beyond the bounds of self-love . . . Well, I'll just leave the ideas with you, and you will make your own judgment.

Two roads diverged in a wood, and I—
I took the one less traveled by,
And that has made all the difference.

Robert Frost,
The Road Not Taken

6

The Awakening

We are moving quite rapidly toward creation of a global wasteland. Whether or not the conditions we have created are already irreversible is a question that is raised frequently. We have heard much of late about the idea of sustainability. Similar terms have been used before without modifying practice. What has been referred to as "sustained yield" in forestry is an example. For many years, while forests stretched over endless hills, the expression could be used with complacency. We now know that the term has had little application to the excessive rate at which forests have been cut.

The recent idea of sustainable development may be much the same. We must identify what level of sustainability is meant. If we mean barely sustainable, just capable of supporting life, then we might have some margin. If we mean to maintain sustainability at our present

167

level of affluence and physical comfort, then we must be certain that we do not add to the burden of carbon dioxide in the atmosphere, or cause further concentrations of toxins in the oceans, or greater increases in parts per million of pesticides in living organisms. Basically we must keep in mind the idea of sustainable development as defined by the World Commission on Environment and Development. To the commission this means that the needs of the present generation must be met without compromising the needs of future generations. It suggests that the limitations involved are set by the ability of the biosphere to absorb the effects caused by human technology and social organization. It hypothesizes that the management and improvement of both technology and social organization can lead to "a new era of economic growth."[1] The serious problem about the idea of sustainability is that it may be another catch phrase which serves as a talking point for politicians and industry, while conditions change very little from what they have been.

We are unfortunately very experienced at making superficial "cosmetic" changes and exaggerating their significance. Upon reflection, it seems dubious that the engineers of the spectacularly unsustainable society we have created have the capability of creating a sustainable one. History reminds us that old habits die hard and leopards rarely change their spots. But that shouldn't be surprising. We are so well-adjusted to the creed of superabundance that it seems positive heresy to even entertain the idea of relative frugality. Of course, it is difficult to believe that real change toward a truly sustainable society could be effected with good cheer.

But we are being told that we need changes and that we need them now. To the World Commission on Environment and Development, "the very survival of the planet" hinges on our ability to change.[2] Realizing that this warning from a political body flies in the face of what is portrayed as pure progress, we should understand its seriousness.

It could be argued that a near revolution would be necessary to produce the formidable changes that we really have to make. We have been quite successful at evading the thought that we have to behave more responsibly toward the earth and if we continue to delude ourselves on that matter, things will be dismally grim. So, revolution it must be; but the kind of revolution needed is something we have never tackled before—a revolution of character.

Will and Ariel Durant observed that violent revolutions, the kind with which we are most familiar, do less to redistribute wealth than to destroy it. They also noted that eventually a new minority with the same instincts as the old group of predators will rise to the forefront and monopolize wealth. As they wrote, "The only real revolution is in the enlightenment of the mind and the improvement of character, the only real emancipation is individual, and the only real revolutionists are philosophers and saints."[3]

If we believe that a major change of thought and attitude is a small price to pay for the continued existence of our species, then we will have to think seriously about what a great number of analysts of the history of events have suggested for years. They have urged nothing less than a major renewal of society. We need to develop goals and purposes that transcend the present acquisitiveness and ambition which now motivate society. What is more, this new form of thought has to penetrate all levels of society, including that level currently controlling the media which so easily influences our values. Lewis Mumford, certainly one of the most published philosophers of recent years, expresses the serious concern of many respected critics in this way: "The wars of our time have only brought out a destructiveness and a denial of life that were latent in this society; they were in a sense the negative alternatives to a general renewal that no ruling class was self-denying enough to sanction."[4]

It has been seriously suggested that our environmental crisis is not merely an unfortunate accident or a necessary outcome of population growth, but is instead the result of a deterioration of human values. As the Rienows suggest in their book *Moment In The Sun,*[5] the only thing

My symphony—To live content with small means;
To seek elegance rather than luxury, and refinement
   rather than fashion;
To be worthy, not respectable, and wealthy,
   Not rich;
To study hard, think quietly, talk gently, act frankly.
To listen to stars, and birds, to babes and sages,
   with open heart;
To bear all cheerfully, do all bravely, await occasions,
   hurry never.
In a word, to let the spiritual, unbidden and uncon-
   scious, grow up through the common.
This is to be my symphony.

William Ellery Channing

that can bring us into equilibrium with our environment and prolong the life of our species, is the "acceptance of a totally new code of values."

A Canadian businessman, W. F. Burditt of Saint John, wrote of the effect of uncontrolled capitalism during the quarter century preceding World War I. He suggested that growth was so rapid that individuals became completely preoccupied with acquiring wealth, and communities were enraptured with population growth and with commercial and industrial expansion. Focus on these issues was so great that "the amenities of life, health and happiness of the masses received scant consideration."[6]

Since that time we have never turned back. Locked into the view that "progress" is materially measurable, the central focuses of profit and material gain have left behind matters of humanity and ethics. Reductionist values have caused us to look upon the magnificent and vital earth as a mere storehouse of resources which exist for the sole purpose of gratifying human whims, whether meaningful or meaningless. People are lumped together as consumers; trees as stems for the lumber industry; the oceans, rivers, lakes, and "unproductive" land as dumps. We subsist with myths that do not withstand serious reflection, and have created a world in which haste precludes the opportunity to reflect. "Getting and spending we lay waste our powers."[7] (For an example of myths, see *The Quiet Crisis* by Stewart L. Udall, U.S. Secretary of the Interior under President John F. Kennedy. Udall makes frequent reference to the Myth of Superabundance which he identified as the myth that our "resources were inexhaustible," [see chapter 4]. Also see *The Hidden Persuaders* by Vance Packard in which he explains how "psychology professors turned merchandisers" use their knowledge of human nature to create a myth that consumers should buy all kinds of products from cakes to cars, regardless of any real need. Similarly, Dr. Samuel Epstein [author of *The Politics of Cancer*, 1979] in a recent journal article, took pains to debunk the cancer establishment's "unfounded and simplistic view that the cure for cancer was just around the corner." Epstein contends that "chemical pollution of our air, water, and food is the major cause of cancer." It is his view that cancer is a preventable disease but unless citizens push for action, little will happen. In the *Politics of Cancer* he suggested that "Cancer prevention must become a major election issue." He also suggests that an "economic boycott" of voluntary contributions to the American Cancer Society "is now well overdue." This money could better be diverted "to public interest organizations and

> "I find it difficult, if not impossible, to justify the use of federal funds to finance research leading to the development of machines or other technologies that may damage the soil, pollute willing workers, and reduce or eliminate competition."
>
> *Bob Bergland*
> *U.S. Agriculture Secretary*

labor groups" more likely to win "the war against cancer." Among the causes of increasing cancer rates he identifies runaway technology which has helped induce "profound and poorly reversible environmental degradation."[8])

Superficially we pretend it is positive thinking to look at short-term advantages and ignore long-term consequences. We decry equity between generations with the old quip, "What has posterity ever done for me?" We vastly aggrandize and prominently display our scientific capabilities, deeming it of no importance that whole dimensions of aesthetic factors, of emotional refinements, of spiritual and philosophical thoughts and intuitions are thrown into the discard because they are neither objectively observable nor quantifiable. A reservation about even a questionable profit-making venture is unacceptable because it is considered "counter-productive."

Mark Twain was probably right, that "Man is the only animal that blushes or needs to."[9]

If our culture is to turn successfully towards a sustainable lifestyle, it will only do so because of a revitalization of long-suppressed metaphysical ideas. People will have to recognize that there is crisis, ponder its meaning, and arrive at the conclusion that the problems manifested are those of our own creation, problems which result from a grossly exaggerated conviction regarding the extent to which we can manipulate nature. Our utilitarian ideals will fall before a growing philosophical comprehension that the mere acquisition of material items is of considerably less importance than the development of wholesome character and devotion to ideals such as recognition of the sanctity of all life. As a society, we are standing at an axial point in which the outcome will likely either be extinction or true civilization. Our pretensions to technological omniscience are clearly unacceptable, simply because the quantity and quality of our toxic waste exceed the self-cleansing ability of planetary systems. If "state of the art" means

171

continued fouling of the world with industrial excretion, then we must belatedly understand that technology is still in its infancy. That the entire planet has served as its swaddling clothes reveals the magnitude of economic indiscretion.

Our whole experience since the dawn of the Industrial Revolution has brought us to an urgent moment of truth. Our hedonistic lifestyles are unacceptable. To attain sustainability we must rethink our aims, aspirations, and expectations, and develop values that lie within the bounds of a healthy, dynamic environment. If we have to rethink even the meaning of life, then we should do so. The function of the planet is obviously something other than to drip milk and honey into unquenchable human mouths. The change in values we face is so immense that our entire social structure must radiate from it as a result of a new comprehensive worldview that will stem from our deepest, most realistic, and studied convictions.

So it is indeed a form of revolution in character that we need. It is overdue. We have focused for too long a while on the difference between ourselves and other living things while ignoring the similarities. We have developed aspirations to rule the cosmos and to use it as our warehouse before learning to dispose of our own wastes, to bring peace to our planet, or to govern our currently ungovernable selves. It is far past time to clean up our own household, and perhaps in so doing, to prepare ourselves for something greater. Our frantic, strident pace has to move toward a more calm and measured approach toward life. That this must happen on the individual level is obvious. Only when we become individually complete and responsible can we expect responsible government and accountable industry. It is our present irresponsibility that is the exact cause of the environmental dilemmas with which we are confronted. The ravager must become the restorer.

From the time of birth, two worlds vie for human attention. One is the technological world that we have created, and quite hastily at that. The other is the natural world which created us and all the other living things that inhabit the earth. As the world has become more mechanized and urbanized, a decreasing percentage of people have had intimate contact with the natural world.

It is unsurprising that the technological world easily claims attention, awe, and even devotion. Its bright lights sparkle in our consciousness, the throb of its power excites the desire for fingertip control of energy, its round-the-clock demands alter biological rhythms, its clamor dulls our senses, and its seemingly rational advocates continually assure us that we live in the best of all possible worlds.

The mind-compelling claims of technology are not entirely without justification. We have all benefited from it in some way. We have had power, opportunity, and material advantage that not even the richest of kings could command but a few centuries ago. But now we are beginning to see the price tag that has been attached throughout the period of techno-industrial growth. There has been an enormous cost to the orderly functioning of the natural world; the one that provides those really essential requirements of our existence—our food, air, water, and favorable climate.

Five Signs of a Failing People

"What are the marks of low condition in a people? I name five. **First,** when people generally look upon the State as a charitable institution, which can be made to supply all their wants by putting enough votes in a ballot-box. That is a sure sign that they are declining in willpower and virility. **Second,** when people generally take to scamping their work in the hours of labour, and to spending their leisure in playing the fool—a sure sign of social incompetence and intellectual poverty. **Third,** when people generally lose discipline, so that, when a big thing has to be done or a difficult manoeuvre performed, instead of marching together, 'one equal temper of heroic hearts,' they get themselves tied up into mobs and bundles and fall to quarreling with one another—a sure sign that they are badly bred and educated. **Fourth,** when people generally buy their pleasures ready-made on the market, in the form of external excitement—a sure sign that personal skill is on the down grade and creativeness passing away. **Fifth,** when religion becomes an interesting speculation, and the existence of right and wrong a vague rumour to be inquired into by experts—a sign that the compass is out of order and the light going out in the binnacle box.

"These are the signs of low condition in a people. Whenever any of the five shows its head let us hit, and hit it hard."

Dr. L. P. Jacks,
One Thousand Famous Things, Arthur Mee, ed.
(London: Hodder and Stoughton Limited, 1937), p. 28.

To be sure, nature has always been able to attract our attention. Few people can ignore a blizzard or raging windstorm. Earthquakes and tornados can make us forget whatever we are doing. Warm spring sunshine beckons us to enjoy basking outdoors and searing summer sun forces us to seek shade. We feel offended, perhaps even betrayed, when onshore winds bring jettisoned garbage to shore and we gag when industrial odors are borne on what otherwise might be fragrant breezes.

If nature's vigorous displays immediately rivet attention, nature also effectively, although quietly, advertises its present distress in ways that are not hard to perceive. Once-clear streams that are brown with spring runoff advertise eroding soil. New avalanche paths often advertise overlogging on steep slopes. Severe algal bloom may announce overburdened waterways suffering from eutrophication. An absence of wasps, robber flies, and carabid beetles proclaims the susceptibility of predaceous insects to pesticides. Blowing and drifting soil calls attention to agricultural practices that do not zealously protect the land. Deformed fish may indicate the presence of lethal chemicals in a body of water. Now dying trees and lakes advertise acid rainfall.

The hard line takes the view that all such signs are inconclusive and irrelevant to progress. The hard line dictates that we should do no more than initiate studies of substantial duration, which, depending on the terms of proof, may be deferred as inconclusive until we are in a totally irreversible situation. This may permit the economic machine to gallop for a furlong or two before it falls into a heap. That "an ounce of prevention is worth a pound of cure" was once considered a tried and true adage. We have muzzled that adage with the modern reservation, "but not if it costs money or causes us to alter our own reductionist definition of what constitutes progress."

We stand in absolute need to reaffirm our bond with the natural world. We need it far more than it needs us.

Society does not immediately change from one worldview to another. It is evident though, that much groping for new ideas is currently happening. Communism, recycling, bioregionalism, and permaculture, organic gardening, banning the bomb, voluntary simplicity: these are but a few of the popular movements that have drawn attention in the years since World War II.

The interesting point is that society is changing from the bottom up. While the drive toward production and profit continues in what may be mistakenly thought of as the higher echelon of society, matters of much more fundamental concern seem to occupy those less preoccupied with a solely business viewpoint of life.

It seems, indeed, that the "unexamined life" is proving itself entirely unsatisfactory and the discomfort of living meaninglessly is sufficient that it has caused people to spontaneously move toward new encounters and new awarenesses.

The existence of various forms of encounter groups is one interesting manifestation of this phenomenon in recent years. The popularity of such groups indicates that there are a considerable number of people who wish to move forth into new modes of thought. At the same time, it is apparent that a certain amount of insecurity exists, which makes individuals want to make this new move in company with other people of similar mind.

Such activity may be a prelude to independent self-examination, which is a necessary step in reconstructing an individual's outlook on life. Although these encounters are valuable, they must not become a substitute for individual reflection. Thoreau's comment that there is likelihood that the person who gets the most mail when he goes to the post-office hasn't heard from himself in a long while, certainly has reference to the extremely busy lives that people tend to live today. The life which involves a constant focus on mere activity is self-defeating to the development of a strong, individual, internal focus.

Dr. Harvey Cox speaks at some length of the need for "interiority" and for the importance of "testimony" in the present straitjacketed condition of society. As he says, "In our society specialization is running amok. The sickness it induces—mastery of the minutiae and neglect of the momentous—now imperils the existence of our species."[10] He claims that when the interiority of individuals begins to decay, and when they lose touch with what they believe, then their place as a cog in the social machine is their only life. They have lost the sense of themselves.

James Michener also touches on the same topic in *Chesapeake*.

"It is testimony that is needed." By some happy chance Rosalind had hit upon the one word that had the power to activate the fighter in the old woman: testimony. A human being, to live a meaningful life, was required to bear testimony; in prayer, in the husbandry of the home, in the conduct of public life, a man or woman must at critical moments testify publicly as to fundamental beliefs. Ruth Brinton had always done so, which was why she was regarded throughout the Eastern Shore as a Quaker Saint, difficult at times, stubborn always, but a testament to man's striving for a saner life.[11]

The importance given to the idea of individuality perhaps reached a peak in the writings of Count Leo Tolstoy. It was his contention that no matter how much we "may have stupefied ourselves by hypocrisy and the auto-suggestion resulting from it," there is no escaping the fact that it is our purpose in life to live according to the rational consciousness which was given us. He saw each individual's responsibility to be "the recognition of the truth revealed to us, and the profession of it, precisely what alone is always in our power."[12]

That we must walk the higher path, with the good of Nature and Humankind in mind—is imperative!

Lewis Mumford warns that in attempting to regain contact with ourselves we must strive to avoid the nonhuman. To dream of traveling from place to place, he suggests, is giving oversignificance to mere change of position and is simply to focus on escape. He feels that the more we fill in activities to keep from confronting ourselves, the more we slip backward. The questions we need to concentrate on are those of deep significance to ourselves. They have to do with the meaning of life, with the kinds of changes that would make life more meaningful, and with positive visions that would replace simple thoughts about one form of security or another.

To regain our own autonomy, we must break with the world's furious haste. Perhaps it would be good to reflect on the matter of whether the quantity of activity in which we indulge is as important as the quality of our actions. We must ask whether we were really intended to live in such hustle and bustle, and ask just where we are going at such a rate of speed. After all, it is not really implicit in our design that we should live in the fashion dictated to Alice in Wonderland by the Red Queen: "Now *here,* you see, it takes all the running you can do, to keep in the same place. If you want to get somewhere else, you must run at least twice as fast as that."

At one time it would not have been necessary to be inventive to find opportunities to ponder about life. Ordinary activities such as hoeing in a garden, cutting firewood by hand, strolling in the woods, or fishing along the bank of a stream or lake; all these provided opportunity to dream, to think, to be alone, and to let the naturalness of a quieter world permeate our being. Now, because so many people

176

Confucius on Creating Harmony in the World

"Things have their roots and their completion. Affairs have their end and their beginning. To know what is first and what is last is the beginning of wisdom.

"Those who desire to create harmony in the world must first establish order in their own communities. Wishing to establish order in their communities, they must first regulate their own family life. Wishing to regulate their own family life, they must first cultivate their own personal lives. Wishing to cultivate their personal lives, they must first set their own feelings right. Wishing to set their feelings right, they must first seek to make their own wills sincere. Wishing to make their wills sincere, they must first increase to the utmost their own understanding. Such increase in the understanding comes from the extension of their knowledge of all things.

"Things being investigated, their own knowledge will become extended. Their knowledge being extended, their own understanding will increase. Their understanding being increased, their own wills will become sincere. Their wills being set right, their own personal lives will become cultivated. Their personal lives being cultivated, their own family life will be properly regulated. Their family life being properly regulated, their communities will become well-ordered. Their own communities being well-ordered, the whole world will become happy and peaceful.

"From the greatest of men down to the masses of people, all must consider the cultivation of the personal life the foundation of every other thing."

Confucius

live in cities, and because so many activities that were once quiet and simple are carried on with mechanical assistance, one has to be deliberate in seeking out opportunities for reflection. It is significant to note that even the common pursuits mentioned above have been motorized: the hoe replaced by a tiller; the crosscut saw, buck saw, or Swede saw by a chainsaw; woodland walking by an ATV or motorbike; and lakeside fishing by a motorized boat of some sort. There are few things as elusive, now, as opportunities for meditative pursuits.

To Gain the Whole World

"All men plume themselves on the improvement of society, and no man improves. Society never advances. It recedes as fast on one side as it gains on the other. It undergoes continual changes; it is barbarous, it is civilized, it is christianized, it is rich, it is scientific; but this change is not amelioration. For every thing that is given something is taken. Society acquires new arts and loses old instincts. What a contrast between the well-clad, reading, writing, thinking American, with a watch, a pencil and a bill of exchange in his pocket, and the naked New Zealander, whose property is a club, a spear, a mat and an undivided twentieth of a shed to sleep under! But compare the health of the two men and you shall see that the white man has lost his aboriginal strength. If the traveller tells us truly, strike the savage with a broad-axe and in a day or two the flesh shall unite and heal as if you struck the blow into soft pitch, and the same blow shall send the white to his grave.

"The civilized man has built a coach, but has lost the use of his feet. He is supported on crutches, but lacks so much support of muscle. He has a fine Geneva watch, but he fails of the skill to tell the hour by the sun . . . His note-books impair his memory; his libraries overload his wit; the insurance-office increases the number of accidents; and it may be a question whether machinery does not encumber; whether we have not lost by refinement some energy, by a Christianity, entrenched in establishments and forms, some vigor of the wild virtue. For every Stoic was a Stoic, but in Christendom where is the Christian?"

Ralph Waldo Emerson
Self-Reliance, p. 166-67.

It is a matter of interest that a nature writer who assembled field guides to birds, mammals, insects, and other living things was once chided about the fact that he made money from his books by helping people escape from reality. His instant response was that he was really helping people escape *into* reality. So distanced have we become from the world of other living things that we hardly recognize that it has a far greater claim on "naturalness" than the mechanical world we have substituted.

If one thinks about the barrage of stimuli to which we are subjected by advertising and by countless exhortations to join in one activity or another, it becomes obvious that there are many external forces which attempt to organize our lives. It is a fair bet that the more we are organized by outside forces, the less self-organization we have. We may thus inadvertently live lives of such intense activity that we hardly know whether we are coming or going. This is reason enough for the process of slowing down and thinking about things. Taking time for reflection is one way of guaranteeing that one does not arrive at the conclusion, in middle-age or later, that life has been wasted and has not been lived in accordance with the inner drives of the individual.

The very mention of the individual brings to mind the fact that each person can find his own way to change routine and bring refreshing insight into the meaning of life. One man, a former mid-level executive in a manufacturing firm and a personal friend of mine, tells his story in this manner.

"I guess I was getting jaded and pretty frustrated. I knew how to be a company man and knew how to get ahead, but more and more I was questioning if it was all worth it. I was working in the daytime, was pretty much on call if there were problems and spent the evening and most weekends watching television—mostly sports. Sometimes when I went to bed at night I lay there and wondered what life was all about and if I was just going to go on being a zombie until it was time to retire and then become some other kind of zombie—maybe have a motor home and travel around here and there to try to keep from being bored.

"One night I guess I'd just had it. I got up from my chair, turned off the TV set and told my wife, 'Let's go for a walk.' She looked at me like I was crazy but she got her coat and we went outside. We lived in a residential area so we walked up and down different streets. It seemed that everywhere we went we saw the flickering light of TV's behind windows with drawn curtains. I couldn't keep from thinking that life was pretty meaningless.

"We did that sort of thing for a while, did a lot of walking and then a lot of talking. I found she wasn't all that happy either. Finally we started looking around weekends, visiting a lot of smaller towns. The upshot was that I found a place where I could get a job—maybe not as good a one—but it was a place we liked from the moment we saw it. It took us over a year to make up our minds, but we finally bought a pleasant house on a couple of acres. I chucked my job and we moved. I wouldn't say that what I did was particularly smart or dumb, but we like it better where we are. The town is small, people are friendly, life is a lot more relaxing. I've started doing some reading, the wife has made friends and the kids too. It just seems like we're living a new life that is a lot closer to the way life should be. We walk in the woods around here. We work in the garden. We look at views. We breathe real air. I heard a loon on the lake a while ago. What a wonderful sound! I think we're all happier."

A surprising number of people who now live in small towns have such stories to tell. In almost all cases they found the standard formula for success to be too inhibiting to their individuality. One of them pointed out that some of his friends in the city felt he had "copped out," but his reflection was, "I feel sorry for them," and "it's amazing how many of them have dropped around and told me I made a wise choice."

In spite of the fact that a principal preoccupation of our society has to do with the acquisition of goods, there is much wisdom in the ancient observation that man does not live by bread alone.

Bay Street and Wall Street are places where business dominates, not centers where wisdom rules. That these are vastly different matters is only beginning to become apparent.

Although a house may be filled with expensive belongings that shout "success" to a world that is not particularly impressed, the hypnotic eye of the television set fixes its glare upon the essentially empty lives of the people who sit before it. In a similar manner, choked weekend highways are visual confirmation of the sad truth that large numbers of people have nothing better to do. The throngs that flock to spectator sports or to some event that might furnish a mere glimpse of a celebrity also indicate the extent of the human search for something to fill time. It is perhaps the ultimate folly that so much time is consumed to little avail in our society, dedicated as it is to consumerism.

Contrary to the prodigious assault of advertising, it is unlikely that humans were born for the express purpose of becoming consumers. If people should, in large numbers, rethink their priorities, and thereby business should founder on the shoals of consumer indifference, the result might be a more meaningful reorientation of our economic philosophy. Would it not be delightful if business could find no more meaningful enterprise than that of unleashing a vigorous campaign to save the planet?

In our world of multiple, similar products and of endless opportunities to buy, to invest, to travel, and to indulge in a variety of activities, the characteristics needed by a wise individual include both skepticism and discretion. If a hundred choices invite expenditure, and only one can be afforded, it pays to act with deliberation and discrimination. The impetuous buyer who must own endless goods and as a result mortgages himself to time payments has surrendered his autonomy and made himself a serf of the consumer machine.

Mumford suggests that we must learn to develop resistance to every suggestion that fosters automatic behavior. We should not do a thing simply because "everybody else is doing it." We should not want a thing simply because it is advertised. We should not extend ourselves into debt simply to be fashionable. We do not need a new gadget simply because it has been invented. We do not need to join the jetset simply because such a life seems glamorous or exciting.

A classic story about resistance to temptation involves an elderly eastern farmer whom I knew. He used to carry his money in a narrow, homemade pouch with a drawstring. The really unusual thing was the length of the drawstring, which permitted him to tie a series of knots in it. Occasionally one might see him in the general store, standing before a showcase, sometimes with his money pouch in hand. Sometimes he would untie a few knots, retie them, and stuff the pouch into his pocket. One morning, after buying gas for his old pickup, and untying and retying the knots to his pouch, the attendant, an old friend, asked him: "Seriously, I've seen you buy gas here for years and have watched you tie and untie the knots in that sack. Why do you carry your money that way?"

For a moment the old farmer's face froze. Then he grinned genially and said, "Well, I'll tell you. I haven't ever made much money and it's a lot easier to spend than to get. These here knots are like my conscience. I think I want something and untie a few knots. By that time I've had time to think about it a little longer, and I guess I don't need it as bad as I thought. So I tie the knots back up. I guess it's kind of funny and all, but it works for me." No impulse buyer that man!

Although the incident is isolated and concerns only one person's way of handling his finances, it does say just a bit about the value of even a moment's reflection, and about how just the slightest bit of sober thought can lead to what is quite likely a wiser choice.

The heart of the matter is that the world is very much a thing of machines that we have made. If we consider ourselves a kind of machine also, as some scientists have suggested, then we must admit that our design is a considerably older vintage and we have, throughout the ages, been accustomed to a significantly different sort of life than we lead today.

Though we hurtle through the world at increasing rates of speed, we were designed to move at a conservative pace of a few miles per hour.

The results of traveling at excessive speed are gathered in appalling statistics and the shortening of numerous lives. Though many try to hurry at life's accelerated pace, more and more statistics tell of neuroses and psychoses that have destroyed many careers and distorted many personalities.

The whole idea of renewal is that of simply taking time to assess life and ask oneself about its meaning. As William Matthews, an American author of the last century, said, "knowledge is acquired by study and observation, but wisdom cometh by opportunity of leisure; the ripest thought comes from the mind which is not always on the stretch, but fed, at times, by a wise passiveness."

We enter the fray of life running full tilt. From the time of youth we are trained to want: cars, homes, boats, wall-to-wall carpet, power lawnmowers, retirement plans—the list goes on endlessly. Most of these things were never heard of even a few generations ago.

Not surprisingly, once we enter the job world we are also expected to run as fast as we can. In addition, individuals are often expected to keep the interests of the employer closest to heart and ideally are expected to espouse company philosophy uncritically. The dutiful individual who follows the company line closely and also indulges in community activities good for the company image, is on his way to success. Sir Joseph of HMS *Pinafore* fame (Gilbert and Sullivan) gives evidence that the road to success, even though it now wanders through a severely polluted world, has changed very little: "I thought so little they rewarded me, by making me the ruler of the Queen's Navee."

Thus we arrive at two demanding reasons for reflection and renewal of life's goals and outlooks. The first is that no matter how accustomed we are to living in the same old fashion as yesterday, we live as individuals as well as members of a community. If we do not take time to assess life carefully, we are all too likely to wind up embittered by opportunities we have missed, by finding out that we have not really lived as we should, and by lamenting the careers we have chosen. If it is all too easy to go through life without thinking deeply about what life should mean to us, then we should be sure that we make time for such a process to occur. The number of people going back to school in their thirties and forties, voluntarily seeking more understanding, is a singular example of how frequently a new path in life is found desirable.

The second reason is that the world desperately needs individuals who have sought enlightenment and who want to break out of the mechanical mold in which they have jelled. There is increasing, even undeniable, evidence that we must nurture our world if we are going to be able to continue our existence as a species. We must move from profligacy to moderation in our expectations. We cannot do this without rethinking our priorities.

In his melodrama *The Petrified Forest* (1935), Robert Emmet Sherwood displayed prescience in describing the way the world has been moving for the last half century:

> . . . Nature is hitting back. Not with the old weapons—floods, plagues, holocausts. We can neutralize them. She's fighting back with strange instruments called neuroses. She's deliberately inflicting mankind with the jitters. . . . She's taking the world away from the intellectuals and giving it back to the apes.

Only by reflecting on what we are doing will we be able to arrive at more meaningful ways of action which will stop this process. Only when we reduce our alienation from the planet will we know the meaning of home. Only when we understand at depth the essential nature of clean air and clean water will we begin to fight to preserve them. Only when we realize that the soil, which is eroding massively throughout the world, supports our life, will we be moved to protect it. Only when we understand the difference between needs and wants will we be able to escape the role of consumers and progress toward being individuals.

Today we worship at the shrine of endless production. We look for more and more of everything. We encourage newer and more efficient ways of doing things, displacing people with machines and computers. Only when we realize that the purpose of life is something other than the creation of profit and the enjoyment of luxuries will we be able to take our place as reasoning citizens.

One thing appears obvious. We are currently devoting our energies toward a war against nature. The carnage is highly visible. However much we may try to shape nature to our wishes, however much we may think we are succeeding, in the long run nature will win. We will win too, and still be around, only if we change our ways. There is no need to live a meaningless life. The world stands in desperate need of protectors.

The Journey and the Dream

For weeks the trees stood robed in white, with branches held tightly by the weight of snow. Yesterday it became mild, and by early afternoon, snow was cascading from the tall conifers, plopping and thudding into the already deep, white mantle that covered the forest floor. As I watched, I could see branches somewhat tentatively elevate themselves, bit by bit, to their more normal positions. One could easily take it to be that the trees were rousing themselves from reverie, throwing off the snow garment, and reawakening to a world from which they had enjoyed a respite.

A certain meditative aspect of the scene brought to mind a biography I had read recently. Its subject was the life of Francis of Assisi, and its title was *Francis: The Journey and the Dream*. Standing among the trees of the living forest, I became aware how appropriate a title

The Journey and the Dream might be for all the individual and collective human lives which have been lived on earth.

No matter how one looks at it, life is a journey—from birth to death, or from "the cradle to the grave." It is a journey in time: so many years . . . and since a year is determined by a planetary revolution about the sun, it is also, literally, a journey through the boundless, untamed leagues of space.

Yes, the journey itself is little short of staggering. I can never be too impressed by anyone's description of a lengthy trip when I realize that in a single year our planetary spaceship takes us on a 300-million-mile (480-million-kilometer) voyage around the sun. An eighty-year-old person, who spent his life on a stump in his farmyard, would have made a 24-billion-mile (38.4-billion-kilometer) journey, in spite of his apparent immobility.

But miles do not really describe the journey, as do experiences. How many smiles, or tears, or happy handclasps would there be in an eighty-year journey? How many hopes fulfilled, how many moments of despair, how many moments of reverence might there be? How many times might there be, when even the most apparently self-sufficient individual would be moved to look to the heavens and say, "God, without You, it doesn't make sense."

In reflection, nothing is stranger than the fact that we are all sharing this journey together, in this exact portion of endless time. Is it not bewildering that the earth is not simply brimful of love—each human for every other human, and also for the tiniest living thing that crawls or swims upon the earth?

A healthy reverence for life is no mystery once you realize the staggering impact of what it means to be alive and conscious of anything at all.

The journey, magnificent as it is, is *nothing* without the dream. It is because we have ignored the dream—in fact turned it into a nightmare—that the world endlessly teeters on the brink of one or another kind of chaos.

What can I tell you about the dream? A little. Not too much, but enough perhaps.

"Where can you find the dream?" someone may ask. If you ask me if it is in churches, I will answer by saying that it could be found in such places, but probably won't be, because too many churches spend their time dogmatically defending dogma. "Can it be found amid governing law bodies?" you may ask. Once again I would say it could be, if most were not too busy covering up past mistakes while perpetrating new ones.

It does not seem unreasonable to suggest that the dream is innate—a built-in affair. It may be something on the order of a gift to humans, which can be ignored at one's own peril. Some call it conscience, and it may be visualized as the natural constitution of the intellect—a sense of justness that is more just than what we call justice. The dream is a thing that can only be found by delving into the core of oneself. Peering through the miasma we make of daily life, one glimpses the dream, covered with dust, perhaps, but as pure as the fact that *it* is the *purpose* of the entire journey.

Light is the task where many share the toil.
                              Homer

7

Steps Toward Reconstruction

Some while ago an alarm bell began ringing. Perhaps it was so muted at first that hardly anyone heard it. Some who assessed the times in which they lived and saw the direction in which society was progressing shook their heads dubiously and wondered how long things could last at the rate with which the planet was being "consumed."

For the past year or two the bell has been ringing stridently. We hear more frequently that action must be taken immediately. The major conclusions of the World Conference on the Changing Atmosphere, Toronto, June 27–30, 1988, offer an example:

> Humanity is conducting an unintended, uncontrolled, globally pervasive experiment whose ultimate consequences could be second only to a global nuclear war. The Earth's atmos-

phere is being changed at an unprecedented rate by pollutants resulting from human activities, inefficient and wasteful fossil fuel use and the effects of rapid population growth in many regions. These changes represent a major threat to international security and are already having harmful consequences over many parts of the globe.

Far-reaching impacts will be caused by global warming and sea-level rise, which are becoming increasingly evident as a result of the continued growth in atmospheric concentrations of carbon dioxide and other greenhouse gases. Other major impacts are occurring from ozone-layer depletion resulting in increased damage from ultraviolet radiation. The best predictions available indicate potentially severe economic and social dislocation for present and future generations, which will worsen international tensions and increase risk of conflicts between and within nations. It is imperative to act now.[1]

We are unequivocally confronted with the fact that international cooperation is going to be essential to solve some of the problems that, wherever they originate, do not confine themselves within the borders of any single country. Suddenly the words of Thomas Paine begin to speak to us: "My country is the world, and my religion is to do good."[2]

It appears that time is going to press upon us a new definition of the word 'good.' Our concept that the word 'good' has greatest significance when applied to things that have positive economic value measurable in dollars has proved to be highly simplistic. Time and events have called forcibly to our attention the fact that things are good which assure the health and long-term sustainability of the planet. In fact, planetary health is the very essence of the concept of sustainability. That the tinkerers are not fully aware of this may be detected in hundreds of articles that may be read daily in the media. For example, in referring to the recent U.S. presidential election, columnist Tom Wicker expressed the reservation, "If the planet's rush to self-destruction is to be slowed in time, Mr. (George) Bush may be the last president to have that opportunity."[3] Can it be that our apathy and unwillingness to change will leave us as no more than spectators at our own demise?

The process called metabolism is a combination of two processes involved in building up protoplasm, the basic life substance. The building up of protoplasm is called anabolism, its destruction is catabolism.

188

Human activities have been breaking down the complex living substance of the planet, acting thus as a catabolic force. This is particularly visible today in the ruination of forests all over the world and in the attendant upheaval of soil that, in many cases, destroys even the mosses or other ground cover. Our actions have already tipped the balances precariously and are threatening to return us to a world suitable only for the simplest of living things. Our whole concept of production and progress has shallowly concentrated on creating and satisfying human wants. In the forest industry, this, in a very real sense, has been done by focusing on the trees as a crop while ignoring the function of forests in stabilizing climate, in regulating moisture, and in many other ways that are pushed aside for the sake of economic priorities.

Our task today is nothing less than to reverse the process of "catabolism on a planetary scale" which we have been carrying out. Instead we need to launch a massive effort to restore the complexity and diversity that we have threatened so effectively with our polarized technology. There is such overwhelming evidence already on hand that we should be able to recognize ourselves as the ravagers and voluntarily strive to become the restorers. The catabolic force must thereby bend its efforts to become anabolic. This is less simple than it sounds but the awareness must necessarily precede the ability to undertake restorative action. It would be a mark of maturity that a society, which has cheerfully greeted change for the sake of change should equally cheerfully welcome necessary change imposed by the conditions that sustain life.

A trenchant awareness of this philosophical necessity was shown in remarks made by Sergio Dialetachi, a speaker from the floor, at the World Conference on Environment and Development public hearing in Sao Paulo in October, 1985:

> We know that the world lives through an international financial crisis, which increases the misery and the poverty in the Third World and we sacrifice even more our environment, though we know that this situation can be reversed, if we can use correctly new technology and knowledge. But for this we have to find a new ethic that will include the relationship between man and nature above all.[4]

Just as a single candle can light a thousand others, so it is that small efforts to recycle, to reduce conspicuous consumption, to cease destruction of the world's remaining forests and to carry out massive reforestation, to do any of thousands of necessary things, are steps on a new road that we must follow to emerge from our present ecological crisis.

As Robert Castanza, editor of The Journal of the International Society for Ecological Economics, suggests, the pursuit of "technological optimism," if it proves erroneous, will lead to "disaster" because it will have caused "irreversible damage to ecosystems." If we adopt a more conservative pace, "technological pessimism," and still find that the pace is too fast, we will be within "tolerable" conditions that will still allow for change.[5]

An Awakening Concern for Forests

To begin with, China is extremely rich in varieties of tree species. Whereas *Native Trees of Canada* lists just under 140 species of trees, there are 679 species in the United States, and *literally* thousands of species in China. The number of tree species in China, according to the *Journal of Forestry* (U.S.) is about 3,000. However, an article written by Zhang Hua for *China Features* claims that China has 7,500 species.

Accounts of deforestation in China may be found in many histories. The resulting erosion, siltation, and drying of soil has been well-reported. When the People's Republic was founded in 1949, only 8 percent of the nation still had forest cover. This was further reduced to about 5 percent due to clearing of large amounts of land under the "grain-first policy."

According to Zhang Hua, a massive tree-planting program instituted in China has resulted in an increase in forest cover from 5 percent to 13 percent over a period of 30 years. Using slogans such as "Green the Nation" and "Cover the Country with Trees," China's target is to increase its forest cover to 20 percent by the end of the century and eventually to 30 percent. The world average is 22 percent and the estimate is sometimes given that about 25 to 30 percent of a country should be covered with forest for climate stabilization in latitudes where this is possible.

In China the task is far more formidable than one would suspect. The size of China means that to move from 13 percent to 20 percent forest cover entails the planting of about 259,000 square miles

(670,000 square kilometers), an area larger than Switzerland and France combined.

To facilitate the plan, the National People's Congress has decreed that all Chinese in good health from the age of 11 to the age of 60 for men and to 55 for women must plant three to five trees every year. In spite of disappointment in some areas where survival of trees may be as low as 10 percent (although in other areas it may be over 90 percent) the Chinese continue to plant or replant to attain their goal.

Part of the plan is an afforestation project that has been called the Green Great Wall. This is a plan to create a 4,300 mile (7,000 kilometers) long belt of trees parallel to large portions of the Great Wall. This project, stretching from Xinjiang in the west to Heilongjiang in the northeast is intended to stop the southward march of the Gobi Desert. Eventually all fields will be criss-crossed with belts of trees on the central, northeast, and north China plains. These trees will serve as windbreaks and are expected to moderate the weather. Tree belts are planned around every village and along roads and stream banks.

Solid rows of trees (called four-around plantings) around cities such as Shanghai and Changsha are proving an asset to cities, reducing noise and winds, making the cities more pleasant, and providing sources of fuel and timber. To facilitate its prodigious efforts, according to Sun Shujin, a forestry ministry official, there are 2,096 nurseries run by counties, tens of thousands run by communes and production brigades, and additional state-run nurseries. More than 950,000 acres (400,000 hectares) in all, are devoted to raising saplings. Over two million workers have full-time employment caring for woodland areas.

It is a matter of pride that even high officials take time from other duties to plant trees.

This is a clear indication of the sort of mobilization of effort that would be of worldwide benefit in climate stabilization and in helping to remove some of the excess carbon dioxide that is produced by the enormous consumption of fossil fuels by our society.

Even with the large-scale efforts at reforestation in China, desertification is still an enormous problem. Since the 1950s deserts in China have grown by 11,500 square miles (30,000 square kilometers) to 69,000 square miles (176,000 square kilometers) and are expected to increase by another 28,000 square miles (73,000 square kilometers)—approximately the area of New Brunswick—by the end of this century. It is very clear that the excessive destruction of forests throughout the world needs to be reversed. We must recognize the vital role of forests in protecting climate and water regimes, and promote the status of reforestation to the level of a global war against those activities which threaten to further reduce the essential conditions that protect all life on this planet.[6] Many countries, including Canada, would be well-advised to start massive, national reforestation efforts which involve the public to the greatest possible extent.

Without this type of serious international commitment, we are very much in the position described by Aldo Leopold, "On the back forty we still slip two steps backward for each forward stride."[7]

If we reflect upon history, and upon the insights of men such as Lowdermilk and Marsh, we can realize that serious afforestation, such as is demonstrated in the Chinese effort, should be carried out globally. Dr. G. M. Woodwell, director of Woods Hole Research Center in Massachusetts, an authority on the vegetative fixation of carbon, has suggested that we are in need of two international protocols. One of these is to stop deforestation all over the world, not just in the tropics. The other is to reforest some 1.55 million square miles (four million square kilometers) on good land, so as to store one billion tons (900,000 tonnes) of carbon annually. This would be done through the removal of carbon from the air by photosynthesis and the resultant growth of trees.[8]

An interesting example of rising consciousness concerning the necessity of this type of action may be found in the "first time ever" initiative of an industrial company to offset its projected production of pollutants by establishing a "carbon sink."

Applied Energy Services (AES) of Arlington, Virginia, which has recently built a small, coal-fired power station, has calculated that it will release about 15 million tons (13.5 million tonnes) of carbon dioxide into the atmosphere during the estimated 40 years it will operate.

The company has calculated that the planting of about 385 square miles (1,000 square kilometers) of forest will absorb about the same amount of carbon dioxide as will be produced by combustion of the coal that the power plant will use. An agreement has been established with the government of Guatemala to reforest an area of this size, precisely for this purpose.

When news of the project was released by Robert Goodland of the World Bank, at a conference arranged by the Royal Geographical Society in London, he said: "Carbon sink forests are not a permanent solution to the greenhouse effect. But they can buy us time—possibly

30 or 40 years—and given the threat facing the world's environment, this time could be all important."[9]

Norman Myers, a British ecologist, claims that as of 1980, some 7 billion tons (6.3 billion tonnes) of carbon dioxide are released into the atmosphere yearly. Roughly 5 billion tons (4.5 billion tonnes) of this comes from burning fossil fuels and 2 billion tons (1.8 billion tonnes) from burning forests. Since 1980, fossil fuel consumption has stayed about the same, but the amount from forest burning has increased. While much of the 2 billion plus tons (1.8 billion tonnes) from forest burning originates in the Brazilian Amazon, substantial contribution is made by slash-burning (avoidable) and forest fires in North America. Mr. Myers believes it theoretically possible to reabsorb about 3 billion tons (2.7 billion tonnes) through reforesta-

---

More about Carbon Dioxide

Canadians, per capita, add slightly in excess of four tonnes (4.4 short tons) of carbon to the atmosphere each year. The carbon produced is a part of the 15 tonnes (16.5 short tons) of carbon dioxide emitted per person. The figure is arrived at by dividing the population into the total annual emissions.

Twenty-five percent of the total annual release of carbon dioxide to the atmosphere is the product of transportation. When a car burns an 80 litre tankful of gasoline (17½ Imperial gallons), 176 kilograms (390 pounds) of carbon dioxide are discharged into the atmosphere. The carbon content of this weight of carbon dioxide is 56 kilograms (123 pounds).

In addition, vehicles exhaust about 70 percent of the world's man-made carbon monoxide and approximately 40 percent of total volatile organic compounds and nitric oxides, precursors of smog.

Although Canada, nationally, emits only about two percent of the planet's total annual carbon dioxide production, its per capita contribution is among the world's highest. Only in the German Democratic Republic and in the United States of America are the per capita amounts substantially higher.

Source: Minutes of Proceedings and Evidence of the Standing Committee on Environment, House of Commons, Tuesday, October 31 1989

tion. This would require the planting of about 1.2 million square miles (3 million square kilometers) of forest, an area approximately the size of Western Europe, at an investment cost of $120 billion.

Mr. Goodland pointed out that the control of greenhouse gases is a huge job, but is nonetheless insignificant compared to the necessity of stopping destruction of the life-support systems of the world.[10]

Israel offers another example of a country which is working toward restorative management of its land. This tiny country of 7,900 square miles (20,000 square kilometers) in area, is about 85 percent as large as Lake Winnipeg. Historically, there once were large forests in Israel, which were cut in previous centuries and not replanted. During the last quarter of the nineteenth century, the Ottoman Turks cut most of the remaining accessible forests to build and provide fuel for a railroad which extended down the Arabian peninsula. When resettlement occurred after World War II, only 99,000 acres (40,000 hectares) of the land were forest covered.

Under guidance of the Jewish National Fund (JNF), a private, nonprofit agency that is the sole land-development agency in Israel, forests had been expanded to 262,000 acres (106,141 hectares) by the end of 1948. The rate of forest cover is increasing by about 6,000 acres (2,500 hectares) per year. While this figure may not seem large, it should be noted that each year an area equivalent to almost one eight hundredth of Israel's total land surface is being reforested. To achieve the same result in Canada, it would be necessary to reforest more than 3 million acres (1.2 million hectares) annually. In the continental portion of the U.S.A., it would require 1.31 million acres (525,000 hectares) of replanting each year. (In Canada, rather than seeing an increase of forested land, only one-fifth of the area harvested between 1975 and 1980 was seeded or replanted. Other areas left to natural regeneration have largely failed to grow new stocks of commercially valuable trees.)

A desirable feature of forest development in Israel is the educational aspect that involves Israeli youth. The JNF runs a number of youth camps which provide children from age eight up with a week or more of life experience in the forest. The children learn why forests should be kept and expanded, learn some basic facts of forest management, and learn about their own responsibility in relation to the forests. The camp experience also involves some useful work maintaining trails and recreational sites.

In grammar school, most Israeli children have the experience of planting trees on one of the JNF afforestation locations. Often the children take great personal pride in the trees they plant and also consider them an important contribution to the improvement of their country. Children frequently visit trees they plant and keep records of growth rate and vigor of the trees. The development of a personal bond with the forest is considered highly desirable.

Social concerns are an important aim of planners for the national fund. One goal is to create 600 square yards (500 square meters) of green space per person in settled regions by the year 2000. This will require 220,000 acres (89,000 hectares) planted near cities and towns, along roads and in other locations that are suitable to create forested zones between industrial complexes and residential areas. There are additional plans for reforestation of recreational areas, many of which are already established youth camps, information centers, and lookout points. Surveys of use indicate that 53 percent of Israeli citizens seek various forms of recreation in the nation's forests.[11]

In spite of its commendable efforts in forestry, Israel, like other nations, is a land of paradox. A recent Associated Press story from Haifa described heavy pollution from more than 2,000 industrial plants along Haifa Bay; blamed were lax emission standards complicated by the fact that compliance with standards does not always occur. As in other nations, the environment ministry calls for the enactment of tougher standards regarding air pollution but contends that industries would be "uneconomic" if forced to use low sulfur oil and to install scrubbers.

According to Uri Merinov of Israel's Environment Protection Service, "There is no real public movement that demands environmental protection as in the United States and Europe."

Social Forestry

A relatively new concept in forestry, which is closely connected to the need to slow down and possibly reverse the rate of tropical deforestation and also to slow down the rate of desertification of arid lands, has been emerging in recent years. The United Nations Food and Agriculture Organization, (FAO) refers to the concept as "forestry for local community development" but in order to emphasize the involvement with local people, it is often called "social forestry."

Social forestry is particularly pertinent to the more than 200 million people in developing countries who live in or near forests and depend on trees for essential needs such as firewood, fodder, or food.

The idea of social forestry is that people who rely on forests may be directly involved in planting trees and in harvesting their own needs, whether they be branches for fuel or leaves to feed livestock. Their direct involvement is intended to assure that replanting takes place at a rate that will compensate for direct use of the trees. Since firewood cutting may be a direct cause of soil erosion, replanting must be a continuing part of the process.

A few examples will indicate the sort of thing that is occurring.

In Nepal, local villages are being given land to serve as community forests. The forestry department provides assistance in management of the land. Other areas of rundown, reserved forests are also being received by the villages and an incentive for improving the condition of the forests is given through a profit sharing program with the government. Since deforestation is also occurring in Nepal, it is unlikely that any net gain in afforested land takes place. What is significant, however, is that large numbers of local people have recognized the problem and have become involved in a "grass roots" movement to help rectify it.

In the Republic of Korea, more than 20,000 village forest associations have been created and these organizations have reforested thousands of acres of both community and private land.

Bangladesh has instituted a project to rehabilitate village woodlots, to establish roadside nurseries, and to create plantations of fuelwood along 3,000 miles (4,800 kilometers) of railways, canal banks, and roadsides.

In the Majjia Valley, Niger, CARE (Cooperative for American Relief Everywhere, Inc.) has planted more than 250 miles (400 kilometers) of neem trees as windbreaks. One result has been improved microclimates in fields protected by the trees. More than a 20 percent increase in millet yield has been recorded in protected fields in spite of intense drought.

Similar efforts have taken place in Thailand, the Philippines, Kenya, Peru, Indonesia, Sudan, Burkina Faso, and other countries.

The choice of neem trees by CARE merits explanation. The neem tree (*Azadirachta indica*) is widely distributed in Asia and Africa. It is a hardy evergreen that grows rapidly to as much as twenty meters in height. It grows well in sub-humid or arid situations, is free from attack by almost all species of insects, and is also unaffected by most plant diseases. It also requires little fertilization or irrigation and very little care.

The hardiness of neem trees is related to synthesis of powerful insecticidal agents in its bark, seeds, fruit, and leaves. Farmers have used preparations of neem seeds for pest control in fields and in crop storage, and the insect species it controls are known to be at least 125 in number and include such economically destructive species as the migratory locust and the rice weevil. Research has shown that substances derived from neem leaves can destroy the larvae of mosquitoes and are effective against Colorado potato beetles, boll weevils, gypsy moths, and also against viruses and fungi. It has been noted that locust swarms do not touch neem leaves and crops sprayed with a neem seed product are also left alone by the swarms.

Neem has also been found to have beneficial medicinal uses against fungicidal and bacterial diseases of humans and is reported to be capable of preventing ulcers and to assist in combating inflammations such as arthritis. Neem oil is an effective contraceptive, apparently without adverse side effects. The trees provide wood that is useful in construction and, as might be suspected, is resistant to insect damage. The seed also contains oil that can be used for lighting and has been found to have other commercial uses as well.

There seems to be little argument that neem trees rank high as a reforestation choice.[12]

Debt Swaps

Another type of activity that can be viewed as anabolic is the move to use the indebtedness of nations to protect resources that would be unlikely to be protected by these underdeveloped countries whose primary concerns are the raising of living standards and the burden of staggering international debt. Conservation organizations have, in some instances, been able to pay off a portion of the debts of these nations in exchange for the preservation of areas that have high biodiversity or are important for the protection of endangered species of animals and plants. Such hopeful, creative action is unfortunately limited by the financial abilities of the environmental groups involved. The first significant program is described in a World Wildlife Fund publication:

A 'first-of-a-kind' debt swap agreement was struck this summer (1987) when Conservation International, a Washington-based environmental group, purchased $650,000 of Bolivia's $4 billion external debt for $100,000. In return, the Bolivian Government committed itself to setting aside 3.7 million acres (1.5 million hectares) in three conservation areas adjacent to the existing Beni Biosphere Reserve in the Amazon Basin. A unique Amazonian reserve in northern Bolivia, the Beni Reserve supports 13 of Bolivia's 18 endangered species, as well as cattle ranching and lumbering. The Beni is also home to the Chimane Indians, a nomadic group of hunters and gatherers.

Signing the agreement in Washington, the Honourable Fernando Illanes, the Bolivian Ambassador to the U.S., said, "The economic health of any nation is ultimately based on its ecological health. This 'debt-for-nature' exchange signifies a major breakthrough, not only as a means to reduce Bolivia's debt burden, but also as an effective way to protect the natural resources upon which our country's long-term economic health depends."

According to Peter Seligmann, executive director of Conservation International, Third World nations have begun depleting their natural resource reserves—fisheries, minerals, forests—in attempts to pay off almost $1.1 trillion in external debt. "The prospects for debt servicing and sustained economic growth are being undermined, not strengthened, by the growing pressures being placed on the resource bases of economically depressed nations," he said.

A market for debt purchases exists because some heavily-indebted developing countries may not be able to pay off their loans. Commercial banks are, therefore, often willing to settle for a percentage of the face value of the loans.

In another debt-swapping venture, World Wildlife Fund (U.S.) committed $100,000 the summer of 1987 to purchase $270,000 of Costa Rica's foreign debt at a discounted rate. In exchange, the government of Costa Rica will purchase and manage 40,000 acres of land in northwestern Costa Rica. The land has been incorporated into Santa Rosa National Park, located in the Guanacaste Province of Costa Rica near the Nicaraguan border. The dry forests of the park are home to more than 350 species of birds and 160 species of mammals. In addition to spider and howler monkeys and peccaries, the park shelters such endangered species as jaguars, ocelots and Ridley sea turtles.

While not a panacea for either debt or deforestation problems, the "debt-for-nature" concept offers an innovative approach to these two thorny issues. Washington based environmental groups are now working with Congressional staffers to introduce legislation which would allow commercial banks to obtain full charitable deductions for the forgiveness of debt. Approval of such legislation would greatly enhance the number of "debt-for-nature" deals. Efforts are also underway to persuade the World Bank and other multilateral development banks to allow developing countries to repay part of their debt by investing in conservation programs. At the heart of these discussions is the mutual realization that sound natural resources management goes hand-in-hand with sustainable economic development.[13]

Individuals, too, can make a difference. Richard St. Barbe Baker, forester and founder of Men of the Trees, traveled worldwide to encourage the planting of millions of trees to prevent the further degradation of arid lands. St. Barbe Baker enjoyed making reference to the fact that people of ancient times believed the earth to be a sentient being which responded in accordance with the behavior of men. He went on to say that there was no scientific evidence that this was not so and it would be the better part of wisdom to act with this in mind. Grave concern about the excessive deforestation carried on by humans caused him to express his fear that we were already approaching the limits to which we could deforest the planet without threatening our own survival. He suggested the possibility that we could cause the water table to "sink beyond recall" and cause life to become impossible. St. Barbe Baker reflected:

How strange it is that communities fail to realize the importance of preserving tree cover on tree slopes. Man has a bad record as a forest destroyer, cutting and burning greedily and recklessly, destroying the built-up fertility that has accumulated through the centuries. He has been skinning the earth alive in his greed and folly.[14]

People-power Alternatives

Not surprisingly it is worth taking a look at agricultural practices in China to find increasing awareness that has been translated into action. To be sure, much that we do by technological means is handled in China by "people power." While this may seem archaic, it must also be realized that automated agriculture in industrialized nations consumes 10 energy units of fossil fuel to produce a single energy unit of food. In China, where 85 percent of people are involved in agriculture, there is obviously less use of fossil fuels with corresponding reduction of pollutants. (In North America, about 70 percent of the population worked in agriculture in 1880, whereas in 1985 the figure was under 3 percent).[15]

In August, 1975, a group of nine U.S. entomologists visited the People's Republic of China to learn as much as possible about insect-control practices there. They traveled 4,700 miles (7,500 kilometers) and visited communes, universities, research institutes, markets, and factories. They noted an extensive pest management scheme designed to manage pest populations in order to avoid economic damage and to minimize environmental side effects. They saw many street signs in crimson letters which carried the message: "Eradicate the four evils, flies, mosquitoes, rodents, and bedbugs, develop good sanitation, change the old traditions, and restructure the world." One of the team, hearing that the housefly had been controlled effectively, kept a diary in which he recorded how many flies he saw. In 27 days of visits to all sorts of communities and farms, he counted only 30 flies.

The entomologists observed that enormous recycling efforts are under way. All human and animal excrement, crop refuse, and organic wastes of all kinds are returned to the land or to fish ponds for food production. One Chinese province, Hunan, had about one million light traps (one for every 10 acres). The electrocuted insects fell into containers which held water from cooked rice. The rice water and electrocuted insects were then used for fish food.

"Agriculture for an honorable and high-minded man, is the best of all occupations or arts by which men procure the means of living."

Xenophon

Many of the most dangerous chemical insecticides are not used at all and very toxic insecticides are not produced in China. A large-scale program for the breeding and distribution of predatory Trichogramma wasps was in place and Chinese entomologists had concluded that wasps offered dependable insect control as good or better than the use of insecticides. Young ducks, which eat about 200 insects each per hour, were also used to reduce the use of chemical insecticides on early rice.

A large-scale interest was evident in the use of insect pheremones and microbial insecticides such as *Bacillus thuringiensis* were also used extensively.[16]

The fact that China is independently concerned with creating sustainability within its own borders was evident during a study mission conducted by the Food and Agriculture Organization of the United Nations. The study, which took place in 1975, established that China had achieved the provision of "adequate food, clothing, shelter, medical care and reasonable security for almost a quarter of the human race." China has successfully put the world's largest agricultural labor force in the field, has reversed the worldwide trend of migration into cities, and has kept most people on the land.

Along with production of food, a great emphasis has been placed on the need to store grain in order to be prepared for natural calamities or such a man-made calamity as war. People are urged to dig deep tunnels and to store grain everywhere. Grain is stored by individual families, by teams, brigades, communes, and at all levels from rural to national level.

A consistently conservative approach is taken to all resources. The FAO study reported that "Waste runs against the ethical grain." The conservative approach extends to the management of land and water resources, to the use of organic residues, to manpower, and the capacity of industrial plants. Every available bit of land is put under crops. New arable land is developed by building terraces and by leveling hills. China utilizes even rooftop gardens to add to food production. When land is not suitable for food production, it is turned over to trees.

The study mission found it a characteristic of China that soil is carefully husbanded. Tremendous amounts of compost and organic material are returned to the soil each year. The mission's conclusion is that the quality of land is improving under intensive care. One member of the mission expressed the view, "There seems to be a love affair between the Chinese farmer and the land." In the pest control and disease area, considerable stress is laid on preventing outbreaks rather than relying on pesticides. Close attention is also paid to breeding for pest and disease resistance.

An interesting innovation in Chinese agricultural schools is the use of "veteran farmers" to provide sound, practical information to supplement the more technical aspects of the agriculture program. A sound basis for sustainable agriculture is implicit in the Chinese approach.

Conservation, Our Greatest Energy Resource

In 1977, Worldwatch Institute researcher Denis Hayes observed that those Americans who had air conditioning used more electricity for that single purpose than 800 million Chinese people used for everything. For lighting alone, the U.S. used more electricity than the total amount generated on the continents of South America, Asia, and Africa.

He identified other areas of waste. The use of wood wastes as fuel, as is done in Sweden, could reduce the use of fossil fuels in some paper mills by as much as 75 percent. Likewise in some European cement plants, the waste heat from kilns is used to preheat the raw limestone. By using waste heat in such a manner, the European plants use only 550,000 BTU's (British Thermal Units) per barrel of cement as compared to 1.2 million BTU's per barrel in the U.S. plants, where waste heat is not utilized.[17]

With bountiful supplies of energy available, little concern for energy conservation was evidenced in the U.S. prior to 1973. Home refrigerators made in the mid-1970s used five times as much energy as those built in the 1940s. The average 1973 model car got ten percent less mileage than did 1961 models.

By 1973, 20 percent of energy used in the U.S. was imported. Rising concerns about energy use resulting from OPEC (Organization of Oil Exporting Countries) manipulated shortages and price increases caused serious attention to energy conservation between 1973 and 1980. Although ex-president Ronald Reagan of the U.S. did not sustain the momentum of those years, since 1973 the conservation policies adopted are estimated to be worth $150 billion dollars a year. This lends credibility to the view that energy conservation efforts were long overdue and are still one of the most effective ways of solving North American energy problems.

The home refrigerator offers an example of means of conserving energy. Between the end of World War II and the early 1970s, home refrigerators more than doubled in size, offered increased freezer space, and offered automatic defrosting as a replacement for manual defrosting. To cut production costs, manufacturers sacrificed efficiency, so that even a small manual-defrost model of the 1970s consumed 70 percent more energy than the same-sized 1940 model.

Lowered efficiency plus the growth in number of American households meant that American refrigerators used the output-equivalent of 34 large coal-fired power plants by the year 1974. Projecting postwar growth rates to the year 1994, it was found that 215 new power plants with a capacity of 500 megawatts per plant would be required simply to supply power for refrigeration.

Faced with this extreme increasing demand for new powerplants, California, with 20 percent of the nation's demand for refrigeration, adopted a requirement that 1980 model refrigerators would have to use at least 20 percent less electricity, on the average, than 1975 models. With improved insulation materials and improved fans and motors, the new requirement was easily met, and by 1985, refrigerators were using 35 percent less energy. Even more stringent regulations in California led to the adoption of national legislation, in 1987, calling for another 15 percent to 20 percent reduction in electricity needs by 1990. The goal is that by 1995, national refrigeration needs will be less than one-fifth of the needs indicated in mid-1970s projections. According to those projections, 107,000 megawatts of power would have been needed to supply refrigeration in 1995, which will now be provided by generation of only 21,000 megawatts.

Refrigeration is just part of the story. More efficient lighting (including fluorescent screw-in bulbs that provide four times as much light as incandescent bulbs of the same wattage), better insulation, and better insulating materials are included among present energy conservation techniques. Improved practices can result in 30 percent to 90 percent less energy consumption than was acceptable even in the late 1980s.[18]

The $150 billion yearly energy saving is equivalent to a savings of almost $2,000 per household.

A forward-looking finding of Public Citizen, a Washington, D.C., research organization, is that renewable forms of energy other than hydro (biomass, wind, direct solar technology, and geothermal) have increased tenfold over the past ten years.

Public Citizen notes that costs of wind systems and solar thermal plants have declined by more than half since 1980, and that the cost of solar photovoltaic cells has dropped by 75 percent since 1980.

The province of Ontario, under its Energy Efficiency Act, has recently set minimum efficiency levels for water heaters, clothes washers, clothes dryers, ranges, dishwashers, and ground-source heat pumps. Energy requirements for water heaters with better insulation will decrease by 20 percent. The savings to the province by these heaters alone would rise from 35 million kilowatt hours in 1990 to 180 million kilowatt hours by the year 2000.

This, coupled with Ontario's finding that environmental protection activities already lead to $2 billion in annual sales and employment of 28,000 people, should help us all to realize that protection of the environment can be good business.[19]

Reducing Synthetic Chemical Use

In Britain, an attempt to encourage more traditional, less intensive farming has been greeted with enthusiasm. Britain has designated nineteen environmentally sensitive areas in which farmers can receive a subsidy if they discontinue use of "synthetic" fertilizers and pesticides and rely on methods of farming that are environmentally sound. The sensitive areas that have been designated amount to a bit more than 4 percent of Britain's agricultural land and extend from undulating chalk downs in southern England to some islands of the outer Hebrides.

The program costs $25.2 million per year, with 25 percent of the amount coming from European Economic Community (EEC) grants. The amount an individual farmer may receive will vary according to the loss of productivity entailed. The amounts range from $250 per acre ($630 per hectare) for returning to traditional agriculture on highly fertile farmland to the minimum of $8 per acre ($20 per hectare) on land having very low productivity.[20]

A similar program has been approved by the EEC and is to take place in the northern federal state of Schleswig-Holstein. This program, costing $7.8 million in 1988 and $10.6 million in 1989, will subsidize farmers who cut back on intensive farming by ceasing to use pesticides and by either leaving fields in fallow condition or turning them into pasture.[21]

The province of Ontario also intends to cut pesticide use in half, by the year 2002. A fifteen-year program, costing $1.4 million, started in 1988, and includes the appointment of four specialists in pesticide management. Pesticide safety will be promoted and research instituted. An annual expenditure of $80,000 will be devoted to research on pesticide alternatives, on management programs, and on reduction of chemical dependency. Ontario's former Agriculture and Food Minister, Jack Riddell, expressed the hope that his province would be able to reduce chemical costs to farmers by $100 million yearly while sustaining crop yields.[22]

Independent companies are also showing disaffection with pesticides. H. J. Heinz Company has informed growers that it will no longer buy produce for baby food processing if that produce has been treated with any of the 12 chemicals that are under "special review" by the Environmental Protection Agency. "Special review" identifies chemicals that may be hazardous and will undergo intensive investigation by the EPA. Heinz declared it would test for residues of these products commencing in 1987. The pesticides identified by Heinz are alachlor, aldicarb, captan, linuron, cyanazine, captafol, carbofuran, carbon tetrachloride, daminozide, ethylene oxide, TPTH, and dinocap. Heinz is the third-largest manufacturer of baby foods in the U.S.A.[23]

Indonesia has become the first nation in the world to adopt integrated pest management as a national pest control strategy. This has come about by decree of President Raden Suharto and comes after increasing complications resulting from massive pesticide applications. The government had subsidized 80 percent of pesticide costs which had totaled $25.4 billion dollars (U.S.) to 1989.[24]

Many contributing factors were involved in this decision. These included the deaths of 31 people in Java, after eating pesticide contaminated food; the deaths of 43 people in the village of Cicadas, the site of a DDT formulation plant; studies by agencies which found excessive pesticide residues in foods as varied as cabbages, mustard greens, fish, shrimp, and crabs; pesticide contamination in all water bodies tested in West Java; and studies by the Indonesian Department of Agriculture which disclosed that in 50 percent of pesticides surveyed in 1987–1988 and 1988–1989, the active ingredient had been misidentified. Research disclosed that 50 percent of chemicals were, in the vernacular, bogus.

During the massive pesticide application period, a small insect called the rice brown planthopper destroyed millions of tons of rice, about 600,000 tons (545,000 tonnes) in 1986. As many as fifteen pesticide applications per month failed to control the planthopper. Scientists determined that pesticides killed natural enemies of the planthopper and some highly poisonous pesticides actually stimulated reproduction of the brown planthopper. A report of the Food and Agriculture Organization of the United Nations said the planthopper "was a pest because of, and not in spite of, pesticide applications."

Integrated pest management (IPM) techniques involve protecting natural enemies of plant-feeding insects, staggering planting times so that there will not always be a steady supply of rice for the planthopper, and using toxic pesticides only when needed. A massive extension program trained more than 15,000 farmers in IPM the first year.

Following the adoption of IPM, pesticide use fell off rapidly and, by the third season, insecticide use was down 90 percent. During the same time, rice yields increased from 2.4 tons per acre (5.5 tonnnes per hectare) in 1986 to 3 tons per acre (6.7 tonnes per hectare) in 1987. Pesticide costs dropped by 70 percent in the same period, in spite of increased costs per unit.[25]

Grassroot Level Action

A surprising amount of activity also exists at the grassroots level in many countries around the world. While we in North America are aware that the ponderous machinery of government and the growth-focused gaze of industry are slowly, and perhaps somewhat grudgingly, beginning to respond to awakening citizen awareness of environmental problems, the reality of these problems is experienced in everyday life in many of the less-fortunate nations of the earth.

In the words of Worldwatch Institute researcher Alan B. Durning, it is those who are actually living and suffering from environmental decline who are the most aware of the peril besetting the planet, and they constitute "the ragtag front line in the worldwide struggle to end poverty and environmental destruction." Throughout the world, he contends, there is a vast grassroots movement taking place to try to reverse environmental decline. He infers that it may not be here in the affluent countries where well-fed people drive personal vehicles to meetings of environmental groups that the most direct action takes place; but it may instead be "the East that could be the environmental boom field of the nineties." Although we might think Soviet Russia an unlikely place for serious environmental action, Durning reports that during "glasnost," citizens' initiatives emerged "like mushrooms after a rain."

In Bangladesh, another nation stirred to movement, 1,200 organizations have formed since 1971, their primary concern being problems of health and income generation.

In Sri Lanka, the influence of Mahatma Gandhi is to be seen in the involvement of three million people and 8,000 villages in the Sarvodaya Shramadana movement. Sarvodaya is a "village awareness" concept and Shramadana means "gift of labor." The movement involves people donating their time to improve life for all. Through the village groups, large numbers of people are mobilized for projects that might include road building, tree planting, or drainage of malarial bogs.

Kenya, by 1984, had 16,232 women's groups with a total membership of 637,000 members. Thousands of these groups, along with youth clubs and harambee (let's pull together) societies have involved themselves in tree planting. In response to a Greenbelt Movement begun by the National Council of Women of Kenya in 1977, more than a million trees have been planted in 1,000 greenbelts and another 20,000 mini-greenbelts have been established. In addition, 670 tree nurseries have been established. Kenya's largest network of women's development groups also began a campaign in 1985 to develop and build cookstoves that would be more efficient and require less wood. What is significant is that a strong partnership is emerging between these groups and government officials.[26]

Thus it is, that some of the most hopeful of human enterprises may be responses to the surge of interest on the part of common people around the world.

That there is paradox in grassroots movements is almost unquestionable. The poorest and weakest of people are acting in accord with convictions which are apparently irrelevant to the streamlined world of technology, the acquisitive habits of the world of high finance, and the pathological preparedness for doomsday that permeates the military sector. Yet the grassroots optimists have more likelihood of creating a world of peace and hope than has the world of finance, technology, and military might, all of which offers little but a divided world of unrest, uncertainty, and inequality.

If the world does not erupt in violence, the surge of consciousness in the small and weak is something akin to the ancient Chinese philosopher, Lao Tzu's observation that although nothing is weaker than water, nothing can withstand it. He expresses his conviction that ultimately weakness prevails over strength, and gentleness over the great hindrances placed in its path. One has only to stand at the edge of some great canyon to see the strength of weakness (water). If it is difficult to imagine the effectiveness of apparently inconsequential factors in human affairs, we have only to think of the cumulative effect of emissions from millions and millions of automobile tailpipes and factory chimneys on the production of acid rain; or the molecule-by-molecule accumulation of PCBs in marine mammals, until we have reached the point where 80 percent of seals in the Baltic Sea are believed to be sterile because of these chemicals and it is hypothesized that marine mammals around the world are facing extinction from our use of this single chemical.[27]

It now seems that a restoration ethic, however rudimentary, is stirring on the planet. Active attempts to heal the earth may stem from self-interest but they display comprehension of what must be done, and it appears that those historically closest to the land are taking the lead. We may be fortunate in that vestiges of Goldsmith's "bold peasantry" (see Chapter 3) may yet exist in every nation on earth, and perhaps in surprising walks of life.

Nongovermental Organizations Activity

Throughout the world, a remarkable amount of positive action has been taken by nongovernmental organizations supported by private donations. World Wildlife Fund Canada offers an interesting example of significant achievement. WWF Canada is one of the 23 affiliates of World Wide Fund for Nature, which has its headquarters in Gland, Switzerland.

WWF Canada (Toronto), founded in 1967, has supported 700 projects worth $35 million, in Canada and around the world. WWF Canada identifies its purpose as the conservation of animals, plants, and habitats for their own sake and for the long-term benefit of people. The achievement of this purpose involves implementation of the World Conservation Strategy, a multi-agency effort launched in 1980, in Canada and internationally, to achieve the goals of maintenance of essential ecological processes and life-support systems, preservation of genetic diversity, and sustainable utilization of species and ecosystems.

Monte Hummel, president and chief executive officer of WWF Canada counts the following among the most important accomplishments of WWF Canada so far:

- Establishment of a national conservation education program, Operation Lifeline, currently involving 5,000 schools and 150,000 students across Canada. Participating classes receive activity books, posters, special tours, and regular newsletters, all of which are designed to fit within existing school curricula. Additionally WWF Canada has helped develop programs along the North Shore of the St. Lawrence regarding seabird conservation and has cooperatively researched and published booklets in Inuktitut on conservation of Arctic resources.

- Outside Canada, WWF Canada has invested $300,000 in education and training programs in China to prepare protected-area managers for administering wildlife reserves, including bamboo-nest habitat for the giant panda.

- Enlisting the support of more than 300 Canadian corporations for conservation, and receiving their support in changing actions and policies with respect to the environment.

- Securing the commitment of the federal government to $100 million for the North American Waterfowl Management Plan, to be matched by $900 million from other sources.

- The raising of $500,000 from Canadians to complete the purchase and protection of the Monteverde Cloud Reserve in Costa Rica. (Monteverde Cloud Forest hosts more than 2,000 plant species, 320 species of birds, and 100 species of mammals).

- A three-year moratorium on logging in the Khutzeymateen Valley in British Columbia while both the wildlife and timber values are more carefully determined.

- The establishment of 155 new parks in Ontario, and a new parks policy which does not permit hunting, logging, mining, or hydro development in Ontario's provincial parks.

- Taking the white pelican off the Endangered Species List in 1987, and the wood bison off the same list in 1988.

- The establishment of major regional and national programs such as Whales Beneath the Ice, the Wildlife Toxicology Fund, Carolinian Canada, and Wild West. Each of these programs includes many sub-projects which tackle issues and produce specific results for wildlife and habitat in Canada.

In its quarter-century of existence, the WWF and its 23 National Organizations have been involved in more than 5,000 projects in 130

Another Comeback

The pronghorn antelope of North America once ranged widely in the Western plains and foothills of North America. Canadian naturalist, Ernest Thompson Seton, estimated that the number of antelope in the late 1860s may have been as high as 100 million. Other more conservative estimates place the primitive numbers between 30 million and 50 million. The pronghorns ranged from the prairies of Canada southward into Mexico.

Seton quoted Newberry's Pacific Railroad Reports (1857) that relentless and incessant war was waged against the pronghorns, making its flesh "cheaper and more abundant" in California markets "than that of any other animal." He also referred to Major J. B. Pond's observation (winter 1868-69) of a band of antelope "huddled together for warmth" that was 20 to 40 rods (100 to 200 meters) in width and 10 to 12 miles long (16 to 19 kilometers). Pond also noted that wagonloads were brought to Denver, Colorado, and sold. The smallest coin in use was a 25 cent piece, and 25 cents was sufficient to purchase three or four carcasses.

Dr. E. W. Nelson's report, "Status of the Pronghorned Antelope, 1922-24," gave the result of this sort of predation and of opening of lands to agriculture. According to his report, antelope had been reduced to 26,604 in the United States, 1,327 in Canada, and an estimated 2,395 in Mexico; in all 30,326 animals.

Restoration of antelope to a present day population of approximately 500,000 in North America is one example of positive success in game management efforts. Efforts commencing with Benjamin Lawton, chief fire and game guardian for Alberta (1909), have led to the establishment of protected areas for the pronghorns. Seton refers to being one member of a committee of two, with "Maxwell Graham of the Wild Life Department at Ottawa," the purpose of the committee being to "select three or four tracts of land as possible Antelope preserves." Later, as superintendent of park animals, Graham did much of the spadework for the establishment of Nemiskam, Menissawok, and Wawaskesy National Parks.

At present there are about 30,000 antelope in southeastern Alberta and southwestern Saskatchewan.

Sources: Ernest Thompson Seton, Lives of Game Animals, vol. III, part II (Boston: Charles T. Branford, Co., 1953), pp. 411-67.

Jim Gibson, "Three Tiny Prairie Parks Saved the Pronghorn," Canadian Geographic, December 1987, January 1988, pp. 59-65.

countries on all the continents in the world. These projects have involved the expenditure of more than $130 million U.S. Projects have ranged from saving Galapagos flora and fauna, including giant tortoises and marine iguanas, to the development, with the United Nations Environment Program and the International Union for Conservation of Nature and Natural Resources, of a "World Conservation Strategy" which demonstrates that conservation is a prerequisite to sustainable economic development. National conservation strategies are being developed in 43 countries.

An interesting example of how a seemingly minor animal may have an impact on natural balance, far beyond that which its size might indicate, may be found in this description of one of the WWF activities.

In 1987, the Indian Government banned the export of frogs' legs. Since the 1960s, India had been exporting 140 million frogs' legs a year to supply the European gourmet trade. But the ecological cost was high; rice-field pests once controlled by the frogs had to be attacked with chemical pesticides. This increased the risk to humans and wildlife, and cost the country more in imported chemicals than the value of exported frogs' legs. WWF India used a traditional scroll, depicting the problems caused by upsetting the natural balance, to alert farmers and villagers to the problem. WWF Traffic's office in Germany led a vigorous campaign in Europe. Announcing the ban, the Indian Government pointed out that 700,000 Rupees a year would be lost in sales of frogs' legs but the saving in pesticides and other costs would be more than 5,000,000 Rupees.[28]

Possibly the most significant of all the WWF enterprises is its focus on conservation in education. Conservation educational programs include such specific projects as a Conservation Awareness in Politicians program in Peru, assistance with an environmental education program that affects 1,500 schools in Ecuador, an In Service Training for Park Personnel program in Thailand, a Training Course in Wetland Assessment in China, and Training Fellowships for Conservation Officers in Africa.

The rapid growth of other organizations such as Friends of the Earth, Greenpeace, and Western Canada Wilderness Committee indicate the rising tide of concern for the health of the planet.

What is now needed is a massive effort on the part of governments and wise use of the media to launch an international effort for the restoration of degraded lands all over the world. This will be no mere cosmetic effort, with a minor curtailment of economic growth and a modicum of concern for environmental protection. Instead, it must be a major effort that will shake the foundations of all nations, goals and objectives and bring runaway development into equilibrium with long-term environmental parameters.

The Conscience of the World?

In 1923, Dr. Albert Schweitzer propounded a scenario for the decay of civilization which now, at last, may be reversing itself; and without question, in what is probably humanity's greatest hour of need. Hypothesizing that a true civilization needs the finest contributions of all its members, he suggested that when collective society influences individuals more than they influence it—in other words, when people behave like sheep and are afraid to be individuals—society is on its way to ruin. This is so because the noblest elements of spiritual and moral worth have surrendered themselves to unthinking conformity. At that point, society cannot even understand the problems it must solve. The fact that individuals are now reversing this trend and are beginning to act with dignity and resolve is a significant change of utmost importance. The political sector now has to realize the wisdom of Gandhi's comment: "There go my followers and I must follow them, because I am their leader."

If the collective spirit of humankind is indeed eroding the shackles of unreflectiveness that have been forged, civilization may be building a base that will yet allow it to flourish. Future hindsight may show that the environmental movement was a first stirring of the conscience of the world.

Campfire Thoughts

The little campfire glowed brightly in the gathering evening shadows. In a nearby thicket a toad called plaintively for the oncoming rain it sensed. From where I sat, with my back against a log, I could look away from the fire and see the shapes of trees, etched in the twilight. I noticed how different the forest appeared when one studied it a bit. Many of the trees leaned at one angle or another. Each seemed to be taking its own path upwards, towards the light. Among the living trees were stark outlines of ones that had died; some of them stiff-limbed to the tip with dead branches and others broken off at varying distances from the top.

Briefly I considered the relationship to human life, wondering whether human individuals are similarly compelled to grow toward a light—perhaps The Light—even though they may not understand either the direction of life or the force that guides it. Like the trees, there are many "leaners" among humans; individuals who have been buffeted by storms, partially uprooted a time or two, yet aiming at the light even though their growth is now "angular." Then too, there are stiff-limbed humans, long dead in spirit, who still stand stalwartly; and if one studies them closely he may find—as one often does in a forest—that a new bit of greenery is hastening upward from roots that yet have a spark of life. Frequently, the growth of such trees, or people, can be prodigious; the dead-seeming top often misrepresenting the living root. Of course, even the storm-blasted hulks, shattered and battered as they are, are contributing their arrested growth to a forest, or a humanity, that is in the future.

I turned back to the campfire, listening to the sizzling and sputtering sounds it was making. I fed it a few sticks and watched the hungry tongues of flame reach for them. In the near-white glow of the coals and in the blues, reds, and oranges of the flames, I could sense the long history of our race, huddled at one time around flames for protection from dangerous things that went thump and bump in the night, or from silent creatures that crept close, but were halted by the winking, glowing eye in the darkness. Now of course, a campfire is little more than a friendly, cheerful companion; or perhaps is the highlight of a recreational outing—but of no greater necessity than that of roasting a few marshmallows, or brewing a pot of "tramp" coffee.

The rocks at the back of the small circle-of-rocks were reflecting heat nicely. I poured a cup of coffee from the can and sat with the cup between my hands, enjoying the warmth of the cup, the heat of the fire, the sound of wavelets lapping the shore of the lake in front of me. I suppose, in a sense, I was also enjoying the thought of the ancient beginnings of our race, and the part that fire had played in sustaining our fragile inner warmth.

My mind drifted back upon other campfires I had enjoyed—in the Appalachians, in the Rockies, the Cassiars, the Ominecas, on the shores of lakes in the Yukon and Alaska. Always, it seemed, the campfires could be associated with moments and places of peace and reflection.

I often ponder these rather simple things, so capable of giving enjoyment. There are those who claim that civilized man has passed the point whereat rustic moments are fruitful. Yet, there are also those, among whom I number myself, who realize that humanity is in dire need of renewing its roots in the simple experiences and settings that nature affords.

No other campfires glowed anywhere around the margin of the lake where I sojourned. Was it, I wondered, that mankind had gone home for the night, and shut itself indoors? Or was it, on the contrary, that mankind had left its real home and shut itself in *away* from that home—away from the soft breezes soughing in the pines? When, I wondered, did man become a stranger to his own world? When, and why, did he cease to love the outdoors save for the monetary wealth it could afford? When did we become aliens in the world which gave us our beginning? And, did we lose sight of a true light—a starlight and sunlight—and begin a new growth toward the false glow of an insatiable ambition to control, to manipulate, to create a world in our own image, twisted image though it may be?

8

*Every virtue gives a man a degree of felicity in
some kind: honesty gives a man a good report;
justice, estimation; prudence, respect; courtesy
and liberality, affection; temperance gives
health; fortitude, a quiet mind, not to be
moved by any adversity.*

Sir Francis Walsingham

The Eleventh Commandment

It has been pointed out, and often seems the case, that the more
things change, the more they remain the same.

Primitive man, in his cave or rudimentary shelter, was subject to all
the vagaries of the "howling wilderness." Death undoubtedly lurked
in the night and the safety and cheer of an open fire must have had
meaning then that stretches beyond our most vivid imagination today.

Modern, urban dwellers, in the labyrinthine web of streets and
ornate, multi-leveled caves of highrises, shut and bar their doors on
another howling wilderness of dangerous streets where it becomes
increasingly unwise to wander, even carefully, at night. Media mes-
sages infiltrate the private caves, bearing constant news of local and
international tension and violence and of a world teetering on the
edge, threatening to slip into one form of embroilment or another.

There seems to be little doubt that the problems of today go far beyond technological and economic considerations. They are problems of the deepest, innermost regions of the human psyche, of that often denied will-o'-the-wisp, the human soul.

They cannot be solved until we have the courage to confront ourselves, to recognize and mend our very real shortcomings.

At the 1988 World Conference on the Changing Atmosphere in Toronto, the Honorable Tom McMillan, then Canada's Minister of the Environment, gave an address in which he referred to a cartoon by Gary Larson, creator of the Far Side cartoon, as "capturing the essence of the human situation."

According to Mr. McMillan,

> He envisioned a conference much like this one filled with dinosaurs at a convention. From the podium, one dinosaur addressed the assemblage.
>
> "Delegates," he said, "the outlook is bleak. We face extinction, an ice age is advancing, meteorites threaten our planet; and we have a brain the size of a walnut."
>
> At our own conference, we, too, are telling ourselves the outlook is bleak. But we have one advantage over the dinosaurs; our brain is not the size of a walnut, it is nature's highest achievement. Unlike that of the dinosaurs, our brain is capable of logic, reason, foresight and judgment.
>
> Will we use those faculties to ensure our survival? The answer has yet to be given.

Begging the question as to whether or not the human brain is nature's highest achievement, we must now earnestly exercise all of the attributes Mr. McMillan assigns the brain, particularly foresight, for we know that the human also has a well-developed habit of learning mainly by hindsight.

Two interesting examples of foresight-hindsight may clarify this point.

Albert Einstein once told Dr. William Hermanns, a German sociologist who interviewed him: "Dr. Hermanns, if you want to do something for me," he said with a faraway look in his eyes, "tell the world that if I had foreseen Hiroshima and Nagasaki, I would have torn up my formula in 1905." In the same vein, Admiral Hyman Rickover, the man who was likely most responsible for the large scale use of nuclear power in North America, told the members of the U.S. Congressional Joint Economic Committee that if he had his hand on the tiller, he would sink the submarines he had responsibility for and try to eliminate dependence on nuclear power. He had been director of the U.S. nuclear submarine program for forty years. When the committee asked him about commercial use of nuclear power, he told them,

> We do not take into account the potential damage the release of radiation may do to future generations. Every time you produce radiation you produce something that has a life, in some cases for billions of years, and I think the human race is going to wreck itself. It's far more important that we get control of this horrible force and try to eliminate it.[1]

In this section we will move back and forth from hindsight to foresight, trying to use the latter to help formulate the former. We have already seen some of the consequences of human interference with systems that were established and quite stable before our intervention. It would probably help considerably if we would dispense with the rather self-satisfying belief that the human brain is natures' superlative effort and look upon ourselves with a bit more humility. More appropriately, we must think of ourselves as one of an unknown number of species that has swelled its numbers until it has put such undue stress on the environment as to cause a serious reaction in the form of environmental resistance. That we have a modicum of intelligence which might be our saving grace is fortuitous. This can be our salvation only if we suppress our unreasonable expectations and behavior and actively strive to rebuild the life-supporting systems we have torn to bits in our haste, and our thus-far remarkable lack of applied foresight.

The Myth of Central Position

This brings us to the point of our greatest need: a self-motivated reawakening from willingly-embraced "technosleep," from a sleep that has been so profound we have allowed the earth to be nearly destroyed. The reawakening must be self-inspired because it must strive against the propaganda barrage of the soothsayers whose control of the phenomenon we mistakenly think of as progress is anchored to the monorail that guides present thought. Out of this vigorous new alertness will arise the realization that what passes for rational behavior today is the most devastating superstition that has ever held humanity enthralled, the superstition that the planet is mankind's puppet, one that will dance and posture at its masters' command.

If we must move the needs of the planet to center stage and assign human aspiration to the wings, it is only because we have been sadly out of step with a genuine realization of our place in the scheme of things. It is an unhealthy paradox that we lavish care on our homes, lawns, cars, and other personal belongings while we ignore the wastelands we have created throughout the world. We must be very confused to think that a mini-paradise created within a fence and four walls is the sum and substance of our responsibility. Eventually the outer world creeps inside as we should have learned from Love Canal, from studies of toxins in drinking water, additives in food, Three Mile Island, and other incidents in recent history.

The necessity of modifying our illusion of central position in the universe is not a new idea. The German zoologist Ernest Haeckel, who coined the term "ecology," defined "anthropism" in 1899: "I designate by this term that powerful and worldwide group of erroneous opinions which opposes the human organism to the whole of the rest of nature, and represents it to be the preordained end of the organic creation, an entity essentially distinct from it, a god-like being."[2]

John Muir, the American naturalist who took the lead in founding the Sierra Club, was one of those who lamented the human demand for center stage in the universe. Muir felt that the biggest obstacle to understanding the correct relationship between humans and other living things lay in the ill-founded assumption that the world was made solely for human purposes. He felt that this was an erroneous conclusion, unjustified by observations of the natural world. As he said, "Every animal, plant, and crystal controverts it in the plainest terms." The once firm friendship between Gifford Pinchot and John Muir dissolved as a result of the disparity of views they held toward the world and man's place in it. Pinchot's utilitarian outlook held that man should be the principal beneficiary of the bounty of nature and Muir's preservationist attitude held that vast areas should be left as God made them, because he believed in the divinity of nature and also felt it would serve forever as an inspiration to all who would live on earth.

John Muir — Man of the Forest

Few men have been as stalwart in defense of nature and wilderness as John Muir. Born in Scotland in 1838, he went to the U.S. in 1849. Although Muir spent four years at the University of Wisconsin, he claimed that the important part of his education was received in what he called the "University of the Wilderness."

Once asked what steps he took to prepare for a sojourn in the wilderness, he replied: "I put some bread and tea in an old sock and jump over the back fence." Deeply immersed in wilderness experiences, Muir enjoyed riding out a Sierra Nevada storm in the topmost branches of a tall tree. He is said to have spoken with "John the Baptist fervor" in defense of his beloved wilderness. In 1879, Muir journeyed to Alaska and discovered Glacier Bay. Muir Glacier, which he also discovered, was named for him.

Both Gifford Pinchot and President Theodore Roosevelt were enraptured by their association with Muir.

Pinchot referred to Muir as "a storyteller in a million." He told of spending "an unforgettable day" on the rim of the Grand Canyon with him. Pinchot related how they had come across a tarantula and how Muir would not let him kill it. "He said it had as much right there as we did." At the close of the day, they had a hard-boiled egg, a small sandwich apiece, and water in their canteens. They made beds of cedar boughs in a thick stand of timber that kept the wind away and "there he (Muir) talked until midnight. It was such an evening as I have never had before or since."

Roosevelt's association with Muir was equally stimulating. After a trip to the Mariposa Grove (sequoias), Muir and Roosevelt camped in a gathering storm. They awakened with four inches of snow covering them and the ebullient president rejoined his own party the next morning shouting, "This has been the grandest day of my life."

Muir's role in the establishment of a number of national parks is significant. He has been accredited a vital role in obtaining park status for Sequoia, Yosemite, Mount Rainier, Crater Lake, Glacier, and Mesa Verde national parks, and also in a number of national monuments, two of which, Grand Canyon and Olympic, later received full park status.

Sources: Paul R. Cutright, Theodore Roosevelt the Naturalist (New York: Harper, 1956).

Gifford Pinchot, Breaking New Ground (New York: Harcourt-Brace, 1947).

Stewart L. Udall, The Quiet Crisis (New York: Holt, Rienhart & Winston, 1963).

Muir contended that "I have never yet happened upon a trace of evidence that seemed to show that any one animal was ever made for another as much as it was made for itself."

Yet he recognized that no animal or plant lived in isolation from other species. He understood that all things shared common existence and depended on each other in ways both obvious and subtle.

> Indeed, every atom in creation may be said to be acquainted with and married to every other, but with universal union there is a division sufficient in degree for the purposes of the most intense individuality; no matter, therefore, what may be the note which any creature forms in the song of existence, it is made first for itself, then more and more remotely for all the world and worlds.[3]

A New Order of Restraint

In our daily lives we have accustomed ourselves to a remarkable number of laws, agreements, and restraints. Often the restraints are designed to protect us from our own clumsiness, impetuousness, ignorance, carelessness, overconfidence, greed, and a host of other frailties. Other restraints may serve to protect individuals and societies from thieves, from swindlers, from the violently inclined, from disease, from dangerous chemicals, and from natural and unnatural hazards.

Here is a random assortment of things which in some way or another fit broadly into the general category of restraints: crib rails, highchairs, banisters on stairs, life jackets, guards around moving parts of machines, seat belts, roll bars, governors, speed limits, stop signs, brakes, one-way streets, guard-rails, quarantine, hunting seasons, bag limits, safety boots, hard hats, safes, safety deposit boxes, vaults, police, armies, navies, early warning systems, burglar alarms, locks, laws, marriage, private property, jails, courts, manned border crossings, noise bylaws, leashes to restrain pets, railroad crossing barriers, passports, job qualifications, pub closing hours, warning signs (e.g. No Swimming —Beach Polluted), strait jackets, manacles, fences, vehicle chains, and warning lights. There will be no trouble adding to this list since it is the product of but a few moment's thought.

It is consistent with society's focus on short-term goals, that the restraints we have devised have to do with health, safety, and prevention of violence in situations that have foreseeable immediacy. Raising our sights to long-term problems has not been our forte.

This is the point at which we seem to have let our thinking founder.

In our particular allegiance to what is sometimes called "speciesism," we ignore our true relationship to the planet. We easily recognize our own importance but fail to recognize that we occupy the surface of a planet, the health of which is the sine qua non of our own health. As long as it is capable of supporting us, we can fantasize whatever illusions we wish as to our own importance. In his highly regarded book, *Soil and Civilization*, Edward Hyams subtitled the second part of his text, "Man As a Parasite on Soil." As a not altogether inaccurate description of our place in the kingdom of life, his subtitle should remind us of the biological axiom that a good parasite does not destroy its host.

Unfortunately that is exactly where we are today. We are well along in the destruction of our host. Consciousness is dawning that we have gone too far, and that we have unwittingly sown the seeds of our own undoing. It is tragic that we remained oblivious for so long a while, although this perhaps does show the extent of the fascination we hold for technology.

It should be noted that a serious proposal for a land ethic was made in 1949 by Aldo Leopold, forester and founder of the discipline of wildlife management. In his essay on the subject, he indicated that a land ethic, ecologically, "is a limitation on freedom of action in the struggle for existence."[4]

The need for restraints of a new order of magnitude is clearly apparent today. We do have a choice of approaches. We could take the Henny-Penny approach, "the sky is falling," or adopt the conservative businessman approach, "It has come to my attention. . . . " We could also be honest and admit we have overstepped our capabilities and launch a serious effort to try to restore the planetary stability we have disrupted. The obviously logical choice is to develop a system of restraints in the form of an *earth ethic* that becomes highly visible and a constant subject of attention. The earth ethic would need to have two components: one for the reduction of our present and future impact on life-support systems, the other for immediate action to be taken to assist in the restoration of the earth. Time is certainly a pressing factor. If, as has been suggested, a million species of plants and animals will likely be extinct by the end of the century, it would be

222

unwise to adopt the bureaucratic model of instituting a study which is twice that number of years in duration.

The value of an earth ethic, if realistically expressed and idealistically conceived, is that it could serve as a moral rallying point in a world of shifting, relative, often meaningless values. It could outline procedures to be followed immediately, which would serve to bend the world away from the suicidal, military, and industrial policies that are leading toward the death of the planet.

Some Needed Changes

Although the "establishment tendency" has long been to brush aside environmental issues as irrelevant and counterproductive, even at times to dismiss them as frivolous, there is a new urgency evident in the media which indicates a change in attitude. In its December, 1988, issue, National Geographic magazine posed the question as to whether we must reach absolute bottom, and crash like alcoholics and drug addicts, before we change our behavior. It referred to the fact that political rhetoric now finds the seriousness of environmental concerns admissable, but at the same time elected officials seem unable to devise any "courageous solutions."[5] It might also be noted that the Globe and Mail, Toronto, produced a supplement on the same subject which it entitled, "To Save The Planet." Time and Maclean's magazines have dedicated significant space to the same topic.

The message is coming across. Despite the blindfolds we have been accustomed to wearing as devotees of the consumer society, our intuition which now strongly tells us that all is not well may yet be our saviour. As Aldo Leopold wrote in a paper which he entitled, "Conservation is a Moral Issue:"

Possibly in our intuitive perception, which may be truer than our science and less impeded by words than our philosophies, we realize the indivisibility of the earth—its soils, mountains, rivers, forests, climate, plants, and animals, and respect it collectively not only as a useful servant but as a living being.

The truth of the matter is that it is at the level of "gut-feeling," or what the philosopher might call "moral intuition," that many people

223

realize we are in grave trouble. Some moral theories, classed as "ethical intuitionism" advise us that moral decisions should be based on "gut-instincts" to a much greater extent than is common.[6]

Let us look for a moment at the changes in attitude and actions the adoption of an earth ethic might entail in just one area, forestry. If we were talking about the expenditure of eight to twelve billion dollars for nuclear submarines, something the Canadian government was seriously contemplating, there would be considerable thought (and there was) that this would be a reasonable sum for a thoroughly worthwhile purchase. If we were to suggest that this enormous expenditure for such life-destroying items should indicate our willingness to spend ten times that amount on reforestation, we would probably encounter outrage. Yet, whereas the nuclear submarines pose a further threat to all life on earth, reforestation is a life-preserving effort.

Reforestation would also be an excellent example of a restorative effort, actively applied. While a massive reforestation effort can only facetiously be called foresight, since it should have been taking place for more than a century, as fast as forests were cut, it is nonetheless foresighted compared to putting it off any longer. It may be noted that in the January 2, 1989, issue of Time magazine, which focused on the "Endangered Earth," one of its agenda items was to "launch a mammoth international tree-planting program."

At this point it is important to remember Woods Hole Research Center director Dr. Woodwell's call for international protocols to stop deforestation and to commence massive reforestation in order to absorb excessive atmospheric carbon.

A similar concern about carbon is expressed by American engineer John D. Hamaker, who writes:

> The increase of carbon dioxide in the atmosphere is man's most urgent problem. In order to save civilization, we will have to take immediate action on a worldwide scale of a magnitude never before undertaken by mankind. *The carbon dioxide curve must be reversed and started downward by about the middle of this decade.* It is so urgent because crop losses due to the carbon-dioxide-induced severity of weather conditions are creating a world that has virtually no food surplus for customers who can pay, let alone for those who are hungry and those who are now starving to death.[7]

It is quite common knowledge that plant photosynthesis produces oxygen as a byproduct. While it is not known how much oxygen the primitive earth atmosphere contained, it is accepted that if it was rich in oxygen, plants have helped keep it so, and if it was deficient in oxygen, as is supposed, then the present proportion of oxygen is probably a result of photosynthesis through the ages.[8] While it is perhaps nearly impossible to determine what man's "most urgent problem" really is, there are many reasons why a truly massive reforestation scheme would be desirable, and would better fit the concept of an investment than of an expenditure. Along with carbon fixation, planting trees would provide such things as better control of soil erosion; better regulation of snow-melt, of stream and spring flow; and stabilization of climate.

Photosynthesis and respiration are, in a sense, reverse but complementary processes that take place in plants. Photosynthesis uses carbon dioxide and water—in the presence of chlorophyll, and with the driving energy of sunlight—to produce sugar and oxygen. The oxygen, which is released into the air, is an important byproduct useful to animals and to other plants. As long ago as 1779, Dr. Jan Ingenhousz, a Dutch physician, performed a series of experiments which proved the emission of oxygen by plants is due to the energy of light itself, and not to the heat of the sun. Today, it is known in greater detail that the intensity of light available determines the rate of photosynthesis.

Respiration uses sugar made by photosynthesis to build and maintain protoplasm, to construct cell walls and protoplasmic membranes. Oxygen is used in this process and carbon dioxide is liberated to the air. Although respiration takes place during day and night (whereas photosynthesis occurs only during daylight hours), respiration is a much slower process. During the daytime the carbon dioxide liberated by respiration is used immediately, and the total carbon dioxide taken in by photosynthesis exceeds the total amount of carbon dioxide produced by respiration.

One of the most alarming prospects of global warming is the fact that respiration is very sensitive to temperature change. A one-degree increase in temperature may increase respiration by 10 percent to 30 percent or more. Since photosynthesis is not affected in a similar manner, there is a serious concern that global warming will increase the decay of organic matter in soils and forests globally without a corresponding increase in the rate of photosynthesis. If these fears are justified, the global warming already being experienced could lead to a release of an additional one to 6 billion tons (.9 to 5.4 billion tonnes) of carbon each year to the atmosphere.

Since land shaded by forests is cooler than deforested land, deforestation, especially clearcutting, may be especially unwise behavior.[9]

While we hear much regarding the importance of the tropical rainforests and the effect on world climate caused by cutting them down, we must also realize that the temperate-evergreen forests, the temperate-deciduous forests, and the boreal forests all contain substantial amounts of the biosphere's total continental plant carbon. Whereas tropical rainforests contain roughly 41 percent of the biospheres' 827 billion metric tonnes (910 billion short tons) of carbon, (excluding the oceans), the temperate-deciduous and evergreen forests combined with the boreal forest contain about 34 percent of the biospheres' total continental plant mass.[10]

Attention that is focused on cutting of the tropical rain forests should in no way minimize our awareness of the cutting of forests in our own country. Focusing attention on tropical forests is one method of diverting attention from the pillage of North American forests. While trees are standing, they are growing, and in this process they remove carbon from the atmosphere. While reforestation is extremely important, the tiny new trees are in no way capable of removing large amounts of carbon. As their size increases, though, they naturally become more efficient atmospheric scavengers. Jerry Franklin, chief ecologist of Region 6, U.S. Forest Service, has pointed out that it is common to think of a Douglas fir of 100 years of age as having passed rotation age. But such a tree has attained only about two-thirds of its eventual height and much less than that amount of its potential growth in diameter. He points out that as these forests attain what is known as old-growth status, they truly become extraordinary in terms of their ability to recycle nutrients and retard erosion. He claims there is no other forest cover that can compare. What is particularly important for carbon removal is the fact that old-growth forests are incredibly efficient atmospheric scavengers because of the huge volume of space they take up, and because of their enormous areas of leaf surface. Their highly efficient root mantle also conserves available food by allowing very little leaching of nutrients into ground water. A single old-growth Douglas fir may have 60–70 million needles with a surface area of about one acre (43,560 square feet or 4,051 square meters). Other old-growth trees which he mentions as having similar important

226

roles are the western red cedar, Sitka spruce, and the noble fir.[11] A fact little advertised by logging companies, which may refer to old-growth forests as "cellulose cemeteries," is that productivity in old-growth forests is typically high, rather than low, in spite of their claims to the contrary. In British Columbia, every 10 days, an area of old-growth forest the size of the entire 16,600-acre (6,730-hectare) Carmanah Valley is clearcut logged. Waste levels of merchantable wood in the clearcuts is often higher than 15 percent.[12] Considering their importance to climate alone, perhaps it is time to stop the removal of our few remaining old-growth forests.

Taking into account atmospheric carbon dioxide concerns such as the greenhouse effect and general destabilization of climate, it truly seems highly justifiable to consider a massive international effort in reforestation as one of the most advantageous actions that may be undertaken in implementation of an earth-restoration ethic. It would be a matter of minimal foresight, now, to engage in this effort without delay before worsening climatic conditions create situations that might make seedling growth far more difficult than it is today.

Reforestation offers an excellent club or group activity. The possibility of buying a logged-over piece of land does exist, and reforestation and care of a tract of land could be a highly worthwhile personal and public service. Organized community effort in reforestation is something we could learn from other nations that have already set out on such a course. Community forestry is becoming a byword in some countries which we often think of as behind the times.

It is interesting to note that the Science Council of Canada, in 1983, pointed out that one-eighth of the productive forest land of Canada has been so deteriorated that huge tracts are devastated and cannot regenerate an economically valuable tree crop in the next 60 to 80 years. Each additional year adds 500,000 to a million acres (200,000 to 400,000 hectares) to this degradation of the forest land base. While the Science Council's agenda for action proposed an increase of the area reforested each year from 250,000 to a million acres (100,000 to 400,000 hectares), this hardly appears adequate in terms of the global effect of forest loss.[13]

From the state of Canada's forests, it is easy to see that other actions should be taken as well. These include a reduction in present forest waste by better utilization and salvage; better management of dead wood in keeping with scientific studies pointing to the valuable role that dead wood has in forest ecosystem ecology (such management would greatly reduce slash-burning, which creates obnoxious smoke and carbon dioxide, and which often causes extensive soil damage); and reduction of site disturbance which accelerates erosion. While rotting produces the same amount of carbon dioxide as burning, decay would also restore valuable nutrients (which are lost in burning) to soil and would be produced on a vastly different time scale, and there is little doubt that we could benefit from added time. The appropriateness of extensive clearcutting should also be reexamined inasmuch as this method of harvesting destroys untold numbers of trees of up to 25 or 30 years of age. These trees, which are being bulldozed into piles and burned after clearcutting takes place, would form a substantial portion of the next standing crop if they were left to grow through selective cutting methods, and they would also serve to store up carbon as they grew. Genetic diversity would also be more efficiently preserved along with recessive genetic characteristics that could be of great value in a time of great climatic change. Time magazine's "Planet of the Year" issue also recommends that forests be harvested without being "obliterated." It points out that selective harvesting of mature trees enables other valuable uses to be encouraged through such strategies as increasingly popular "ecotourism."[14]

If, as it appears, clearcutting is one more instance of available technology dictating how things are done, it is the technology that needs to be changed, rather than to allow premature destruction of tomorrow's trees. Review of numerous forestry reports indicates that new things are being learned all the time and that there is a growing understanding if not a widespread appreciation for the order and intricacy of the forest established by nature. It wasn't widely known until the mid-1950s, for example, that the nonleguminous tree, red alder, has the capability of nitrogen fixation. This tree often serves as a pioneer species, appearing in burns or clearcut areas, rebuilding soil and increasing the soil nitrogen supply, by a conservative 1,700 pounds (780 kilograms) of nitrogen per acre every five years, with a value of $100 per acre every five years.[15] Yet for years it has been regarded as a weed species and systematically destroyed by herbicide application. Similarly, during the past ten years, two other important sources of nitrogen have been discovered: symbiotic relationships with blue green algae in crown and ground lichens, and bacterial fixation of nitrogen in rotting logs. Such evidence suggests that we are cutting at rates above sustainable yield while we are still unaware of many of the important relationships within forests.

Ecotourism:
A Rea$on to $ave Nature

A joint study of "Tourism as a Generator for Regional Economic Development," held at Whistler, B.C., in May, 1987, indicated that the demand for outdoor opportunities will "intensify in the decades ahead" due to peoples' concern about stress on the family and also due to the fulfillment that individuals are finding in leisure activities rather than in traditional forms of work.

Some indication of this trend is found in statistics from a Canadian federal fisheries survey in 1985 which indicated that revenue from the freshwater sport fishery totalled $144 million. (Of this amount, $31.5 million came from visitors to B.C.). Saltwater anglers spent an even greater amount, $166 million.

Revenue from other leisure activities has likewise increased. Within a period of 15 years, companies sponsoring river-rafting trips grew from one to 50. A 12-day river trip costs $2,225 (1987), and the trip-cost does not include additional money spent on air fares before and after the trip, on accommodations, personal equipment, and various purchases.

When Canadian Mountain Holidays introduced heli-skiing in 1965, 13 guests were taken into the Bugaboo Mountains. In 1987, 3,500 guests paid an average of $2,800 per week for heli-skiing experiences.

Adventure travel is being promoted as therapy and re-creation of the individual self. Reduction of stress and a restoration of the self, mentally and physically, are some of the benefits sought by individuals. Corporate participation in adventure experiences is growing as companies recognize the benefits such trips can provide to their executives.

Source: "Tourism as a Generator for
Regional Economic Development,"
Proceedings of the
First Annual Advanced Policy Forum on Tourism,
Whistler, B.C., May 1987.

Certainly attention to harvesting at or below sustained yield would fit the other component of the earth ethic we need, the component which would reduce our impact on life-support systems. Although we now know that the rate of deforestation should be slowed, our devotion to market forces has accelerated forest removal. As University of Manitoba physicist Jovan V. Jovanovich has pointed out, it may be too late when we find out for sure that deforestation is changing global climate. He recognizes the possibility that cutting down the Amazon jungle and British Columbia's forests may eventually result in the Prairies being as dry as the Sahara. Certainly we should act with prudence and decrease the rate at which we remove our forests—and our options.[16]

We can also look at reducing the impact of our actions in still another way, one which could cause a substantial reduction in the amount of carbon produced. This one might violate what we consider one of our sacred rights, to exploit potential wealth as we choose, though it is questionable what such sacred rights will amount to if we continue to play brinkmanship with the well-being of the planet.

In the 1960s and early 1970s, secondary school students studying chemistry in British Columbia learned that one U.S. gallon of gasoline can be considered to be about 25 moles of octane, C^8H^{18}. They learned that the combustion of a gallon of gasoline required 22 pounds (10 kilograms) of oxygen from the atmosphere, and as a result of combustion, 19.4 pounds (8.8 kilograms) of carbon dioxide was produced and emitted to the atmosphere. In other words, for every 100 gallons (378 liters) of gasoline completely combusted by vehicles, almost one ton (1,940 pounds) (880 kilograms) of carbon dioxide replaces oxygen in the atmosphere. Of course, not all the carbon dioxide that enters the atmosphere remains there. About half is absorbed by the oceans and taken up by the growing plants on earth, which again indicates why reforestation on a very large scale can be considered beneficial at this time.

Two things are quite obvious. One is that a substantial reduction in the use of vehicles would help curb the release of carbon dioxide to the atmosphere. The other obvious thing is that many people would be upset if restrictions were put on the right to drive, wherever, whenever, and as much as one feels like driving.

Gasoline rationing, at present, seems unacceptable in self-indulgent societies. Yet we must face the fact that we are not in a situation that is going to solve itself, and that changing lifestyles are going to result from things we must do in order to try to prolong life on this planet.

It might help if we were aware of some important facts regarding the consumption of gasoline. In 1968, when a UNESCO conference came to the conclusion that it would only be about 20 more years before the planet started to reach a condition of uninhabitability due to air pollution alone, the 90 million motor vehicles in the U.S.A. were contributing vast tonnages of pollutants to the atmosphere. In the late 1960s the U.S. Public Health Service calculated that American automobiles annually polluted to the extent of 66 million tons (60 million tonnes) of carbon monoxide, 1 million tons (910 thousand tonnes) of sulfur oxides, 6 million tons (5.5 million tonnes) of nitrogen oxides, 12 million tons (10.9 milllion tonnes) of hydrocarbons and 1 million tons (910,000 thousand tonnes) of particulates, plus other inimical substances. This amounted, on a daily basis, to pollutants that weighed more than a bumper-to-bumper line of cars reaching from Chicago to New York.[17] Calculations for 1967 indicated that passenger cars in the U.S. consumed 55.3 billion gallons (209 billion liters) of gasoline, an average of 671 gallons (2,540 liters) per car per year. Buses used about 2,755 gallons (10,428 liters) per year per bus, and trucks and other combinations used about 1,324 gallons (5,012 liters) per unit. The automobile was credited with 60 percent of U.S. air pollution, and with as much as 85 percent in some cities. Altogether, automotive use contributed 91 percent of all carbon monoxide to total air pollution.[18]

One often hears the statement: "I'd like to do something, but what can I do?" The answer becomes quite obvious when a person realizes that the great environmental problems of our day are the sum total of millions of individual incidents in which injurious substances are released into the environment. This has been realized for some time and led individuals such as philosopher Lewis Mumford to suggest that we should use machines as little as possible. To be sure, many things are beyond an individual's control, but it is still possible to curb one's own driving and one's use of fossil fuels in general. Self-imposed rationing of fossil-fuel use could certainly be considered as evidence of individual foresight and become part of our personal earth ethics.

Sometimes the opportunity for less polluting travel is readily available. GO (Greater Ontario) Transit in Toronto is an example. Although 780,000 cars enter Metro Toronto each day, the number is reduced by the fact that GO trains carry 16 million passengers yearly, while the city's bus fleet carries another 11 million. Ian Allaby points out that the comparative cost of using a GO train or a private car from Oakville to downtown Toronto, one-way, is $3.45 by train compared to $8.15 by car. In addition, the car user may pay up to $10 per day for parking his private vehicle. Mass transit is less polluting than private

> "Restore human legs as a means of travel. Pedestrians rely on food for fuel and need no special parking facilities."
>
> *Lewis Mumford*

vehicles and also consumes less energy, while "packaging" people far more efficiently than one or one-and-a-fraction to the car.[19]

Recycling, a highly constructive activity for organizations, constitutes another effective way to reduce the quantity of polluting gases while reducing impact on our battered forests. Paper made from recycled materials rather than from new wood cuts the energy requirement by 35 percent to 50 percent and reduces air pollutants that would be created by making new paper by 95 percent. Sandra Postel points out that significant reductions in worldwide carbon emissions could also take place if the three largest users of coal, China, the U.S.S.R., and the United States were to take vigorous, concerted action.[20]

Clearly, there are many things an individual can do, just in connection with the things we have mentioned, which are generally centered around the issue of carbon. Cutting down on personal transportation is the most evident of these actions. Associated activities may involve lobbying for mass transit, lobbying for more efficient vehicles, relying less on vacation activities that involve extensive travel and thereby getting to know better one's own locale, bicycle holidays, walking tours, doing things manually that are usually done with machines (i.e. spading the garden instead of tilling it), and, in general, being very conscious of the overuse of all forms of energy. It is equally obvious that one can plant trees when the opportunity exists, encourage the observation of Arbor Day by schools and community, reduce one's own use of paper in all forms, urge higher postal rates for junk mail, encourage recycling, make others aware of conservative actions, lobby for increased tree planting, for less wasteful logging, and for vastly increased reforestation.

Only through the effect of a massive groundswell of public opinion can we make our politicians aware of the fact that they are supposed to represent the long-term well-being of society rather than the short-term profit of industry. Only through absolute refusal to accept the obtuseness of industrial forces that devastate the land and threaten all life on earth can we awaken the frozen indifference of those who

One Obvious Solution

Recycling materials reduces the extraction of resources, reduces garbage disposal (landfill and incineration), and also reduces air pollution and energy consumption.

In Canada and the U.S., per capita consumption of paper is about 600 pounds (275 kilograms) per year (direct and indirect use). The Sunday edition of a large newspaper, the New York Times, consumes about 150 acres (60 hectares), some 75,000 trees. In Canada alone, more than 20 million trees were cut down last year to keep Canadian newspaper presses rolling.

Worldwide about 25 percent of waste paper is recycled. This includes 18 percent of waste paper in Canada and 27 percent in the U.S.A. During World War II, when recycling was a priority, the U.S. recycled 40 percent to 45 percent of its paper.

The recycling of a 36-inch-high (90 centimeters) stack of newspaper saves one tree, thus reducing the harmful effects of deforestation. Paper recycling also saves from 30 percent to 55 percent of the energy required to make paper from virgin pulp and can decrease air pollution from pulp mills by about 95 percent. Construction of a mill to process waste paper is 50 percent to 80 percent cheaper than building one to process virgin pulp. Grades of paper that can be recycled range from the highest quality office stationery to newspapers and corrugated cardboard. After being recycled several times, fibers become too short to make paper but are still of value in the production of insulation, roofing felt, or animal bedding.

Ways in which individuals can help to reduce wasteful paper uses include:

1. Buying recycled paper products.
2. Encouraging local recycling efforts and supporting them by sorting and saving paper for recycling.
3. Avoiding the purchase of paper napkins, paper towels, paper diapers, paper cups and plates.
4. Avoiding purchase of overpackaged items.
5. Reusing paper bags.
6. Lobbying for reduction of junk mail.
7. Writing on both sides of paper and urging schools to adopt this practice.
8. Carrying lunches in a lunch box rather than in a paper sack.
9. Saving large mailing envelopes for reuse.

Sources: G. Tyler Miller, Jr., Living in the Environment (Belmont, CA: Wadsworth Publishing, 1985), pp. E69-E71.

Cynthia Pollock-Shea, "Realizing Recycling's Potential," State of the World 1987 (Washington, DC: Worldwatch Institute, 1987), pp. 109-11.

consider profit more important even than the death of the planet. Our individual actions will therefore lead to those changes which society as a whole must make.

Most of us are aware of the Biblical line, "They shall beat their swords into plowshares, and their spears into pruning hooks; nation shall not lift up sword against nation, neither shall they learn war any more." (Isaiah, 2:4). There is no activity we could contemplate that would be as optimally beneficial to humanity as the maturation of our species to the extent that it could dispense with warfare. Not only would this be a tremendous reduction of resource use for entirely wasteful purposes but also it would be a means of releasing huge sums of money for the rebuilding of the planet.

The traditional approach has been to label the pursuit of peace on earth as utterly impractical and foolishly idealistic. If we take a really hard look at our claim that we are an intelligent species and at just where we are and just what sort of prognosis there is for the survival of our species, we will have to realize that we must solve the problem of our own bellicose nature. By any sensible standard of thought, it is our pathological devotion to mayhem that we must curb and extinguish if we are to have a single hope of saving our lives. It could be hypothesized that it is impossible to stop warfare. Then we might as well say that it is impossible to continue to exist. If we cannot unleash our intelligence against our own defects in character, our extinction is just a matter of time. Our fascination with newer and more destructive weapons leaves no room for doubt in this matter. It would be interesting to tally the number of military academies throughout the world in comparison to the number of schools for training people in ethical statesmanship or in solving the problems of bringing peace to our planet. Is it simply the fact that war is a profitable venture for the manipulators of human fate?

The preoccupation with weaponry seems almost an inbred characteristic and has led to the suggestion that man became the dominant species only by developing weapons which compensated for his lack of physical strength and speed compared to that of other predatory animals. If, as playwright and author Robert Ardrey suggests, we have been shaped by our weapons to the extent that "from handaxe to hydrogen bomb, (our) best efforts have been spent on the weapon's perfection," we can no longer afford to continue in the same vein. Ardrey's argument that man's specialty is the weapon is all too convincing.[21]

 An annual edition of the Manhattan (New York) phone directory requires the paper from 43,000 trees. In addition, 100,000 pounds (45,454 kilograms) of ink are used and more than 35,000 pounds (15,900 kilograms) of glue. In 1974, 1.5 million Manhattan telephone directories were printed. If they were piled in a single stack, it would be 40 miles (64 kilometers) high.
Source: Common Sense, no. 5, 1979, p. 10.

Considering the likely outcome of military posturing all over the world, we invite our own demise—particularly if we ponder seriously the theory of paleontologist Richard Swann Lull that "extreme specialization" is a significant fact in the extinction of species.[22] Lull states that paleontology offers repeated evidence of evolved characteristics which have led to extinction; the huge size and awkwardness of sauropod dinosaurs, the huge antlers of Irish deer, and the excessive tusks of the Jefferson mammoth.

So we must assume that we can get over the hurdle of being predisposed to warfare, and if we do, then very much becomes possible.

In 1970, Richard St. Barbe Baker—founder of Men of the Trees, the man who started the Save the Redwoods campaign in California,

> "Do you know what amazes me more than anything
> else? The impotence of force to organize anything. There
> are only two powers in the world, the sword and the spirit.
> In the long run the sword will always be conquered by the
> spirit."
>
> *Napoleon*

and also a man who devoted his life to reforestation—suggested that
if the standing armies of the world (then 22 million men) were de-
ployed to planting trees in the deserts, within 8 years 100 million
people could be rehabilitated and provided with life-sustaining food
grown in lands that are now unproductive. His own experience suggests that techniques he developed could be adequate to this process.

Instead of rubbing our hands ruefully and fruitlessly over the
problem of spreading deserts, we should mobilize human effort to
reclaim these areas. This seems a far more worthwhile course than
many that are undertaken and also constitutes a meaningful challenge
to human ingenuity—a first step in the restoration of Eden. In many
instances, land has been so savaged by human activity that it is unlikely
that much of it can grow any crop that we consider "economic." This
is because we have not yet realized that healing of the land has any
economic value. Because we are so closely tied to immediate benefits,
or profits, we often cannot comprehend, at least at any depth, that
while individuals live in the short term, species survival is more than a
short-term matter. If the fertility of land must be restored under grass
and weed cover that we consider useless, it is simply because the land
was initially overstressed by our ignorance. It must be allowed to
rebuild itself with the help of our wisdom.

With a 1989 figure of 5.6 billion tons (5 million tonnes) of carbon
added to the atmosphere by the consumption of fossil fuels and up to
3 billion tons (2.7 billion tonnes) of carbon being added by deforestation annually, it is past time that we separate frivolous uses of fuel
from necessary uses, and the convenient mechanical methods of clear-
cutting forests from careful, selective logging methods which leave
growing trees on the land.[23]

Although we have a conviction that the world is, in addition to
being our workplace, also our playground, we need ask ourselves
whether we can continue to hurl carbon into the atmosphere from
countless activities that contribute to unsustainability—in ecological

terms rather than in economic terms—simply because in the long run we cannot manipulate the environment the way we can readjust our economic imperatives. Do we absolutely need automobile races at Lemans or at the Indianapolis Speedway? Are helicopter skiing and helicopter hiking valuable uses of a diminishing resource and justifiable activities in a world in which global warming is possibly leading to planetary disaster? Is jet tourist travel essential? What about pleasure boating, pleasure driving, use of ski tows to haul exercise-seeking individuals up steep hills? These may be questions we do not wish to confront, and it may be comforting to hide our heads in the sand and pretend that they are irrelevant. However, if we cannot confront the necessity of curbing our infatuation with motorized play, it may turn out that we have blinded ourselves to a truly terminal addiction.

We prefer to dismiss serious consideration of relevant issues by lumping them as alarmist. This is akin to ignoring a fire in the back hall because we are sitting in the living room. Our environmental crises are a function of the sum total of all contributing issues, none of which are unimportant; and if we dismiss any of them summarily we are as irresponsible as Aesop's grasshopper who mocked the busy ants by skipping and playing while they went about the business of storing food for winter. We can say that of course the grasshopper was preprogrammed and didn't know any better but it is unlikely that we have a right to claim the same excuse.

As for technology specifically, a vast filtering of good technology from bad technology is a serious necessity. We are long overdue in deciding that no industrial process should come into being until it has proved beyond doubt that its development includes the full ability to render its wastes harmless. Dream solutions such as shooting wastes into orbit, dumping them in oceans, or storing them in salt mines until some never-to-arrive day in which they can be safely handled comes about are simply ridiculous. If we cannot control what we create, we have no business creating it. Much of the wealth of today exists because environmental costs have been ignored. To continue our folly any longer is ignorance. The grandiose megaprojects that result from the desire to master nature must be replaced by micro-projects designed for minimum impact on natural systems; a much greater challenge to engineering technique.

We are overdue in another sphere where we need to take action. The few remaining wilderness areas of the planet have shrunken to the point where limitations should be put on further exploitation.

Given our business mentality, this will be hard to achieve. The human is so utterly committed to "development" that it is considered "heretical" to point out that much of what we call development is simply glib misuse of the language. Destruction would be a far better word to describe what often happens. In our hopes to rebuild the world to some level of sustainability, we need to protect substantial portions of our undisturbed land, wherever it may be, for many reasons including the fact that we need to understand what functioning natural ecosystems are really like. Both because of what we have done to the environment and because of the rising awareness that we must change, we need to save such areas before those who would "develop at any cost" have put them forever beyond our reach. This is an issue on which society is quite divided but a move towards preservation of

---

Yes, in Our Backyards!

The difficulty of disposing of toxic wastes invites us to question how much longer we can gear societies' wants to production processes which leave behind offal of such dangerous character that no safe method of disposal is known or can be afforded. Present handling of such material is little more than "out of sight, out of mind" dumping.

Toxic wastes are a menace to life on earth. Instead of working to reduce the quantity of toxic wastes, industrial nations attempt to avoid the high costs of safe disposal by exporting waste to countries that will allow low cost dumping.

The U.S.A., which generates about 300 million tons (273 million tonnes) of hazardous waste yearly, has successfully opposed United Nations Environmental Program efforts to control transboundary shipments of hazardous wastes.

Trade in toxic wastes is sufficiently alarming that more than forty nations have banned waste imports and provided for criminal penalties to deter waste importers.

At present, between 75 and 90 percent of hazardous waste exported by the U.S.A. goes to Canada.

Source: Mary Deery Uva,
"Where In The World Shall We Send Our Hazardous
Waste Today?",
Journal of Pesticide Reform, vol. 9, no. 2,
Summer 1989, pp. 10-12.

generous portions of these lands may be of absolute and indispensable value in a very short while.

Another hard-to-tackle problem is that of ever-increasing numbers of humans on earth. Lester Brown, president of Worldwatch Institute, has spoken of the need to limit populations by encouraging two-child families for the world as a whole and in some countries to a single child per family.[24] Third world countries are almost all committed to curtailing population growth. Surveys by the United Nations and other agencies have shown that more than 200 million women in developing countries do not want any more children; and yet, in many instances they have little, if any, access to effective means of birth control. Given the fact that we seem subject to the general conditions that face other organisms, a natural check to human population looms darkly on the horizon.

In speaking of population control, English economist and theologian Thomas Malthus referred to three obvious checks on human population: war, famine, and disease. Certainly the propensity for war that is evidenced in daily news reports gives clear warning that the hounds of war may not long be held in abeyance. Famine already stalks many lands and disease has leveled populations before. We have no alternative but to do the best we can to make birth control available globally as quickly as possible and at the same time to try to rebuild a world which is steadily losing its ability to support life. Consideration of the fact that Africa's population of 531 million is increasing at a rate of 3 percent per year, and will thus multiply twentyfold within a century, shows that we cannot delay on the provision of birth-control availability. That 140 million of that 1984 African population were fed with imported grain should give added impetus to our efforts.[25]

Of all the areas in which we have been remiss, the area of education is the one which has spun its wheels most deeply into a morass of trivia. Anchored to the trailing edge of culture, the educational system has ignored all signs of decay of the planet and toddled willingly behind the purveyors of the idea that affluence and progress are the same thing. During the Future Environments of North America conference, held in April, 1965, economist Kenneth Boulding pointed out the necessity of making ecology the "guiding principle of elementary and secondary education"[26] He spoke of the fact that the educational system of the whole world needed to be revised within an ecological framework.

At the same conference, Lewis Mumford also spoke of the need to reeducate ourselves "to get on top of a technological system that is destroying both organic variety and human choice."[27] Actually, the topic of education was referred to often by the many gifted participants in the conference.

Since that time, there have been repeated calls for environmental education from well-respected organizations. The United Nations Conference on the Human Environment recognized the great need for education to focus on environmental issues;[28] The Standing Committee on Agriculture, Fisheries and Forestry, in its report to the Senate of Canada (June, 1984), recommended "That Provincial Governments commit themselves to the introduction of soil degradation and conservation studies at the primary and secondary school levels through the addition of environmental courses;"[29] the 21-nation report of the World Commission on Environment and Development stated, "Environmental education should be included in and should run throughout the other disciplines of the formal education curriculum at all levels—to foster a sense of responsibility for the state of the environment and to teach students how to monitor, protect, and improve it;"[30] and The Changing Atmosphere—Implications for Global Security conference statement (1988) recommended that it would be desirable for governments to "Allocate financial support for environmental education in primary and secondary schools and universities."[31] Time magazine's "Endangered Earth" issue in January, 1989, also called for programs of environmental education to be immediately introduced worldwide in schools and workplaces and suggested that governments give central focus to environmental issues.[32]

While individual teachers do attempt to insert some environmental awareness in cluttered educational curricula, the dynamic thrust needed to bring vital knowledge to those who will be directing the world in its most trying times is truly conspicuous by its absence. The educational machine, at this point, seems both unaware of the needs of its students and hopelessly shackled to the prevailing commercial mentality.

Without question, the ethical foundation missing in the collapsing years of great economic prosperity must be reintroduced to education; and that will be a difficult prospect, inasmuch as we are only beginning to recognize it as an essential, but missing, component.

The key to instigating action on points so far mentioned, and on others, is to make the environment and its health a matter that is kept in the forefront of consciousness. An involved citizenry can forcefully call for more enlightened actions on the part of government and industry. Staying asleep at the switch guarantees the continuation of actions that are leading us all down a very dismal path. There is no substitute for personal enlightenment and the adoption of a personal ethic that will enable us to turn the corner and foster conditions that will restore health to the earth. Self-interest, alone, should be a sufficient motivating force but for many it will be more than that: a genuine, deeply felt concern for the earth that is our home.

The Need for Personal Ethics

The paramount importance of developing a personal ethic can better be realized by considering the resistance to change on the part of entrenched industry and elected politicians whose main concern is the maintenance of apparent prosperity in order that they may be assured reelection. By and large, resistance to change is enormous and society has a great facility for shutting out information it does not want to hear. Yet, there is growing awareness that nature is both rebelling and succumbing due to human assault.

Only through development of personal ethics, leading to active individualism, can we produce the stretching and flexing of limbs that will eventually awaken the constructive energy of society and remove our own species, as well as many other species, from the threat of extinction.

The cumulative effect of a personal ethic is made apparent in a thought of American psychologist and philosopher William James:

> I am done with great things and big things, great institutions and big success, and I am for those tiny, invisible, molecular moral forces that work from individual to individual, creeping through the crannies of the world like so many soft rootlets, or like the capillary oozing of water, yet which, if you give them time, will rend the hardest monuments of man's pride.[33]

Dr. Albert Schweitzer also recognized the individual as the sole agent that might lead to the renewal of civilization. He felt that it was only possible for ethical thoughts to develop in the minds of individuals. To rescue society from the "slough of barbarism" in which he saw it wallowing, enough individuals would have to become ethical individually to eventually change the collective attitude of society.[34]

The Valdez Principles — Corporate Guidelines

One of the signs of our times is the effort to increase responsible behavior at all levels of society. The significant impact upon lives caused by the tanker Exxon Valdez running aground on Bligh Reef in Prince William Sound, with a resultant oil spill of 240,000 barrels of oil, now lends its name to a series of principles intended to improve corporate conduct in an increasingly threatened world.

The Valdez Principles, drafted by a number of environmental organizations, including the National Audubon Society (U.S.), public pension-fund managers in New York and California, and the Social Investment Forum, are an attempt to develop standards which openly commit corporations to the acceptance of environmental responsibility. Corporations which subscribe to the principles acknowledge that they and their stockholders have responsibility for the environment and place voluntary limitations on actions that may be undertaken in the quest for profit. Potential investors and graduates seeking employment with corporations may check to find out which of these organizations subscribe to the Valdez Principles and accept the responsibility of assuming a role which involves stewardship toward the earth.

Corporations which subscribe to the Valdez principles agree to move measurably toward implementation of each of the following ten principles: (Guidelines and criteria for measurement to be established.)

- Protection of the Biosphere—minimize and eliminate emission of pollutants which cause environmental damage.
- Sustainable Use of Natural Resources—insure sustainable use of land, water, and forests; conserve non-renewable resources through efficient use; protect biodiversity.
- Reduction and Disposal of Waste—recycle wherever possible; employ safe disposal methods.
- Wise Use of Energy—employ safe and sustainable energy sources; conserve and maximize energy efficiency of products.
- Risk Reduction—minimize environmental, health and safety risks.
- Marketing of Safe Products and Services—sell products that minimize adverse environmental impacts; inform consumers of the impacts of products and services.
- Damage Compensation—restore the environment from harm caused; provide compensation to persons adversely affected.
- Disclosure—disclose accidents and hazards; protect employees who report them.
- Environmental Directors and Managers—have at least one board member qualified to represent environmental interests; appoint a senior executive to be responsible for environmental affairs.
- Assessment and Annual Audit—conduct annual self-evaluation to determine progress in implementing principles; create independent environmental audit procedures.

Knowledge of the Valdez Principles, and of which corporations subscribe to them, is important in the fostering of consumer discretion. An enlightened public will have the opportunity to buy stock in and make purchases from corporations which affirm these basic principles of environmental responsibility.

Source: "The Valdez Principles," Audubon, November 1989.

242

We must reject an economic system that counts in its ever-increasing Gross National Product the manufacture of thermonuclear bombs, napalm, billions or trillions of dollars for military purposes in general, the destruction of the world's forests, the precarious health of the Great Lakes and the North Sea, the saturation of the earth with biocides, the medical and funeral expenses of victims of air disasters, the treatment of cancer victims whose cancer is caused in 85 percent to 95 percent of cases by environmental pollution, the costs of terrorism, the profits from alcoholism and cigarettes, advertising designed to " 'stimulate' consumer buying by creating wants,"[35] and a host of other things that could be better lumped under another heading such as the "Cost of the Diseases of Society."

That people with a personal ethic must rise in passive resistance is a necessary fact, simply because those who develop a real personal ethic reject the studied violence inherent in military might and in the obsessive greed that has been accepted as a justification for ruthlessness in the business world.

By ones, by tens, and by hundreds and thousands, individuals must arrive at personal decisions that it is far more ethical to moderate our expectations than it is to pursue the path we have been following.

The Four Cardinal Virtues

Much as we are familiar with the sort of restraints mentioned earlier in this chapter, we have kicked into a cocked hat those once formidable restraints that were called the Seven Deadly Sins and we also ignore the time-honored Four Cardinal Virtues.

Suppose that we did still accept the four cardinal virtues cited by Plato. These virtues, prudence, courage, temperance, and justice, applied to today's world, would impose considerably more circumspect behavior in our treatment of the earth as well as in our daily, personal lives than we have been practicing.

Fortitude, or courage as it became more commonly known, is both the bravery of the hero who faces death in dangerous encounter and the strength of mind required to discipline oneself to face the truth.[36] William James points out that life presents many dark abysses in which it is difficult to face the truth. The heroic individual, according to James, is the one who can face the problems that exist; "He can stand this Universe."[37] If, as Aristotle declared, it must be "for a noble end that the brave man endures and acts as courage directs,"[38] then we must adopt the noble end of preserving not just our own ways but also those of many other species that function in little known ways to maintain the integrity of this planet. If we could adopt this sort of courage unflinchingly, then we could wholeheartedly face the truth and react fully to our plight. We would be ready to deny ourselves some of the material things we think we need in order that we might attain the greater good for times yet to come.

Temperance is the virtue which concerns itself with the moderation of overindulgence in all its forms of excess. The absence of temperance is particularly to be noted in our society where excess has been encouraged to the point of becoming habitual.[39] Freud's theory of the reality principle suggests that an individual whose chief quest is pleasure is infantile in his behavior. According to psychologist Sigmund Freud, it is not until one learns to postpone immediate gratification and to altogether renounce certain sources of pleasure that the quality of *reasonableness* is attained.[40] While it is often true that individuals are driven by intense pride and ambition, the ancient maxim "Nothing overmuch" must be followed to live a life of principle. Obviously, temperance is the antithesis of what is encouraged as appropriate behavior in a consumer society. It is not at all surprising that contemporary thinking has discarded, virtually buried, any contemplation of the virtues which were considered desirable before production and consumption became the end-all and be-all of the industrial mode of existence.

Justice, as a moral virtue, has had to contend with two distinct extremes. One is the view expressed by Thrasymachus in Plato's *Republic*, "that justice is nothing else than the interest of the stronger." This view that "might makes right," is one that governing bodies still often find tempting, and too much of its flavor still permeates society. The other view holds that power can be either rightly or wrongly exercised and involves greater responsibility than using it merely as a simple tool in the practice of "expedient" leadership. What this amounts to is, in the first instance, the view that governments are above the law, and, in the second, that laws made by governments can themselves be unjust, that there is a higher natural principle of justice that applies to all peoples in all places. This higher principle is more clearly expressed by the term "original justice" used by theologians. The Catholic philosopher, Thomas Aquinas, saw this as a condition stemming from one's "reason being subject to God," and "the lower powers subject to reason."[41]

There apparently is much more to the concept of "original justice" than we have explored here. No matter how much we wish to run the world according to our own tastes, our knowledge of the intricacy of life, rudimentary though it is, suggests that we are being extremely careless in erasing life forms at our convenience. As Aldo Leopold suggested, the first requirement of intelligent tinkering is that we should save all the parts.

It is evident that original justice must be involved in our relationship with our planet, as well as in our relationships with one another. We know, if only at the level of self-interest, that we are rendering extinct species that might prove to be of great value to us directly. They may also be of great value indirectly, in relationship to the whole fabric of nature. Thus they deserve protection under both of the interpretations we hold of justice. Certainly in terms of original justice, they have the right to existence because they are a functioning part of the entirety of nature.

Whether or not we give various life forms "standing" in our courts, they apparently have standing in a higher court. Rivers, lakes, forests, mountains, prairies, and deserts, along with nitrogen-fixing bacteria, stratiomyid flies, chipmunks, Canada geese and slime molds—all of these and multitudes more are functioning components of the dance of life. There is a great probability that in denying *them* standing, let us say within the principle of necessity, that our own species is flood-lighting itself in the eye of original justice.

Of the four cardinal virtues, it bears mention that prudence is considered to be the intellectual virtue whereas temperance, courage or fortitude, and justice are referred to as moral virtues. Prudence is distinguished from cleverness by Aristotle, who points out that it is sometimes clever to set a goal and attain it, but if the goal that is set is not good in itself, then cleverness is merely smartness. To be truly prudent, an act of cleverness must also have the quality of nobility. As far back as Roman times, a distinction was made between prudentia, which signified that wisdom derives from experience, and sapientia, which referred to knowledge gained from science. Action upon knowledge without experience and memory of similar things, when used to determine likely consequences, may sadly lack in prudence. For instance, immediately applied innovative knowledge may produce unforeseen problems, as we are learning today.

As might be expected, it is generally agreed by philosophers that a harmony among all the virtues is needed. As the philosopher Immanual Kant states, prudence by itself only advises us what to do. Without the impetus of the other moral virtues, it may only result in acting along the line of self-interest. However, "the law of morality commands" that prudence be translated into action.[42]

It seems evident that to be truly prudent, we should greatly reduce the industrial and personal impact we are causing upon the environment. There is strong evidence that no matter what prudence might advise, we are bereft of the moral conviction that might command us to heed such wise counsel.

Prudence involves not only calculation, foresight, and forethought, but also implies caution, circumspection, or economy, especially in practical affairs. Whereas calculation, in itself, might suggest coldness or selfishness, foresight means that careful concern for the future is an essential aspect of prudence.

With the new broom of this virtue, actively used, it would be necessary to sweep our short-term values out the window and replace them with long-term (thereby sustainable) considerations. Wherever we looked, at forests for example, we would know better than to raze them to the ground. Or if we appraised the massive air and water pollution as it is condoned today, we would reject such further behavior immediately because our foresight would recognize it as folly. We would also be aware that soil erosion is a staggeringly serious problem because our concern for environmental health would make us aware of what is happening.

The Vale of Soul Making

The poet Kahlil Gibran once stated, "Your reason and your passion are the rudder and sails of your seafaring soul." He went on to point out that the lack of either rudder or sail can cause chaos in life. In our society, where we have exalted the rational approach (so called) and disdained all other influences as counter-productive and inconsequential, we are dangerously unbalanced. Our only hope is that a latent awareness will advise us to retrace our path and pick up some of the scattered historical gems of greater understanding that we have discarded in our haste to create a technological Utopia.

We need to look again at our poets and philosophers and contemplate whole areas of thought and possibilities of meaning that we have swept under the rug. Did the poet John Keats have an insight we

246

lack when he wrote to his brother and wife in North America that the world is a "vale of soul-making" in which humans forge their identities? He went on to say: "There may be intelligence or sparks of the divinity in millions—but they are not Souls till they acquire identities, till each one is personally itself." And later, "Do you not see how necessary a World of Pains and troubles is to school an Intelligence and make it a soul?"[43]

This is typical of much thought that we reject in our conviction that a thing which cannot be weighed, measured, recorded on an oscilloscope, or shaken in a test tube is a mere figment of imagination.

The English poets William Blake and William Wordsworth also recognized the growth that could ensue from restoring harmony to lives focused so narrowly they had become meaningless and chaotic. Their ideal human was the embodiment of reconciled opposites: the logical mind and the understanding heart, the philosophic vision and the enjoyment of the physical senses. This is the beginning of "holism," so studiously analyzed in the following comment of statesman and philosopher, J. C. Smuts:

> This is a universe of wholemaking, not merely of soul-making, which is only its climax phase. The universe is not a pure transparency of Reason or Spirit. It contains unreason and contradiction, it contains error and evil, sin and suffering. . . . is profoundly complex and replete with unsearchable diversity and variety. . . . It is forever evolving new and higher wholes . . . whose inner freedom and creative metabolism transform the fetters of fate and the contingencies of circumstance into the freedom and harmony of a more profoundly cooperative universe.[44]

There are reputable scientists who are alarmed at our lack of ethical concern. The writings of Dr. Erwin Chargaff express his own serious doubt about the direction science is taking. Chargaff, a biochemist, did research and taught at Mt. Sinai hospital and at Columbia University in New York. The concept of "complementarity" which he formulated is known as Chargaff's Law; it preceded his demonstration of "pairing of the bases," which is considered the major proof of the double-helix structure of DNA, the molecular basis of heredity.

In his book *Voices in the Labyrinth*, Chargaff expresses his view that we are living in one of the truly bestial centuries in human history.

Referring to such vicious events as took place at Auschwitz, Dresden, Hiroshima, and in Vietnam, he laments the way in which scientific imagination has been brutalized. What sort of humanity would invent "napalm" as a substance to be used against other humans? He sees many modern scientists as individuals who possess a Ph.D. but have had not time to grow up; and he questions the convictions of scientists who are "undecided between making a Leonardo da Vinci in the test tube or planting a Coca Cola sign on Mars." He contends that if we reach the stars and their planets, we will rapidly make them as uninhabitable as we have made the earth. In another of his books, *Heraclitean Fire,* he comments, after having devoted the most important investment a man can make, *his own life,* to science, that he had to speak out against the misdeeds in which science has involved itself. It is his conviction that the goals of science have become vastly altered since he entered the discipline, some fifty years ago.

In an interview with author Michel Salomon, Chargaff lamented the lack of intellectual development in people, suggesting that while people may survive as statistics, they do not survive as intellects. The lack of a philosophical view among scientists is also evident and it disturbs him that scientists are so detached from reality that their concerns are principally materialistic and they function without appreciation of philosophical or religious thought.[45]

Nor is Chargaff the only scientist with serious reservations about the direction we are taking. In Salomon's interview with Nikolass Tinbergen, who received the Nobel Prize for medicine in 1973, Tinbergen holds that although science is a potential tool for improving life, it is being used in a shortsighted and reckless fashion. It is Tinbergen's conviction that unless human lifestyles are drastically changed, the physical and mental health of humanity, and its very survival, are in great danger. Like many others who fret in anguish at human behavior, he feels that we have the insight to do what we must but we lack, tragically, both the will and the foresight.[46]

There is no longer an excuse for our lack of foresight. We have been provided with extremely alarming information as to what will happen to our earth if we do not change our ways. Our instinctive desire to survive should surely be enough to activate our will to change. In the past, we have rarely thought of environmental responsibility as individual responsibility. It has been much more convenient for us to think of it in terms of an obligation of society, forgetting that society is made of individuals—and that each of us is one of those individuals.

When we drive our vehicles needlessly, we pollute everyone's air. When we buy extravagantly, we utilize resources that belong to the whole world. We have been cheerfully living with a double standard. Whatever we do is permissible, but what the other fellow does may be wrong.

A striking thing about the great religious systems of the world is their common focus on what we know as the Golden Rule. Judaism says, "What is hurtful to yourself, do not to your fellow man. That is the whole law, and the remainder is but commentary." Buddhism says, "Hurt not others with that which pains yourself." The Brahmans taught: "Do naught to others which if done to thee, would cause thee pain." When asked about perfect virtue, Confucius said: "Not to do unto others as you would not wish done unto yourself," And Jesus said, "Whatsoever ye would that men should do to you, do ye evenso to them."

Thus religions throughout time have recognized our personal responsibility toward our fellow man. To extend this responsibility to the entire earth should be a natural outcome of our religious heritage. When we harm the earth, we harm the living creatures which all depend on the earth. For all who think of this as Divine Creation, our treatment of earth is nothing less than disrespect for its Creator. If we recognize the importance of a clean environment for all life, we must make certain that we take responsibility for our individual actions which contribute to the pollution of that environment. In the final analysis, if we get by the environmental and political crises that beset the age, we will get by them because of a strengthened morality, for in reality, environmental problems are not strictly technological and political, they are moral problems. When Christ said, "He that is not with me is against me," (Matthew 12:30) He stated a simple truth—there are no neutral positions in life; one has to choose to be part of the problem, or part of the answer.

Don't we overdo our neutrality today? Isn't our "don't rock the boat," "yes-man" philosophy evidence of the fact that we are scared stiff of expressing real convictions? What has happened to us that we are so loath to say that a thing is wrong? It is a simple truth that we are as sick as the planet. It is possible, however, that we will restore our own character and mental health in the process of tackling an overdue responsibility. And it would not be surprising that in dedicating ourselves to something, and in rebuilding our own essences, we could also restore the earth to verdancy and to near pristine grandeur.

As the maxim goes, "Tis better to have loved and lost, than never to have loved at all." If there is any love that is needed, it is love for the earth that is our home. Win or lose, we may attain our finest hour in transcending our personal goals and in trying to restore health to an ailing world. We could do worse than lose ourselves in labor and might even find ourselves in joy.

Calls for an Earth Ethic

Long before our present day, dire predictions had been made as to the outcome of our rapacious attitude toward the earth. More than fifty years ago, an American Indian won first prize in a farm magazine contest for the best 100-word analysis of a picture which showed a deserted farmhouse in a badly gullied field. His description may be all too close to the naked truth:

> Picture show white man crazy. Cut down trees, make big tepee. Plough hill. Water wash. Wind blow soil. Grass gone. Door gone. Whole place gone. Money gone. Papoose gone. Squaw too. No chuckaway. No pigs. No corn. No plough. No hay. No pony. Indian no plough land. Keep grass. Buffalo eat grass. Indian eat buffalo. Hides make tepee. Make moccasin. Indian no make terrace. No make dam. All time eat. No hunt job. No hitch hike. No ask relief. No shoot pig. Great Spirit make grass. Indian no waste anything. Indian no work. White man crazy.[47]

Among the calls for a land ethic, in one form or another, is an interesting *Eleventh Commandment* proposed by Dr. Walter Lowdermilk, who was the first associate chief of the U.S. Soil Conservation Service. During his lifetime, Dr. Lowdermilk studied the relationship of man to the earth in twenty-eight countries on four continents. Much of his work focused on determining the reasons why land that had been productive turned into "man-made deserts." In short, he learned that the suicidal use of resources, particularly overgrazing and overcutting of forests, led to soil erosion and siltation and turned the formerly productive lands to deserts.

Contending that if Moses had foreseen the sins of civilization against the environment, he would have been inspired to offer an eleventh commandment to regulate human behavior on earth, Dr. Lowdermilk proposed an eleventh commandment. This was aired on Radio Jerusalem in 1939 and was dedicated to the settlers in Israel who were trying to reclaim the desert and return it to productivity.

This is what Dr. Lowdermilk hypothesized the eleventh commandment might have been:

> Thou shalt inherit the holy earth as a faithful steward, conserving its resources and productivity from generation to generation. Thou shalt safeguard thy fields from soil erosion, thy living waters from drying up, thy forests from desolation, and protect thy hills from overgrazing by herds, that thy descendants may have abundance forever. If any shall fail in this good stewardship of the earth, thy fruitful fields shall become sterile, stony ground or wasting gullies, and thy descendants shall decrease and live in poverty or perish from off the face of the earth.[48]

There has been rising awareness for more than a century of the desperate need for some kind of ethical stance that will limit our human tendency toward self-destruction. This would include the "good stewardship" spoken of by Walter Lowdermilk and would also aim at the preservation of undisturbed areas which would serve as indications of what natural communities are and how rebuilding might take place.

In 1958, ecologist Charles Elton addressed some of the criteria that must be kept in mind.

> From now on, it is vital that everyone who feels inclined to change or cut away or drain or spray or plant any strip or corner of the land should ask themselves three questions: What animals and plants live in it, what beauty and interest may be lost, and what extra risk will changing it add to the accumulating instability of communities. . . . This outlook may enable us to put into the altered landscape some of the ecological features of wilderness.[49]

Dr. Marston Bates likewise pondered upon an ecological morality, expressing his thought thus:

In defying nature, in destroying nature, in building an arrogantly selfish, man-centered, artificial world, I do not see how man can gain peace or freedom or joy. I have faith in man's future, faith in the possibilities latent in the human experiment: but it is faith in man as part of nature, working with the forces that govern the forests and the seas: faith in man sharing life, not destroying it.[50]

Lewis Herber also referred to the need for a land ethic, asking whether we really believed we could, "by aimless and uninformed tinkering," improve upon a planet in which a million and a half species lived in a dynamically balanced equilibrium, using and reusing the same molecules of soil and air.[51]

Now we are receiving the message, loudly and clearly, that modification of our behavior is no longer merely desirable. It is imperative!

Ethics and Employment

A change in worldview means that we will have to look upon the world with newly opened eyes. Industry often tells us that the cost of more conscientious behavior will be the loss of a certain number of jobs. It is then customary to blame increasing unemployment on those unspeakable environmentalists. This sort of behavior is often referred to as the scapegoat technique. The truth of the fact is that we should have heeded environmentalists (so-called) long ago. They just happened to have been some of the people who have utilized foresight. As for the matter of jobs, it would be considerably more appropriate to blame this situation on technology, if we really feel it necessary to blame anyone other than our collective selves and all our frailties. To find that we have forged the chains that have increasingly shackled us, we can look back to an article in *Technology Review* in 1975. The article pointed out that manufacturing systems controlled by central computers would be demonstrated by 1985. The same article quoted an executive of a leading automation company as predicting that with a continuation of current trends, only two percent of the labor force in the United States would take part in manufacturing operations by the year 2000.[52]

This also says a lot about the energy crisis, about the continual need for power plants, new hydroelectric dams, new nuclear generating plants, and also about tremendous additional pollution. As David Brower and Steve Lyons of Friends of the Earth expressed it: "The primary function of energy in the American economy is to power machines, whose purpose is to replace labor, not to provide it. Between 1959 and 1969, jobs in the steel industry dropped from 450,000 to 100,000, but production rose 45 percent. This feat was possible because men were put out of work by machines which ran on cheap oil, demanded no benefits, staged no strikes."[53]

In many ways, it has been convenient that the activities of people whose foresight made them aware of growing environmental problems have served as a diversion for the fact that automation and technological innovation have steadily reduced job opportunity.

Technological sophistication has had a similar impact in the logging industry in British Columbia. In 1950, the average production per forest worker stood at 379 cubic meters per job, whereas in 1986 the average production per job was 1,280 cubic meters. Another way of expressing this is to point out that in 1950 there were 2.64 persons employed for each 1,000 cubic meters of production, whereas in 1986, each 1,000 cubic meters harvested employed only seventy-eight one-hundredths of one employee.

Automation and employment opportunity obviously do not make good bedfellows.[54]

In short, this adds up to a strangely comforting fact that by reducing our technological impact upon the planet—with all its attendant pollution and exotic chemicals—we would also be employing more people.

This is, no doubt, a staggering thing to assimilate: that we might have to move toward less sophisticated means of activity. However, we do have the opportunity to make use of whatever excellent technology is appropriate and not environmentally destructive, and it is very likely

Grossman and Daneker's report, "Jobs and Energy," made available the information that increased electrification has always meant lost jobs. For every quadrillion BTU's of fuel changed to electricity (an amount equivalent to 1.3 per cent of U.S. annual consumption of energy), there has been a corresponding job loss over the U.S. economy of 75,000 jobs.
Source: Common Sense, vol. 3, no. 3, October 1981.

that, given a more sensible mandate, we could adapt technology to the realities we have never before seriously considered an obligation.

The cumulative effect of human activity during the period since the Industrial Revolution began has been such that our ability to innovate technologically has outstripped our social conscience. We have impoverished the many for the sake of material affluence for a small segment of the world population. There is also no question that we have the ability to accumulate data. There is less evidence of ability to recognize a true crisis therein and the necessity of curbing immediate appetites and passions to solve that crisis.

Naturalist Joseph Wood Krutch noted that the world has advanced to the extent of sitting on a hydrogen bomb instead of sitting on a powder keg, and suggested that our technicians may be likened to sorcerer's apprentices rather than to the master magicians they think they see revealed in the mirror of achievements.

Our continued existence depends upon our ability to control the conditions we create and our past performance gives no indication that this is within our present capability. Thomas Henry Huxley's analogy of the world as a chessboard (*Adventures in English Literature*) is indeed apt. Perhaps we should pay attention to the increasing vulnerability of our king.

Wisdom

One of the great quests of history has been the philosophical search for wisdom. Some philosophers have divided wisdom into two parts, the one called prudence having to do with *practical wisdom,* and the other having to do with *speculative wisdom* which can be thought of as theology or the search for divine knowledge. Opposed to true wisdom is foolish wisdom which is referred to as folly. Theologians have sometimes referred to "worldly wisdom" as a counterfeit of true wisdom.

In Homer's *Iliad,* Agamemnon refers to folly in the following manner: "Folly, eldest of Jove's (Jupiter's) daughters, shuts mens' eyes to their destruction. She walks delicately, not on the solid earth, but hovers over the heads of men to make them stumble or to ensnare them." At one time, Folly even tricked her own father, at which point he became enraged and "caught Folly by the hair and swore a great oath that never should she again invade starry heaven and Olympus, for she was the bane of all." Jove threw her from heaven so that she was cast upon the fields of mortal men.

Sir William Temple, an English statesman of the seventeenth century, summarized the relationship between wisdom and folly by saying, "A Man's wisdom is his best friend; folly his worst enemy."

The important thing about wisdom, particularly for us today, is that its primary characteristic is that true wisdom cannot be misused. We know it is possible to use artistic skill and scientific knowledge for evil purposes. But wisdom is marked by the fact that it does not fly at short-term solutions or short-term gains. It involves deliberate judgment and understanding of right action that considers all available facts. It consists of something more than being well-learned because it also gives great consideration to the appropriate application of what is known.

Plato felt that the attainment of wisdom was so difficult that he would not refer even to philosophers as wise, calling them instead "lovers of wisdom." In his *Laws,* he described wisdom as the leading virtue, as "chief and leader of the divine class of goods. . . . Next follows temperance; and from the union of these two with courage springs justice, and fourth in the scale of virtues is courage."

In spite of the many references made to the modern knowledge explosion it is becoming apparent that items of knowledge can be stacked up to the stars without making men any wiser. Our zealous haste to acquire new bits of knowledge without taking time to assimilate or reflect upon this knowledge is analogous to the avid eater at a Smorgasbord who must sample everything in spite of predictably massive indigestion that will follow upon the heels of such unselective eating.

It is not at all surprising that we do hear many references to modern knowledge but that when we refer to the topic of wisdom it is more often thought of as ancient than modern. The inference that wisdom has been lost, rather than gained over the centuries, is not inconsistent with the environmental plight that is now so highly visible and so much a subject of concern.

The implementation of practical wisdom in the political forums of the world might well lead to radical measures to attempt restoration of the earth's health before such time as all efforts become inadequate. This would necessitate a renewal of interest in areas of thought which have been swept under the carpet in pursuit of the very narrow concept of progress which is held today.

We are sadly unfit for solving complex environmental problems. Unlike the mechanical problems proficiently solved by humans, the interacting organisms, micro-environments, and micro-climates in nature are so many and so varied that our understanding of them is rudimentary. What is more, we, as a species, are trying to understand a wholeness of which we ourselves are a part. If we could devise ten or a dozen mechanical procedures which would solve environmental dilemmas, we would undoubtedly do just that.

Unfortunately, things are not that simple. Whether or not we like the idea, it does appear that the universe is some sort of moral ground which requires obedience to immutable laws. Our materialistic pursuits have involved us in putting on blinders in order to concentrate on the very narrow goal of producing and using goods. This has been done without reference to other dimensions of our own being.

Now it looks very much as though we may succumb to our own denial of deep meaning in a universe we have arbitrarily labeled meaningless except as it pertains to our own wishes.

Any palliative efforts we may make could well prove to be meaningless mechanical motions unless we once again concern ourselves with right thinking. This is very likely the central problem that we must address. We must indulge in soul-searching and make innumerable individual decisions to storm the "high ground" of nobler thoughts and establish a fresh vantage point from which to view the world. Our self-serving goals are too shoddy for a species that possesses as many talents as our own.

Folly flits over our head and lures us to the brink. Wisdom, silenced, can only brood and await our call with all the hidden strength we must activate to meet our needs.

The cultivation of wisdom, and its attendant moral virtues, is the prerequisite to all that we must do to regain our foothold on the beautiful blue and green planet that is our home.

The chains of habit are too weak to be felt
until they are too strong to be broken.
Samuel Johnson

Signposts on the Path

Think of the Chinese symbol for crisis. It involves two apparently contrary ideas: danger and opportunity.

We are now familiar with a number of the dangers that face society. Toxic wastes and nuclear holocaust would be but two of hundreds, perhaps thousands, of problematical issues that would appear in a modern lexicon of dangers. Most insidious among them are the dangers we have created for ourselves.

We are less familiar with the opportunity side of the equation; less familiar with the things we might do which will increase our chances of making a safer and saner world, one that we now think of as being a sustainable world.

Whether or not we think of the earth as a single living entity—which many have held it to be throughout the recorded history of our species—it will help, for our purpose at this moment, to think of it as a single living organism. Cell by cell, we have torn apart the fabric of the organism. Forest by forest, watershed by watershed, stream by stream, lake by lake, and ocean by ocean, we have disrupted its wholeness. Having gorged at the banquet of life to the extent of baring the cupboard of our host, we must now curb our appetites and work with might and main to replenish the larder.

As a wound rebuilds tissue cell by cell, so we must rebuild the planet.

This is why individual action is so important. We, in a very real sense, have been individual cells of the earth that have been out of step with the needs of the earth. Now we must control, first of all, our demands on a weakened earth, helping it wherever we can, but above all desisting from demanding those things that we know, at the bottom of our hearts, are superficial, and are of no real consequence to a meaningful life.

Rampant technology will not save the day. There are those who think it will. Specific technology designed for very low impact can certainly be of assistance. Such technology must stem, however, from a different philosophy than we hold today. The massive saddle sores of our making will heal themselves if we loosen the cinches and protect the wounds from further harm. They will not heal from "more of the same" or by spurring our planetary steed to new levels of production.

Whatever metaphors we employ, mixed or unmixed, whatever graphic expressions we must adopt to convince ourselves, it is our species that is threatening the elastic limits of the earth. Space exploits may be enthralling, but our destinies will be worked out here on terra firma. As Emerson questioned the traveler to Europe who really had nothing exceptional to give to Europeans when he got there, so we might ask the same about our intended sojourns in the outer universe. We have not yet learned to be good citizens of this planet. What message do we have for anyone else in the universe? Or would we merely be looking at the universal export-import business—shipping our garbage to the outermost reaches and importing everything we could find that might have value?

The luxury of saying "let somebody else worry about the problems because I don't want to think about them" is one that we can no longer afford. What we must strive for is that essential courage which involves the ability to "face the dark abysses" which are part of the times in which we live. The "externalities" of economic single vision (such as

> "Cultivate poverty like a garden herb, like sage. Do not trouble yourself much to get new things, whether clothes or friends. Turn the old; return to them. Things do not change; we change. Sell your clothes and keep your thoughts."
>
> *Henry David Thoreau*

air and water pollution) have never been irrelevant and the longer we pretend they are, the less chance we have to survive the mess we have created.

The more that we know individually, the more it will be possible to look at the world—in our homes, communities, provinces or states, in our nations and internationally—with a new realization that the health and sustainability of all things depends on the mutually interlocking web of all the components of the functioning earth. If we are capable of fostering a sense of "earthism" to which we could subordinate our divisive nationalisms, and to which religions might pay more heed, we might be able to take large steps toward eliminating war, terrorism, and many of the other problems which have resulted from the ill-advised belief that the world is primarily a place of business.

Learning more as individuals can prepare us for an active and enlightened role in advocating a caring and restorative attitude toward the earth. We are already perilously close to Thoreau's foresight-filled admonition that it will not make any difference whether or not one has a beautiful house if there isn't a decent planet to put it on.

Given understanding, there is opportunity to help others to understand. If each individual enables two others to develop this type of awareness and if each of those two were to influence two more . . . such is the rate of geometric progression that by the end of 33 doublings, more than 8 billion people would be germinating an enlightened attitude toward the planet. For those who would point out that the world does not yet have a population of eight billion, it might be said, "Wait a minute!"

A life of principle that transcends the mainly materialistic considerations of the present age has moved from being "nice" to being essential. The importance of such principles was recognized by Marcus Aurelius, who spoke of the close correlation and intermingling of things that are human and divine:

259

As surgeons keep their lancets and scalpels always at hand for the sudden demands of their craft, so keep your principles constantly in readiness for the understanding of things both human and divine; never in the most trivial action forgetting how intimately the two are related. For nothing human can be done aright, without reference to the divine and conversely.[1]

And so, we append here a list of things which might be incorporated into our lives as actions which can be put into practice and can stand as a testament to the idea that human ethics and treatment of our earth are inseparable. Included are things both practical and spiritual; specific enough to give us things to do at once, and broad enough to encompass our every action; basic enough for even the youngest members of the family to understand, and complex enough for community, family, or group discussion and action; an attempt to blend the human and divine:

1. Honor the earth
2. Treasure all life
3. Live modestly
4. Know your water source
5. Waste nothing
6. Encourage recycling
7. Cultivate wisdom
8. Plant trees
9. Use public transportation
10. Walk whenever possible
11. Plant a garden
12. Insist on truth from government
13. Exercise prudence
14. Defend nature
15. Demand pure foods
16. Encourage diversity
17. Simplify your wants
18. Know your own area
19. Don't litter
20. Conserve the soil
21. Protect watersheds
22. Make good use of wealth
23. Conserve energy
24. Become involved
25. Compost wastes
26. Vacation close to home
27. Learn!
28. Repair when possible
29. Pause to reflect
30. Share rides
31. Teach the young
32. Use a bicycle
33. Work for peace
34. Use no pesticides
35. Protect the forests
36. Demand clean industries
37. Turn off lights
38. Pray for insight
39. Turn down thermostats
40. Buy recycled paper
41. Take family walks
42. Reduce travel
43. Learn about nature
44. Speak your concern
45. Buy durable goods
46. Seed waste places

47. Reject overpackaging
48. Encourage small farms
49. Trade and share goods
50. Support cottage industry
51. Join an environmental club
52. Be skeptical of advertising
53. Turn down hot water tanks
54. Read more, Watch TV less
55. Respect others
56. Dispense with disposables
57. Slow down
58. Share your knowledge
59. Be gentle
60. Value truth
61. Avoid the superficial
62. Be a good example
63. Cultivate dependability
64. Tithe to nature
65. See beauty
66. Appreciate the seasons
67. Be temperate
68. Repair leaky faucets
69. Write to politicians
70. Reduce driving by 20 to 50 percent

In almost every case the real problem we face is the problem of *restraint*—the problem of how to restrain ourselves. We have to restrain ourselves from making too much impact on our fragile planet, from overcutting forests, from overpopulation, from overdevelopment, from overconsumption, from overexpectation, from overuse of fossil-fuel consuming vehicles, from greed beyond need, from ruthlessness beyond reason, from reckless willingness to express hostility and foster militarism, from overdependence on the quick solutions and overcommitment to short-term benefits at the expenses of long term costs.

We can heal the planet only if we first heal ourselves.

 # An Afterword for Policy Makers

This book has predicated that our ability to create a truly healthy, sustainable world is dependent upon the formulation of a new, life-supporting worldview. The world at present is dominated by the dictates of concentrated wealth in the form of corporations, banks, and private fortunes. For the most part, these forces are blindly devoted to profit, power, and often life-threatening enterprises labeled "development."

Throughout the world, politicians have been weak-willed and have succumbed to these power structures, to the point where it is frequently admitted that the forces of concentrated wealth rule the world.

In reality, politicians have an entirely different mandate than to blindly collaborate with the self-seeking goals of this relatively small segment of society. It is the responsibility of elected officials to protect the land; to promote the health and well-being of the populace; and to *govern*—which means to regulate and restrain opposing forces for the greatest good of the many, and certainly for the protection of the planet, which is the source of life for all. The terrible position in which we find ourselves is a dilemma of modern politics. Politicians who have been impressed by wealth and who have fawned and carped at the feet of the mighty, have allowed a society of blinded and trained consumers to develop, a society in which propaganda rules over intelligence. One of the greatest "renewals" that must occur is in the development of political will based on a deep sense of responsibility and a reaffirmation of the determination to live a life of principle. From adherence to election promises, to avoiding automatic deference to those who can support lobbies, government need immediately put itself on a plane of behavior which is unquestionably one of devotion to the solution of the greatest problem that has befallen humankind. As Dr. David Suzuki has so aptly stated, "It's a matter of survival."

To think of where we are heading if we continue upon our present course, we can use Newton's laws of motion as an analogy. For linear motion, his first law states that a body at rest remains at rest or if in motion continues in motion at a uniform velocity in a straight line unless it is acted upon by an unbalanced force.

If we apply that to the current pattern of industrialization, technological experimentation and development, we will continue to lose massive amounts of soil, continue to put hundreds of millions of pounds of toxic chemicals into the air each year, continue to ravage forests, poison oceans, and likewise continue to weaken human immune systems, increase cancer rates, and precipitate serious environmental catastrophes each year. The end result is expressed in the third law of motion, which states that for every action there is an equal and opposite reaction. That equal and opposite reaction would be the death of the planet with extinction of our own species as part of that episode.

Our hope, to continue the analogy, lies in action along the lines of the second law of motion. This states that if a mass is acted upon by an unbalanced force, it will accelerate in the direction of that force, and the rate of acceleration will be proportional to the force and inversely proportional to the mass of the body. Let's consider our degraded planet as the mass, and that the unbalanced force is a supreme effort on the part of humankind to restore the health of the planet. The energy with which we act upon this goal will determine the rate at which we may help the planet mend itself. It will take time and effort to overcome the effects of what has already been done to jeopardize the health of the planet, but the rate of healing will gradually increase just as one recovers, at first slowly and then more rapidly, from a major illness. In this instance we might avoid third law calamity by redirecting our own actions and ambitions so that they fit within the self-renewing capabilities of the earth. No other course will really suffice. Considering the bulging larder of our own continent when the first white men arrived it is obvious that the earth's own dynamic equilibrium was one of teeming health. That our own "improvements" have been inept is not surprising inasmuch as we were loath to conform with those parameters which had enabled the earth to function well before we were a gleam in the eye of some primordial ape or perhaps a slight electrical impulse in some gaglion of a precocious tunicate ... or recipients of a Divine Creation which had been deemed "very good" at the end of the sixth day.

Yes, there is difficulty involved in real acceptance of a more environmentally benign worldview. Certainly one thought would be that the economy would fall apart. If we think about things carefully, we might recognize that the economy is close to falling apart anyway, and certainly if we consider the environmental destruction wrought by our economic aspirations it can be recognized, as Dr. Paul Ehrlich has pointed out, that economic progress as we have viewed it, has been "imbecilic." We can no longer maximize so-called "benefits" and ignore "real costs." That we have been doing so is reason enough to reorder our priorities entirely, and start off on a much safer path, one in which it will not be considered "uneconomic" to give maximum priorities to safeguarding land, restoring forests, virtually eliminating toxic emissions, and cleaning waterways. "Uneconomic" has served as a weasel-word for those blinded by ambition, focused on their own affluence, and content to consign future generations to lingering death on a maimed earth. To play the game which posits that it is not conclusive that acid rain is killing forests and lakes, and that global warming is noIt proved beyond doubt, is simply disgraceful.

For those politicians who have not forgotten who it is they are really supposed to represent, the following items are a few of many which are overdue for their consideration and rectification. Indeed, it is every politician's duty to do something positive in each of these areas.

1. Why is it that government has worked overtime to assure that there are no loopholes for small taxpayers, but allowed "Concentrated Wealth" the status of privileged parasites on the rest of society? Corporations and other high income earners should pay taxes at the appropriate rates to the earnings involved. Rights to avoid taxation should be consistent with the rights of the smallest of earners—who basically have no such rights. Much lack of credibility for government exists when society is fully aware that there is one law for the rich and another for the poor, or, in short, feudalism in the twentieth century. It is currently the theory that tax benefits to corporations allow them to reinvest in further industrialization and that such industrialization is a benefit to society as a whole. Our experience, however, has shown that our environmental crisis is largely a result of uncontrolled industrial expansion. Funds accruing to government through lawful taxation of corporations would finance environmental cleanup campaigns and other projects which may pull us out of the morass we have been cast into through unbridled industrialization.

2. Since the purpose of industry is to make profit and the purpose of government is to *govern,* let there be separation of industry and government as there has been separation of church and state. Since campaign contributions and lobbying activities are psychological impediments to objective *governing,* the format and extent to which these can occur should be reviewed.
3. Stop funding megaprojects with taxpayers' money. (Hibernia and OSLO projects will initially result in carbon dioxide emissions equal to 240 percent of Canada's total carbon dioxide emissions in 1985). Alternatively, offer support to small, local, labor intensive industries with full pollution control.
4. Decentralize government by empowering communities. For example: In forested areas, communities should be given the power to practice true sustained yield in surrounding forests and to protect watersheds by long-term, limited cutting plans. Strong communities are the strength of a nation and communities are far more concerned with protection of their immediate environment than are multinational corporations.
5. Approve no new plans for industrialization unless plans show clearly that "zero toxic emissions" will occur. We can no longer afford to play Russian roulette with the health of the planet and its cargo of living organisms. We do not need a growth society but a stable society.
6. Enact stringent regulations on toxic emissions, without providing for long periods of delay. If regulations are not met, shut down plants involved. If "studies" show that "X" number of jobs will be lost, it is equally true that over five billion human lives will be lost if we continue to foul the air, water, and soil of the planet. Slackness in employment can be taken up by elimination of technologies that are not sufficiently labor-intensive, as it is better to employ people than to employ machines. Re-employment projects can be funded through corporation taxes which have been avoided for so long.
7. Immediately stop exporting pesticides to Third World Countries when these pesticides have been banned in North America. This, at best, is a cynical practice; at worst, it is murderous. For example: The highly toxic pesticide toxaphene has been banned in the U.S. and Canada for 15 years. Depositions of this pesticide are routinely monitored, at present, in Canada, by Environment Canada. The source for deposition in Canada is assumed to be Mexico,

where it is still used. Toxaphene is now found in the flesh of fish throughout Canada.

Toxic waste shipments to other countries are equally to be disparaged. The best place to stop toxic substances is at the source. If we do not know how to dispose of them, we should not produce them.

8. Since it is commonly agreed that we must move away from fossil fuels, provide subsidies for development of alternative, renewable forms of energy—wind, solar thermal, photovoltaic, and the like.

9. Require industries to provide full disclosure of kind and quantities of pollutants emitted and fully enforce existing pollution control laws.

10. Freeze pesticide use to present levels with emphasis on major reduction through Integrated Pest Management.

11. Declare a two-year to five-year moratorium on all new energy projects and during that period make 100 percent effort to put serious energy conservation measures into effect.

12. Encourage energy conservation by reversing energy pricing formulae so that preferential rates are given to low energy users and high rates to high users.

13. Institute a nationwide educational program to reverse the effect of advertising that has made people "trained consumers." Keynote of this program would be "cautious consumption based on real need."

14. Educate the public as to the environmental necessity of the use of public transit, car pools, bicycling, and walking where distances are reasonable.

15. Make soil conservation a national priority on more than a lip-service basis. Refuse development or urban encroachment on good farmlands anywhere in Canada on the basis that Canada's farmland base is so small that further removal of such lands is inimical to national security.

16. Use military forces and institute Civilian Conservation Corps organizations and make it a national goal to reforest Canada's 24 million hectares of Not Sufficiently Restocked (NSR) forest lands. Give this project priority status because of global warming, fully realizing that this is a conservation matter that has been a political oversight for a full century.

17. Adopt forest harvesting plans which are truly sustainable and fully within the principles of sustained yield, and which put health and

preservation of complete forest ecosystems and protection of watersheds as primary forest management objectives. Modify forest practices such as clear-cutting which set the stage for massive infiltration of brush and thereby lead to the call for herbicides to compensate for poor forestry practices.

18. Promote a program which would allow tax deductible "Gifts to Canada" in the form of donations for a national reforestation program. These funds would be in addition to funds that might ordinarily be set aside for this purpose.
19. To encourage Canadian self-sufficiency in manufactured forest products, place a prohibitive tax on raw material exports such as whole log exports.
20. Support World Wildlife Fund's Endangered Spaces campaign by meeting the Bruntland Commission recommendation that at least 12 percent of national lands be set aside as true wilderness, free from resource extraction. This issue should not be delayed, considering the rate at which such lands are diminishing.
21. Institute extensive recycling programs in all communities at least as thorough as the program in Neunkirchen, Austria. Provide nationwide facilities for production of recycled paper throughout Canada.

Serious consideration must be given to many issues such as the foregoing. Our problems arise from the roots of long-held convictions which we now know have been erroneous. The problems we now face will not go away by continuing "business as usual" with a cosmetic coating of green oratory.

People in political office today might well pay heed to Longfellow's words:

> Humanity with all its fears,
> With all the hope of future years,
> Is hanging breathless on thy fate!

Endnotes

Chapter 1

1. Dr. Paul Ehrlich, "Eco-catastrophe," *The Everlasting Universe*, eds. Lorne J. Forstner and John H. Todd (Lexington, Mass.: D.C. Heath and Company, 1971), p. 163.
2. *Webster's New Twentieth Century Dictionary, Unabridged*, 2nd ed., s.v. "integrity."
3. Robert Service, "The Men That Don't Fit In," *The Shooting of Dan McGrew and Other Poems* (Surrey, B.C.: Hancock House Publishers Ltd., 1989), p. 5.
4. Jacqueline Murray, *The First European Agriculture—A Study of the Osteological and Botanical Evidence Until 2000 B.C.* (Edinburgh: University Press, 1970), pp. 36, 80, 81.
5. Edward Hyams, *Soil and Civilization*, Harper Colophon edition (London: John Murray, 1976), pp. 69-71.
6. Ibid.
7. Raymond F. Dasmann, *The Last Horizon* (New York: The Macmillan Company, 1963), pp. 58-59.
8. R. O. White, *Grasslands of the Monsoon* (New York: Frederick A. Praeger Publisher, 1968), pp. 167-73.
9. Thomas L. Green, "Organic Farming in India," *Alternatives,* (Waterloo, Ont.: Faculty of Environmental Studies, University of Waterloo, December, 1987), p. 9.
10. J. Bandyopadhyay and V. Shiva, "Chipko: Rekindling India's Forest Culture," *The Ecologist*, vol. 17, no. 1 (Cornwall, England, 1987), pp. 26-34.
11. Sumanta Banerjee and Smitu Kothari, "Food and Hunger in India," *The Ecologist*, vol. 15, no. 5/6 (1985), pp. 257.
12. Sir Percy Sykes, *A History of Afghanistan*, vol. 1 (London: Macmillan & Co., 1940), p. 224.
13. S. D. Amedee, *Histoire d'Attila et de ses successeurs; suivie des legendes et traditions* (Paris: Thierry, 1856), quoted in George Perkins Marsh, *Man and Nature*, David Lowenthal, ed. (Cambridge, Mass.: Harvard University Press, Belknap Press, Originally published 1864, 2nd printing 1967), p. 352.
14. Paul Hanley, ed., *Earthcare: Ecological Agriculture in Saskatchewan* (Indian Head, Sask.: Earthcare Information Center, 1980), p. 14.
15. Theophrastus, *Enquiry Into Plants,* trans. Sir Arthur Hort (Cambridge, Mass.: Harvard University Press, 1916), p. 463. (Original manuscript written about 300 B.C.).

16. Tom Dale and Vernon Gill Carter, *Topsoil and Civilization* (Norman: University of Oklahoma Press, 1955), pp. 42, 52, 53.

17. Walter Clay Lowdermilk, "Lessons from the Old World to the Americas in Land Use," *Annual Report of the Smithsonian Institution* (Washington, D.C.: U.S. Government Printing Office, 1943), pp. 413-28.

18. J. V. Thirgood, *Man and the Mediterranean Forest* (New York: Academic Press, 1981), pp. 102-06.

19. L. Delaporte, *Mesopotamia* (London: 1925), quoted in Will Durant, *The Story of Civilization,* 11 vols. (New York: Simon and Schuster, Inc., 1963), 1:268-69.

20. *The Holy Bible,* Deut. 8:7-9.

21. Lowdermilk, "Lessons from the Old World," p. 416.

22. Dale and Carter, *Topsoil and Civilization,* pp. 64-68.

23. Macrobius, *The Saturnalia,* bk. 7, ch. 5, (9), trans. P. V. Davies (New York: Columbia University Press, 1969), p. 463.

24. P. K. Hitti, *Lebanon in History* (London and Toronto: Macmillan & Co., 1967), pp. 33-34.

25. Lowdermilk, "Lessons from the Old World," p. 416.

26. Dale and Carter, *Topsoil and Civilization,* pp. 64-68.

27. Plato, *Critias,* trans. Rev. R. G. Bury (Cambridge: Harvard University Press, 1929), pp. 273-75.

28. Robert Rienow and Leona Train Rienow, *Moment in the Sun* (New York: Ballantine Books, Inc., 1967), p. 78.

29. Thucydides, *History of the Peloponnesian War,* trans. C. F. Smith (Cambridge, Mass.: Harvard University Press, 1918), bk. VIII, p. 181, XIX, p. 297.

30. Thompson King, *Water, Miracle of Nature* (New York: Collier Books, 1961), pp. 202-13.

31. Lester Brown, "Forest Talk," *Silviculture (Toronto: Maclean Hunter, May/June/-July 1988), p. 21.*

32. Lowdermilk, "Lessons from the Old World," pp. 419-21.

33. Edward Gibbon, *The History of the Decline and Fall of the Roman Empire,* 5th ed., J. B. Bury, ed. (New York: Methuen & Co., 1909), 1: 185.

34. Lowdermilk, "Lessons from the Old World," pp. 419-21.

35. Th. Monod, "Conservation of Natural Resources in Africa," *Man and Africa,* eds. G. Wolstenholme and M. O'Connor (London: J. & A. Churchill Ltd., 1965), pp. 258-74.

36. Philip Appleman, *The Silent Explosion* (Boston: Beacon Press, 1965), p. 32.

37. Ibid.

38. George Perkins Marsh, *Man and Nature,* ed. David Lowenthal (Cambridge, Mass.: Harvard University Press, Belknap Press, 1967. Originally published in 1864, New York: Charles Scribner), pp. 205-14.

39. Jérome A. Blanqui, "Rapport sur la situation economique des departments de la frontiere des Alpes: Isere, Hautes-Alpes, Basses Alpes, et var" (Académie des Sciences Morales et Politiques, Séances et Travaus, 1843), quoted in *Man and Nature,* p. 211.

40. Marsh, *Man and Nature,* p. 253.

41. Ibid., p. 336.

42. Alfred Russel Wallace, *Island Life* (London: Macmillan & Co., 1892), p. 295.

43. A. H. Emsmann, in the notes to his translation of Pierre Foissac, *Meteorologie,* (Liepzig: 1859), p. 654, quoted in *Man and Nature,* p. 114.

44. Kenneth B. Cumberland, "Man's Role in Modifying Island Environment in the Southwest Pacific: With Special Reference to New Zealand," *Man's Place in the Island Ecosystem—A Symposium,* ed. F. R. Fosberg (London: British Museum Press, 1965), pp. 187-205.

45. Ibid, p. 191.

46. Henry W. Haygarth, "Recollections of Bush Life in Australia during a Residence of 8 years in the Interior" (originally published in 1848), quoted by W. K. Hancock, *Discovering Monaro—A Study of Man's Impact on His Environment* (London: Cambridge University Press, 1972), pp. 60-61.

47. Durward Allen, *Our Wildlife Legacy* (New York: Funk and Wagnall, 1962), pp. 31-32.

48. Hyams, *Soil and Civilization,* pp. 220-29.

49. Dasmann, *The Last Horizon,* p. 23.

50. Dale and Carter, *Topsoil and Civilization,* p. 208.

51. B. Moser and D. Taylor, *The Cocaine Eaters* (New York: Taplinger Publishing Co., Inc., 1964), pp. 65, 122.

52. Paul R. Ehrlich, Anne H. Ehrlich, and John P. Holdren, *Ecoscience: Population, Resources, Environment* (San Francisco: W. H. Freeman & Company, 1977), pp. 624-25.

53. Rafael Herrera, "Amazon Rain Forest Fires," cited in Peter Bunyard, "World Climate and Tropical Forest Destruction," *The Ecologist,* vol. 15, no. 3 (1985), pp. 125-36.

54. Kenneth C. Boulding, "The Economics of the Coming Spaceship Earth," cited in Paul R. Ehrlich and Anne H. Ehrlich, *Population, Resources, and Environment* (San Francisco: W. H. Freeman & Company, 1970), pp. 282-83.

Chapter 2

1. J. Talman, ed., *Basic Documents in Canadian History* (Princeton, N.J.: D. Van Nostrand, 1959), p. 7.

2. Ibid., p. 11.

3. John Bakeless, *The Eyes of Discovery* (New York: Dover Publications, Inc., 1961), pp. 105, 267, 317, 397.

4. Ibid., pp. 267, 317, 397.

5. William Cody, "True Tales of the Plains," quoted in *America: A Library of Original Sources,* 12 vols., n.p., quoted in Peter Mathiessen, *Wildlife in America* (New York: The Viking Press, 1959), pp. 148-49.

6. Wayne Lynch, "The Return of the Swift Fox," *Canadian Geographic* August/September 1987, p. 28.

7. Jean Dorst, *Before Nature Dies,* trans. Constance D. Sherman (Baltimore: Penguin Books, 1970), pp. 49-51.

8. Peter Mathiessen, *Wildlife in America* (New York: The Viking Press, 1959), p. 151.

9. William T. Hornaday, *The Extermination of the American Bison with a Sketch of*

its Discovery and Life Story, reprinted from Report of National Museum, 1887 (Seattle: The Shorey Book Store, Facsimile Reproduction, 1971), p. 525.

10. Mathiessen, *Wildlife in America,* p. 151.

11. Farley Mowat, *Sea of Slaughter* (Toronto: McClelland and Stewart, 1984), pp. 179-86.

12. Anthony Netboy, *The Atlantic Salmon* (Boston: Houghton Mifflin Co., 1968), pp. 353-66.

13. Ibid., p. 354.

14. Ibid., p. 366.

15. H. B. Bigelow and W. C. Schroeder, "Fishes of the Gulf of Maine," *Fisheries Bulletin* of the Fish and Wildlife Service, vol. 53 (Washington, D.C.: U.S. Government Printing Office, 1953), pp. 121-31.

16. John L. Culliney, *The Forests of the Sea* (New York: Doubleday and Co., Inc., 1979), pp. 331-64.

17. "Sportsman's Journal," *Outdoor Canada,* (Don Mills, Ont., September 1988), p. 22.

18. F. E. Carlton, "Biting the Bullet," *Atlantic Salmon Journal,* vol. 37, no. 1 (Montreal: Atlantic Salmon Federation, Spring 1988), p. 50.

19. Ibid., p. 52.

20. L. C. Cole, "Our Man-Made Environmental Crisis," *Canadian Audubon* (Toronto: Canadian Audubon Society, November/December 1968).

21. John S. Hoffman, "Carbon Dioxide and Future Forests," *Journal of Forestry,* vol. 82, no. 3 (Bethesda, Maryland: The Society of American Foresters, March, 1984), p. 164.

22. A. Marsh, "Air Pollution," *Technological Injury,* ed. J. Rose (New York: Fordon & Breach, 1969), pp. 17-27.

23. Samuel Taylor Coleridge, *Omega,* ed. Paul K. Anderson (Dubuque, Iowa: Wm. C. Brown Company Publishers, 1971), p. 128.

24. Dorst, *Before Nature Dies,* pp. 206-15.

25. Paul R. Ehrlich, Anne H. Ehrlich, and John P. Holdren, *Ecoscience: Population, Resources, Environment* (San Francisco: W. H. Freeman & Company, 1977), pp. 544-58.

26. Lester R. Brown, *The Twenty-Ninth Day* (New York: W. W. Norton & Company, 1978), pp. 42-45.

27. *Canada's Environment, An Overview* (Ottawa: A publication of Environment Canada, Supply and Services, 1986), p. 16.

28. Samuel S. Epstein, "Losing the War Against Cancer," *The Ecologist,* vol. 17, no. 2/3, 1987, pp. 91-99.

29. Cynthia Pollock, "Realizing Recycling's Potential," *State of the World 1987* (New York: W. W. Norton & Company, 1987), pp. 101-21.

30. C. Lundberg, ed., *The West Coast Environmental Law Research Foundation Newsletter,* vol. 13 (Fall 1987), p. 1.

31. Allen E. Boraiko, "The Pesticide Dilemma," *National Geographic,* February 1980, p. 150, quoted in *Earthcare: Ecological Agriculture in Saskatchewan,* ed. Paul Hanley, (Indian Head, Sask., Earthcare Information Centre, 1980), p. 12.

32. Ross H. Hall, *A New Approach to Pest Control in Canada,* report no. 10 (Ottawa: Canadian Environmental Advisory Council, July 1981), p. 1.

33. Jan M. Newton, "Herbicides and Economics," *NCAP News*, vol. 3, no. 4 (Eugene, Oregon: 1984), pp. 10-11.

34. J. Altman and C. L. Campbell, "Effect of Herbicides on Plant Diseases," *Annual Review of Phytopathology* 15 (1971): 361-85.

35. Francis Chaboussou, "How Pesticides Increase Pests," *The Ecologist*, vol. 16, no. 1 (1986), pp. 29-35.

36. Robert van den Bosch, *The Pesticide Conspiracy* (Garden City, N.Y.: Doubleday and Co., Inc., 1978), p. 28.

37. Hall, *Pest Control*, pp. vi, 2, 36.

38. Eric P. Eckholm, *Losing Ground* (New York: W. W. Norton & Company, 1976).

39. R. F. Harrington and R. C. Passmore, *Learning About Environment* (Ottawa: Carlton-Green Publishing Company Ltd., 1972), pp. 42-43.

40. Ehrlich, Ehrlich, and Holdren, *Ecoscience*, pp. 634-36.

41. Kenneth Mellanby, *Pesticides and Pollution* (London: Wm. Collins Sons & Co., 1967), pp. 137-40.

42. "Canadian Notes," *Alternatives*, October/November 1989, p. 2, and September /October 1988, p. 2.

43. J. F. Castrilli and T. Vigod, *Pesticides in Canada: An Examination of Federal Law and Policy* (Ottawa: Law Reform Commission of Canada, 1987), p. 9.

44. Ehrlich, Ehrlich, and Holdren, *Ecoscience*, pp. 855-58.

45. Samuel S. Epstein, *The Politics of Cancer* (Garden City, New York: Doubleday and Co., Inc., 1979), pp. 273-81.

46. Hall, *Pest Control*, p. 12.

47. Castrilli and Vigod, *Pesticides in Canada*, p. 85.

48. van den Bosch, *Pesticide Conspiracy*, p. 29.

49. Jonathan King, *Troubled Water* (Emmaus, Pa.: Rodale Press, 1985), pp. 53, 55-56, 97.

50. Christie McLaren, "Damage to Immune System Cited, Potato Insecticide Called Health Peril," *Globe and Mail*, September 19, 1986.

51. R. F. Spalding, G. A. Junk, and J. J. Richard, "Water, Pesticides in Groundwater Beneath Irrigated Farmland in Nebraska," *Pesticide Monitoring Journal*, vol. 14, no. 2 (September 1980), pp. 70-73.

52. R. Frank, G. J. Sirons, and B. D. Ripley, "Herbicide Contamination and Decontamination of Well Water in Ontario, Canada, 1969-78," *Pesticide Monitoring Journal*, vol. 13, no. 3 (December 1979), pp. 120-27.

53. Randall F. Perkins, coord., *Methods of Managing Competing Vegetation, Pacific Northwest Region*, Forest Service, U.S. Department of Agriculture, May 1981, pp. 125-39.

54. Barbara Wallace, MLA, Cowichan-Malahat, personal correspondence with Linda Harrington, October 29 1985, quoting source as: A. J. Hudson, Department of Clinical Neurological Science, University Hospital, Ontario, 1978.

55. *Earthcare: Ecological Agriculture in Saskatchewan*, Paul Hanley, ed. (Indian Head, Sask.: Earthcare Information Center, 1980), p. 13.

56. "World Notes," *Alternatives*, Winter 1985, p. 61.

57. "Knowledge on Chemical Risks is Lacking," *Infotox, vol. 2, no. 2 (Ottawa: Friends of the Earth*, August 1985), p. 2.

58. Bill Blaikie, MP, Winnipeg-Bird's Hill, *Newsletter*, no. 1 (Winnipeg: June 1985),

p. 4.

59. Peter Farb, *Living Earth* (New York: Harper & Row, Publishers, 1959), pp. 5-15.
60. E. S. Shaler, *Nature and Man in America* (New York: Charles Scribner & Son, 1906), p. 184.
61. H. O. Buckman and N. C. Brady, *The Nature and Properties of Soils*, 7th ed. (New York: The Macmillan Company, 1969), pp. 223-36
62. *National Wildlife Magazine*, February/March 1983.
63. Hon. H. O. Sparrow, Chairman, *Soil at Risk*. Report on Soil Conservation by the Standing Committee on Agriculture, Fisheries, and Forestry, to the Senate of Canada (Ottawa: 1984), pp. 3-8.
64. Durward L. Allan, *Our Wildlife Legacy* (New York: Funk and Wagnall, 1962), pp. 18-23.
65. Louis Bromfield, *Malabar Farm* (New York: Ballantine Books, Inc., 1970), pp. 343-76.
66. "This Is No Way to Grow," *Time*, September 18, 1989, p. 55.
67. Paul B. Sears, *Deserts on the March* (Norman, Okla.: University of Oklahoma Press, 1935), p. 168.
68. *Complete Mother*, Fall 1987.
69. King, *Troubled Water*, pp. x-xii.
70. Castrilli and Vigod, *Pesticides in Canada*, p. 11.
71. *Canada's Environment, An Overview*, p. 11.
72. Eckholm, *Losing Ground*.
73. J. P. Sprague and C. P. Ruggles, "The Impact of Water Pollution on Fisheries in the Atlantic Provinces," *Pollution of Our Environment*, Background Paper A4-1-3 (Ottawa: Queen's Printer, 1966), 1:4.
74. D. A. Monro and V. E. F. Solomon, "The Impact of Water Pollution on Wildlife," *Pollution of Our Environment*, Background Paper A4-1-3 (Ottawa: Queen's Printer, 1966), 1:3.
75. M. L. H. Thomas, "Effects of Bunker C Oil on Intertidal and Lagoonal Biota in Chedabucto Bay, Nova Scotia," *Journal of the Fisheries Research Board of Canada*, vol. 30, no. 1 (January 1973), pp. 83-90.
76. Ehrlich, Ehrlich, and Holdren, *Ecoscience*, p. 658.
77. Ross H. Hall and Donald A. Chant, *Ecotoxicity: Responsibilities and Opportunities*, report no. 8 (Ottawa: Canadian Environmental Advisory Council, August 1979), p. vi.
78. Jeremy Rifkin, *Entropy* (New York: Viking Press, 1980), p. 163.
79. "World's Forests are Shrinking," *Christian Science Monitor*, in *The Western Producer*, February 16, 1984 Newspaper, p. B9.
80. Stewart L. Udall, *The Quiet Crisis* (New York: Avon Books, 1964), p. 151.
81. G. Tyler Miller, Jr., *Living in the Environment: An Introduction to Environmental Science*, 4th ed. (Belmont, Calif.: Wadsworth Publishing Co. Inc., 1985), p. 178.
82. Udall, *The Quiet Crisis*, pp. 67-70.
83. Jamie Swift, *Cut and Run* (Toronto: Between the Lines, 1983), pp. 31-49.
84. G. W. Weetman, "Forestry Practices and Stress on Canadian Forest Land," *Stress on Land in Canada* (Ottawa: Environment Canada, Government Printing Office, 1983), pp. 259-302.
85. Roger Hart, "The Questionable Practice of Slash Burning," *NCAP News*, vol. 4,

no. 3 (Fall, 1984): pt. 1, pp. 17-21; vol 4. no. 4 (Winter 1985): pt. 2, pp. 19-24.

86. Gordon Robinson, *The Forest and The Trees* (Washington, D.C.: Island Press, 1988), p. 194.

87. William Vogt, *People!*, p. 66, quoted in Philip Appleman, *The Silent Explosion* (Boston: Beacon Press, 1965), p. 41.

88. Roger Hart, "The Questionable Practice of Slash Burning," *NCAP News*, vol. 4, no. 3 (Fall 1984), pp. 17-21.

89. Christie McLaren, "Quest for profit leaves coastal timber to rot," *Globe and Mail*, December 31 1987, n.p.

90. Bob Williams, Speech to the 45th Annual Truck Logger's Convention, Vancouver, January 13, 1988.

91. *Canada's Environment, An Overview*, pp. 6-7, 16-17.

92. George Perkins Marsh, *Man and Nature*, ed. David Lowenthal (Cambridge, Mass.: Harvard University Press, Belknap Press, 1967. Originally published in 1864, New York: Charles Scribner), p. 280.

93. Abraham Lincoln, "Second Inaugural Address," March 4 1865. In *Great Thoughts of Great Americans*, Constance Bridges, comp. (New York: Thomas Y. Crowell Company, 1951), p. 121.

Interlude 2

1. Ernest Thomson Seton, *Lives of Game Animals*, 8 vols., (Boston: Charles T. Branford Company, 1953), 1:417.

Chapter 3

1. R. B. Blakney, *The Way of Life, Lao Tzu* (New York: New American Library, Mentor Books, 1955), pp. 13-49; Manly Palmer Hall, *Twelve World Teachers* (Los Angeles: Philosophical Research Society, Inc., 1973), pp. 125-44.

2. Lao Tzu, *The Way of Life*, (New York and Toronto: New American Library, Inc., Mentor Books, 1955), no. 29, p. 81; no. 64, p. 117.

3. Will Durant, *The Story of Civilization: vol. 1, Our Oriental Heritage* (New York: Simon and Schuster, Inc., 1935), pp. 652-58. Copyright 1935, 1963 by Will Durant. Reprinted by permission of Simon & Schuster, Inc.

4. Robert Mayne Hutchins, ed., *Great Books of the Western World*, 54 vols. (Chicago: Encyclopaedia Britannica, Inc., 1952), 10:9-19.

5. Ibid, 8:499-626, 9:7-339.

6. Ibid., 9:148, 248.

7. Vergil, "The Joys of Farm Life," *Latin Literature in Translation*, trans. John Dryden (New York: Longman's Green and Co., 1954), p. 327.

8. Columella, *De Rustica.* Book I, ii, pp. 3-4, Book II, i, pp. 5-7.

9. Lucretius, *Of the Nature of Things*, trans. W. E. Leonard (London: J. M. Dent and Sons Ltd., 1921), pp. 10, 12.

10. *Pliny's Natural History*, comp. Lloyd Haberly (n.p.: Frederick Ungar Publishing Co., 1957), pp. 177-79.

11. *Pliny, The History of the World,* trans. P. Holland and selected Paul Turner, (New York: McGraw Hill Book Co., 1962), pp. 431-32.
12. Brooks Atkinson, ed., *Walden and Other Writings of Henry David Thoreau* (New York: Random House, Inc., The Modern Library, 1950), p. 74.
13. Marcus Aurelius, *Meditations,* trans. Maxwell Staniforth (Harmondsworth, England: Penguin Books, 1964), p. 78.
14. Ibid., p. 73.
15. Ibid., p. 106.
16. Will Durant, *The Story of Civilization, vol. II, The Life of Greece* (New York: Simon and Schuster, Inc., 1939), p. 137.
17. Dom. Cuthbert Butler, *Benedictine Monachism* (Cambridge: Cambridge Speculum Historiale, 1923, reprinted 1961), pp. 319-20.
18. A Monk of Dubai Abbey, col., *The High History of St. Benedict & His Monks* (London: Sands and Co., 1945), p. 228.
19. René Dubos, "Conservation, Stewardship, and the Human Heart," *Audubon,* September 1972.
20. Ibid.
21. William E. H. Lecky, *The History of European Morals,* vol. 2 (London: Green & Co., 1910), p. 172.
22. Lynn White, "The Historical Roots of Our Ecological Crisis," ed. Lorne J. Forstner and John H. Todd, *The Everlasting Universe* (Lexington, Mass: D. C. Heath and Company, 1971), p. 7-18.
23. Murray Bodo, OFM, *The Way of St. Francis* (New York: Doubleday and Co., Inc., 1984), p. 145.
24. John Ray, *The Wisdom of God Manifest in the Works of His Creation* (London: n.p., 1691).
25. Rewey Belle Inglis, Donald A. Stauffer, and Cecil Evva Larsen, *Adventures in English Literature* (Canadian Edition: W. J. Gage and Company Limited, 1952), p. 310.
26. Alexander Pope, *Selected Works,* ed. Louis Krenenberger (New York: Random House, Inc., The Modern Library, 1951), p. 34.
27. Ibid., p. 105.
28. Inglis, Stauffer, and Larsen, "The Tables Turned," *Adventures in English Literature,* p. 352.
29. Ibid., p. 360.
30. Roderick Nash, *Wilderness and the American Mind* (New Haven: Yale University Press, 1967), pp. 23-66.
31. Thomas Henry Huxley, "A Liberal Education," *Adventures in English Literature,* p. 465.
32. The World Commission on Environment and Development, *Our Common Future* (New York: Oxford University Press, 1987), p. 1.

Chapter 4

1. Robert L. Heilbroner, *An Inquiry Into The Human Prospect* (New York: W. W. Norton & Company, 1980), p. 11.

2. Charles Alexander Eastman (Ohiyesa), *The Soul of the Indian* (Boston: Houghton, Mifflin, 1911), p. 45, quoted in T. C. McLuhan, comp., *Touch The Earth* (New York: Simon & Schuster Inc., Pocket Books, 1972), p. 36.

3. Gifford Pinchot, *Breaking New Ground* (Originally published New York: Harcourt, Brace and Co., 1947. Reprinted: Washington D.C., Covelo, Calif.: Island Press, 1987), pp. 24-25.

4. Grant MacEwan, *Tatanga Mani: Walking Buffalo of the Stonies* (Edmonton: Hurtig Publishers, 1969), p. 190.

5. Stewart L. Udall, *The Quiet Crisis* (New York: Avon Books, 1964), p. 20.

6. Albert Schweitzer, *Goëthe, Five Studies,* trans. Charles R. Joy (Boston, Beacon Press, 1961), pp. 56, 117-18.

7. R. M. Hutchins, ed., *Great Books of the Western World,* 54 vols., *Goëthe* (Chicago: Encyclopaedia Britannica, Inc., 1980), 47:281.

8. Walt Whitman, "Song of Myself," *Leaves of Grass and Selected Prose* (New York: Random House, Inc., The Modern Library, 1950), p. 49.

9. Brooks Atkinson, ed., "Walking," *Walden and Other Writings of Henry David Thoreau* (New York: Random House, Inc., The Modern Library, 1950), p. 627.

10. Clifford Dowdey, *The Land They Fought For* (New York: Doubleday and Co., 1955), p. 386.

11. Udall, *The Quiet Crisis,* pp. 66-67.

12. George Perkins Marsh, *Man and Nature,* ed. David Lowenthal (Cambridge, Mass.: Harvard University Press, Belknap Press, 1967. Originally published in 1864, New York: Charles Scribner), p. title page.

13. Bernhard & Michael Grzimek, *Serengeti Shall Not Die* (New York: E. P. Dutton and Co. Inc., 1959), pp. 205-42.

14. Marsh, *Man and Nature,* p. 37.

15. Wallace Stegner, *Beyond the Hundredth Meridian* (Boston: Houghton Mifflin Co., 1953).

16. Donald Mackay, *The Crisis in Canada's Forests* (Toronto: Macmillan of Canada, 1985), p. 26.

17. Mackay, *Crisis in Canada's Forests,* p. 27.

18. Jamie Swift, *Cut and Run* (Toronto: Between the Lines, 1983), pp. 48-52.

19. Gifford Pinchot, *The Fight for Conservation* (Seattle: University of Washington Press, 1910), p. 4.

20. Ibid, p. 81.

21. Ibid, p. 124.

22. R. F. Harrington, "Theodore Roosevelt—Conservationist With a Big Stick," *Commonsense,* vol. 2, no. 3 (July 1980), pp. 12-15.

23. Theodore Roosevelt, *Literary Essays* (New York: Charles Scribner's Sons, 1926), p. 420.

24. Liberty Hyde Bailey, *The Holy Earth* (New York: Charles Scribner's Sons, 1915; reprinted ed., Ithaca, N.Y.: State University of New York, 1980), p. 13.

25. Ibid., p. 23.

26. Ibid, p. 56.

27. Nathan Miller, *F. D. R., An Intimate History* (New York: Doubleday and Co., Inc., 1983), pp. 89-90.

28. Havelock Ellis, *Little Essays of Love and Virtue,* quoted in John Bartlett, *Familiar*

Quotations, 13th ed. (Boston & Toronto: Little, Brown and Company, 1955), p. 783b.

29. Ralph D. Bird, *Ecology of the Aspen Parkland of Western Canada* (Ottawa: Research Branch, Agriculture Canada, Publication #1066, Queens Printer, 1961), reproduced courtesy of Agriculture Canada and by permission of the Minister of Supply and Services Canada, p. 42.
30. Hon. H. O. Sparrow, Chairman, *Soil at Risk.* Report on Soil Conservation by the Standing Committee on Agriculture, Fisheries, Forestry, to the Senate of Canada (Ottawa: 1984), p. 45.
31. Barry Commoner, *The Closing Circle* (New York: Bantam Books, Inc., 1972), p. 125.
32. *Water 2020: Sustainable Use for Water in the 21st Century,* report no. 40 (Ottawa: Science Council of Canada, June 1988), p. 15.
33. Commoner, *The Closing Circle,* pp. 78-90.
34. Stephen H. Schneider, *The Genesis Strategy* (New York: Dell Publishing Co., A Delta Book, 1977), p. 193.
35. World Commission on Environment and Development, *Our Common Future* (New York: Oxford University Press, 1987), pp. 36, 307.
36. Anne Chisholm, *Philosophers of the Earth: Conversations With Ecologists* (London: Sidgewick & Jackson, 1972), p. 8.

Chapter 5

1. Paul R. Ehrlich and Anne H. Ehrlich, *Population, Resources, Environment* (San Francisco: W. H. Freeman & Company, 1970), p. 324.
2. Bradford Torrey and Francis H. Allen, eds., *The Journal of Henry D. Thoreau* (New York: Dover Publications, Inc., 1962); Brooks Atkinson, ed., *Walden and Other Writings of Henry David Thoreau* (New York: Random House, Inc., The Modern Library, 1950).
3. Brooks Atkinson, ed., "Walking," *Walden and Other Writings of Henry David Thoreau* (New York: Random House, Inc., The Modern Library, 1950), p. 82.
4. Ibid., p. 33.
5. Ibid., p. 32.
6. Ibid., p. 613.
7. Ibid., p. 617.
8. Ibid., p. 86.
9. Ibid., p. 288.
10. Brooks Atkinson, ed., *The Selected Writing of Ralph Waldo Emerson* (New York: Random House, Inc., The Modern Library, 1950), pp. 913-14.
11. Atkinson, *Walden and Other Writings,* p. 297.
12. George Perkins Marsh, *Man and Nature,* ed. David Lowenthal (Cambridge, Mass.: Harvard University Press, Belknap Press, 1967. Originally published in 1864, New York: Charles Scribner), p. 52.
13. Ibid., pp. 273-80.
14. Ibid., pp. 41, 42, 43.
15. Ibid., pp. 250-53.
16. Ibid., pp. 251-55.

17. Ibid., pp. 464-65.
18. Ibid., p. 352.
19. Ibid., pp. 274-80.
20. Ibid., pp. 45-46.
21. Norman Cousins, *Albert Schweitzer's Mission—Healing and Peace* (New York: W. W. Norton & Company, 1985), pp. 111-12.
22. Lewis Mumford, *The Conduct of Life* (New York: Harcourt Brace Jovanovich, Inc., 1970), p. 181.
23. Chief Luther Standing Bear, *Land of the Spotted Eagle* (Boston and New York: Houghton, Mifflin, 1933), p. xix, quoted in T. C. McLuhan, *Touch the Earth* (New York: Pocket Books, ed., 1972), p. 45.
24. Albert Schweitzer, *The Decay and the Restoration of Civilization* (London: Unwin Books, 1956), p. 15.
25. Ibid., p. 15.
26. Albert Schweitzer, *Civilization and Ethics* (London: Unwin Books, 1956), pp. 212-44.
27. Schweitzer, *Decay and the Restoration of Civilization,* pp. 75-77.
28. John Milton, "On His Blindness," Sonnet XV, *Adventures in English Literature,* (Canadian Edition: W. J. Gage and Company Limited, 1952), p. 230.
29. Atkinson, *Walden and Other Writings,* p. 597.
30. Marsh, *Man and Nature,* p. xxv.
31. Atkinson, *Walden and Other Writings,* p. 68.

Chapter 6

1. World Commission on Environment and Development, *Our Common Future* (New York: Oxford University Press, 1987), p. 8.
2. Ibid., p. 23.
3. Will and Ariel Durant, *The Lessons of History* (New York: Simon and Schuster, Inc., 1968), p. 72.
4. Lewis Mumford, *The Conduct of Life* (New York: Harcourt Brace Jovanovich, Inc., 1951), p. 13.
5. Robert Rienow and Leona Train Rienow, *Moment In the Sun* (New York: Ballantine Books, Inc., 1967), p. 285.
6. Michael Simpson, "Thomas Adams in Canada, 1914-1930," *Urban History Review,* vol. xi, no. 2 (n.p.: n.d.), p. 3, quoted in W. F. Burditt, "Civic Efficiency and Social Welfare in the Planning of Land," *Urban and Rural Development in Canada* (Ottawa: Commission of Conservation, 1917), p. 78.
7. William Wordsworth, "The World Is Too Much With Us," *The Norton Anthology of English Literature,* 3rd ed., M. H. Abrams et al., eds. (New York: W. W. Norton & Company, Inc., 1975), p. 1441.
8. Stewart L. Udall, *The Quiet Crisis* (New York: Avon books, 1964), pp. 66-67. Vance Packard, *The Hidden Persuaders* (New York: Pocket Books, 1973). Samuel S. Epstein, "Losing the War Against Cancer," *The Ecologist,* vol. 17, no. 2/3, (1987), pp. 91-97.
9. John Bartlett, *Familiar Quotations,* 13th ed. (Boston and Toronto: Little, Brown

and Company, 1955), p. 679a.
10. Harvey Cox, *The Seduction of the Spirit* (New York: Simon and Schuster, Inc., 1973), p. 103.
11. James A. Michener, *Chesapeake* (New York: Random House, 1978), p. 383.
12. Leo Tolstoy, *The Kingdom of God is Within You* (New York: Farrar, Straus and Giroux, The Noonday Press, 1905), pp. 379-80.

Chapter 7

1. World Conference on the Changing Atmosphere: Conference Statement. Implications for Global Security, Toronto, June 27-30, 1988.
2. Thomas Paine, *The Rights of Man* (1915; reprinted ed., London: J. M. Dent & Sons Ltd., Everyman's Library, 1969), p. 233.
3. Tom Wicker, "Time to Tackle the Threat," *The Globe and Mail,* November 29, 1988.
4. World Commission on Environment and Development, *Our Common Future* (New York: Oxford University Press, 1987), p. 71.
5. Robert Costanza, "What is Ecological Economics," *Journal of the International Society for Ecological Economics,* vol. 1, no. 1 (Solomons, Md.: University of Maryland), pp. 1-7.
6. James Rusk, "Deserts Winning Battle of the Land," *The Globe and Mail,* April 25, 1988.
7. Aldo Leopold, *Sand County Almanac* (New York: Ballantine Books, Inc., 1966), p. 243.
8. Robert H. Boyle, "Will There be a Next Year?" *Sports Illustrated,* November 1987.
9. Sue Branford, London Observer Service, "Business Can Buy Time Against Greenhouse Effect," *Globe and Mail,* December 2, 1988.
10. Ibid.
11. S. I. Cohen, "The Afforestation of Israel," *The Journal of Forestry,* February 1985, pp. 95-99.
12. Gail Hepburn, "Pesticides and Drugs from the Neem Tree," *The Ecologist,* vol. 19, no.1, January/February 1989, pp. 31-32.
13. "Swapping Debt For Nature," *Working for Wildlife,* Fall 1987.
14. Richard St. Barbe Baker, *My Life My Trees* (Forres, Scotland: Findhorn Publications, 1979), pp. 157-67.
15. "Agriculture—An Unsolved Problem," *Manas,* vol. XLI, no. 46 (Los Angeles: Manas Publishing Company, November 16, 1988), p. 1.
16. Robert L. Metcalf, "China Unleashes Its Ducks," *Environment,* November 1976.
17. Denis Hayes, *Rays of Hope* (Washington, D.C.: Worldwatch Institute, 1977).
18. Ralph Cavanagh, David Goldstein, and Robert Watson, "One Last Chance For a National Energy Policy," *The Challenge of Global Warming,* ed. Dean Edwin Abrahamson (Washington, D.C., Covelo, Calif.: Island Press, 1989), pp. 279-90.
19. "Renewing Energy Efficiency" and "Ontario Becomes More Energy Efficient," *Probe Post,* September 1989, pp. 39-40.
20. David Jones, *The Western Producer,* September 15, 1988.
21. "Germany Pays for Conservation," *The Western Producer,* November 24, 1988.

22. "Pesticide Cuts Promoted," *Alternatives,* November/December 1988, p. 3.

23. "Heinz Gets Tough," *Mother Earth News,* July/August 1987.

24. Riza Tjahjad, "PAN Indonesia: A Grassroots Organization Moves Its Country Toward Alternatives to Pesticides," *Journal of Pesticide Reform,* vol. 9, no. 2 (Summer 1989):20-21.

25. Kay Treakle and John Sacko, "Where There's a Will There's a Way: Indonesia, Rice and Alternatives to 57 Pesticides," *Journal of Pesticide Reform,* vol. 9, no. 2 (Summer 1989):18-19.

26. Alan B. Durning, *Action At the Grassroots—Fighting Poverty and Environmental Decline.* Worldwatch, Paper 88 (Washington, D.C.: Worldwatch Institute, January 1989), p. 38.

27. Nicholas Lenssen, "The Ocean Blues," *Probe Post,* vol. 12, no. 2 (September 1989):10.

28. "Achievements and Priorities in Conservation," *World Wildlife Fund, Awareness Training and Education,* p. 5.

Chapter 8

1. "The Ecologist Digest," *The Ecologist,* vol. 12, no. 3 (1982), p. 1.

2. Ernest Haeckel, *The Riddle of the Universe* (London: Watts and Co., 1929), p. 9.

3. John Muir, *Steep Trails* (Boston: Houghton Mifflin Company, 1918), p. 11.

4. *Sand County Almanac,* p. 238.

5. Wilbur E. Garrett, "Editorial," *National Geographic,* December 1988, p. 764.

6. E. D. Klemke, A. David Kline, and Robert Hollinger, eds., *Philosophy, The Basic Issues* (New York: St. Martin's Press, Inc., 1982), p. 413.

7. John D. Hamaker, *The Survival of Civilization* (Seymour, Mo.: Hamaker-Weaver Publishers, 1982), quoted in "A Question of Relevance," *Manas,* December 22, 1982, p. 1.

8. Carl Wilson and Walter E. Loomis, *Botany* (New York: Holt, Rinehart & Winston, Inc., 1957), pp. 65-101.

9. George M. Woodwell, "Biotic Causes and Effects of the Disruption of the Global Carbon Cycle," ch. 5, *The Challenge of Global Warming,* ed. Dean Edwin Abrahamson (Washington, D.C.: Island Press, 1989), pp. 71-81.

10. R. H. Whittaker, and G. E. Likens, "Carbon and the Biota," *Carbon in the Biosphere,* eds. G. M. Woodwell and E. Pecan (Washington, D.C.: Technical Information Center, USAEC), p. 281-300; Paul R. Ehrlich, Anne H. Ehrlich, and John P. Holdren, Table 4-6, *Ecoscience* (San Francisco: W. H. Freeman & Co., 1977), p. 132.

11. Jerry Franklin, "Old Growth, Its Characteristics, and its Relationship to Pacific Northwest Forests," A talk presented at the Old Growth Conference, Corvallis, Oregon, August 25, 1988.

12. *Western Canada Wilderness Committee Education Report,* Winter 1988/89, p. 4.

13. *Canada's Threatened Forests* (Ottawa: Science Council of Canada, 1983), p. 5.

14. Eugene Linden, "The Death of Birth," *Time,* January 2, 1989, p. 33.

15. Gordon Robinson, *The Forest and the Trees* (Washington, D.C.: Island Press, 1988), p. 228.

16. Jovan Jovanovich, "Is Man Meddling?" *The Globe and Mail,* January 10, 1989, p. A7.
17. Paul R. Ehrlich and Anne H. Ehrlich, *Population Resources and Environment* (San Francisco: W. H. Freeman & Co., 1970), p. 118.
18. Paul Swatek, *The User's Guide to Protection of the Environment* (New York: A Friends of the Earth/Ballantine Book, 1970), p. 250.
19. Ian Allaby, "GO Transit Moves a City," *Canadian Geographic,* December 1988, pp. 30-36.
20. Sandra Postel, *Altering the Earth's Chemistry—Assessing the Risks.* Worldwatch, Paper 71 (Washington: Worldwatch Institute, 1986), p. 45.
21. Robert Ardrey, *African Genesis* (New York: Dell Publishing Co., Inc., 1961), pp. 204-7.
22. Richard Swann Lull, *Organic Evolution* (New York: The Macmillan Company, 1938), pp. 190-94.
23. Woodwell, *Challenge of Global Warming,* pp. 71-81.
24. Lester R. Brown, *The Twenty-Ninth Day* (New York: W. W. Norton & Company, Inc., 1978), pp. 277-78.
25. Lester R. Brown and Edward C. Wolf, *Reversing Africa's Decline.* Worldwatch, Paper 65 (Washington, D.C.: Worldwatch Institute, June 1985), pp. 7-9.
26. F. Fraser Darling and John P. Milton, eds., *Future Environments of North America* (Garden City, N.Y.: The Natural History Press, 1966), p. 404.
27. Ibid., p. 728.
28. The United Nations Conference on the Human Environment, Stockholm, Sweden, 1972, Principle #19.
29. Hon. H. O. Sparrow, Chairman, *Soil at Risk.* Report on Soil Conservation by the Standing Committee on Agriculture, Fisheries, Forestry, to the Senate of Canada (Ottawa: 1984), p. 18.
30. The World Commission on Environment and Development, *Our Common Future* (New York: Oxford University Press, 1987), p. 113.
31. Statement from the World Conference on the Changing Atmosphere, Toronto, Canada, June 1988.
32. Thomas A. Sancton, "Hands Across the Sea," *Time,* January 2, 1989, p. 52.
33. "The Ethical Sense," *Manas,* June 22, 1988.
34. Albert Schweitzer, *The Decay and the Restoration of Civilization* (London: Unwin Books, 1967), pp. 68-69.
35. Vance Packard, *The Hidden Persuaders* (New York: Pocket Books, 1973), pp. 6, 15.
36. Robert Mayne Hutchins, ed., *Great Books of the Western World,* 54 vols., *The Great Ideas* (Chicago: Encyclopaedia Britannica, Inc., 1978), 2:252-67.
37. Ibid., 2:253-54.
38. Ibid., 2:255.
39. Ibid., 3:866-81.
40. Ibid., 3:867.
41. Ibid., 2:850-79.
42. Ibid., 3:472-87.
43. John Keats, "Letters to George and Georgiana Keats, February 14-May 3, 1819," *The Norton Anthology of English Literature,* 4th ed. (New York: W. W. Norton & Company, Inc., 1979), 2:876-77.

44. General the Right Honorable J. C. Smuts, *Holism and Evolution* (London: Macmillan and Co., 1926), p. 337-38.

45. Michel Salomon, *Future Life* (New York: The Macmillan Publishing Company, 1983), pp. 102-19.

46. Ibid., pp. 269-79.

47. Inez Marks Lowdermilk, *All in a Lifetime* (Berkeley, Calif.: Lowdermilk Trust, 1983), pp. 134-35.

48. Lowdermilk, *All In a Lifetime,* p. frontispiece.

49. Charles S. Elton, *The Ecology of Invasions by Plants and Animals* (London: Methuen & Co., 1958), p. 159.

50. Marston Bates, *The Forest and the Sea* (New York: Random House, 1960), p. 262.

51. Lewis Herber, *Our Synthetic Environment* (New York: Alfred A. Knopf, Inc., 1962), p. 30.

52. "The Coming Age of Automatic Factors," *Technology Review,* 1975.

53. David Brower and Steve Lyons, "A Misstep on A Hard Path," *Not Man Apart* (San Francisco: Friends of the Earth, March, 1978).

54. "Sharing British Columbia," *Factsheet* (Victoria, B.C.: Sierra Club of Western Canada, 1988).

Chapter 9

1. Marcus Aurelius, *Meditations,* trans. Maxwell Staniforth (Harmondsworth, Middlesex, England: Penguin Books, 1964), p. 60.

Bibliography

Abrams, M. H., gen. ed. *The Norton Anthology of English Literature*. 4th ed. New York and London: W. W. Norton & Company, 1979.

Allaby, Ian. "GO Transit Moves a City." *Canadian Geographic,* December 1988, pp. 30-36.

Allan, Durward L. *Our Wildlife Legacy*. New York: Funk and Wagnalls, Inc., 1962.

Altman, J., and Campbell, C. L. "Effects of Herbicides on Plant Diseases." *Annual Review of Phytopathology* 13 (1971): 361-385.

Appleman, Philip. *The Silent Explosion*. Boston: Beacon Press, 1965.

Ardrey, Robert. *African Genesis*. New York: Dell Publishing Co., Inc., 1961.

Atkinson, Brooks, ed. *Walden and Other Writings of Henry David Thoreau*. New York: Random House, Inc., The Modern Library, 1950.

Atkinson, Brooks, ed. *The Selected Writings of Ralph Waldo Emerson*. New York: Random House, Inc., the Modern Library, 1950.

Bailey, Liberty Hyde. *The Holy Earth*. New York: Scribner, 1915. Reprint. Ithaca, New York: State University of New York, 1960.

Bakeless, John. *The Eyes of Discovery*. New York: Dover Publications, Inc., 1961.

Bandyopadhyay, J., and Shiva, V. "Chipko: Rekindling India's Forest Culture." *Ecologist,* vol. 17, no. 1 (1987), 26-34.

Banerjee, Sumanta and Kothari, Smitu. "Food and Hunger in India." *Ecologist,* vol. 15, no. 5/6 (1985), 257-260.

Bartlett, John. *Familiar Quotations*. 13th ed. Boston and Toronto: Little, Brown and Company, 1955.

Bates, Marston. *The Forests and the Sea*. New York: Alfred A. Knopf, Inc., 1962.

Blakney, R. B. *The Way of Life, Lao Tzu*. New York: New American Library, Inc., Mentor Books, 1955.

Bodo, Murray, OFM. *The Way of St. Francis*. New York: Doubleday and Co., Inc., 1984.

Bodo, Murray, OFM. *Francis: The Journey and the Dream*. Cincinnati, Ohio: St. Anthony Messenger Press, 1988.

Boraiko, Allen A., "The Pesticide Dilemma," *National Geographic.* February 1980. In *Earthcare: Ecological Agriculture In Saskatchewan*. Edited by Paul Hanley. Indian Head, Sask.: Earthcare Information Center, 1980.

Bosch, Robert van den. *The Pesticide Conspiracy*. Garden City, New York: Doubleday and Co., Inc., 1978.

Boulding, Kenneth C. "The Economics of the Coming Spaceship Earth." In Paul R. Ehrlich and Anne H. Ehrlich. *Population, Resources and Environment*. San Francisco: W. H. Freeman and Company, 1970.

Bromfield, Louis. *Malabar Farm.* New York: Ballantine Books, Inc., 1970.

Bromfield, Louis. *From My Experience: The Pleasures and Miseries of Life on a Farm.* New York: Harper & Brothers, Publishers, 1955.

Brown, Lester R. *Reversing Africa's Decline.* Worldwatch, paper 65, Washington, D.C.: Worldwatch Institute, 1985.

Brown, Lester R. *The Twenty-Ninth Day.* New York: W. W. Norton & Company, 1978.

Buckman, H. O., and Brady, N. C. *The Nature and Properties of Soils.* 7th ed. New York: The Macmillan Company, 1969.

Canada. Law Reform Commission of Canada. J. F. Castrilli, and T. Vigod. *Pesticides in Canada: An Examination of Federal Law and Policy,* Ottawa, 1987.

Canada. Environment Canada. *Canada's Environment, An Overview,* Ottawa, 1986.

Canada. Senate. Standing Committee on Agriculture, Fisheries, and Forestry. Report to the Senate of Canada on Soil Conservation. *Soil at Risk.* Chairman of reporting committee, Hon. Herbert O. Sparrow. Ottawa, 1984.

Canada. Environment Canada. Policy Research and Development Branch. Lands Directorate. G. W. Weetman. "Forestry Practices and Stress on Canadian Forest Land." In *Stress on Land in Canada.* Folio no. 6, Ottawa, 1983.

Canada. Agriculture Canada. Ralph D. Bird. *Ecology of the Aspen Parkland of Western Canada.* Publication no. 1066, Ottawa, Ottawa, 1961.

Canada. Science Council of Canada. *Canada's Threatened Forests: A Statement by the Science Council,* Ottawa, March 1983.

Canada. Canadian Environmental Advisory Council. Ross H. Hall. *A New Approach to Pest Control in Canada.* Report no. 10, Ottawa, July 1981.

Canada. Science Council of Canada. *Water 2020: Sustainable Use for Water in the 21st Century.* Report no. 40, Ottawa, June 1988.

Canada. Canadian Environmental Advisory Council. Ross H. Hall and Donald A. Chant. *Ecotoxicity: Responsibilities and Opportunities,* Report no. 8, Ottawa, August 1979.

"Canadian Notes." *Alternatives,* September/October 1988, 2; October/November 1989, 2.

Carlton, F. E. "Biting the Bullet." *Atlantic Salmon Journal,* Spring 1988, 50-52.

Cavanagh, Ralph; Goldstein, David; and Watson, Robert. "One Last Chance For a National Energy Policy." In *The Challenge of Global Warming,* edited by Dean Edwin Abrahamson. Washington, D.C., and Covelo, Calif.: Island Press, 1989.

Chaboussou, Francis. "How Pesticides Increase Pests." *Ecologist,* vol. 16, no. 1 (1986), 29-35.

Cody, William. "True Tales of the Plains." In *America: A Library of Original Sources,* 12 vols. In Peter Mathiessen. *Wildlife in America.* New York: The Viking Press, 1959.

Cohen, S. I. "The Afforestation of Israel." *The Journal of Forestry,* February 1985, pp. 95-99.

Cole, L. C. "Our Man-Made Environmental Crisis." *Canadian Audubon,* November/December 1968.

Coleridge, Samuel Taylor. *Omega.* Edited by Paul E. Anderson. Dubuque, Iowa: Wm. C. Brown Company Publishers, 1971.

Commoner, Barry. *The Closing Circle.* New York: Bantam Books, Inc., 1972.

Cousins, Norman. *Albert Schweitzer's Mission: Healing and Peace—With Hitherto*

Unpublished Letters from Schweitzer, Nehru, Eisenhower, Khrushchev, and Kennedy. New York: W. W. Norton & Company, 1985.

Cox, Harvey. *The Seduction of the Spirit.* New York: Simon and Schuster, Inc., 1973.

Culliney, John L. *The Forests of the Sea.* New York: Doubleday and Co., Inc., 1979.

Cumberland, Kenneth B. "Man's Role in Modifying Island Environment in the South-West Pacific: With Special Reference to New Zealand." In *Man's Place in the Island Ecosystem—A Symposium.* Edited by F. R. Fosberg. London: British Museum Press, 1965.

Dale, Tom and Carter, Vernon Gill. *Topsoil and Civilization.* Norman, Okla.: University of Oklahoma Press, 1955.

Darling, F. Fraser, and Milton, John O., eds. *Future Environments of North America.* Garden City, New York: The Natural History Press, 1966.

Dasmann, Raymond F. *The Last Horizon.* New York: The Macmillan Company, 1963.

Delaporte, L. *Mesopotamia.* In Will Durant. *The Story of Civilization.* Vol. 1. *Our Oriental Heritage.* New York: Simon and Schuster, Inc., 1963.

Dickens, Charles. *Little Dorrit.* Edited by John Holloway. First published in 1857. Harmondsworth, Middlesex, England: Penguin Books Inc., 1967.

Dieren, W. van, and Hummelinck, M. G. W. *Nature's Price: The economics of Mother Earth.* Translated by Joyce E. Houwaard-Wood. Edited by Jon Barzdo. London and Boston: Marion Boyars Publishers Ltd., 1979.

Dorst, Jean. *Before Nature Dies.* Translated by Constance D. Sherman. Baltimore: Penguin Books, 1970.

Dowdey, Clifford. *The Land They Fought For.* New York: Doubleday and Co., 1955.

Dubos, René. "Conservation, Stewardship, and the Human Heart." *Audubon,* September 1972, np.

Durant, Will. *The Story of Civilization.* vol. 1. *Our Oriental Heritage.* New York: Simon and Schuster, Inc., 1935.

Durant, Will. *The Life of Greece.* vol. 2. New York: Simon and Schuster, Inc., 1939.

Durant, Will, and Durant, Ariel. *The Lessons of History.* New York: Simon and Schuster, Inc., 1968.

Durning, Alan B. *Action At the Grassroots: Fighting Poverty and Environmental Decline.* Worldwatch, paper 88. Washington, D.C.: Worldwatch Institute, 1989.

Eckholm, Eric P. *Losing Ground.* New York: W. W. Norton & Company, 1976.

Ehrlich, Paul. "Eco-catastrophe." In *The Everlasting Universe.* Edited by Lorne J. Forstner and John H. Todd. Lexington, Mass.: D. C. Heath and Company, 1971.

Ehrlich, Paul R.; Ehrlich, Anne H.; and Holdren, John P. *Ecoscience: Population, Resources, Environment.* San Francisco: W. H. Freeman and Company, 1977.

Elton, Charles S. *The Ecology of Invasions by Plants and Animals.* London: Methuen & Co., 1958.

Epstein, Samuel S. "Losing the War Against Cancer." *Ecologist,* vol. 17, no. 2/3 (1987), 91-99.

Epstein, Samuel S. *The Politics of Cancer.* Garden City, N.Y.: Doubleday and Co., Inc., 1979.

Farb, Peter. *Living Earth.* New York: Harper & Row, Publishers, 1959.

Franklin, Jerry. "Old Growth, Its Characteristics, and its Relationship to Pacific Northwest Forests." Paper presented at Old Growth Conference, 25 August 1988, Corvallis, Oregon.

Garrett, Wilbur E. "Editorial." *National Geographic,* December 1988, p. 764.

Gibbon, Edward. The History of the Decline and Fall of the Roman Empire. 5th ed. Edited by J. B. Bury. New York: Methuen & Co., 1909.

Green, Thomas L. "Organic Farming in India." *Alternatives,* vol. 15, no. 1 (December/January 1987 and December/January 1988), 4-13.

Grzimek, Bernhard, and Grzimek, Michael. *Serengeti Shall Not Die.* New York: E. P. Dutton and Co., Inc., 1959.

Haeckel, Ernest. *The Riddle of the Universe.* London: Watts and Co., 1929.

Hall, Manly Palmer. *Twelve World Teachers.* Los Angeles: Philosophical Research Society, Inc., 1973.

Hamaker, John D. *The Survival of Civilization.* Seymour, Mo.: Hamaker-Weaver Publishers, 1982.

Hanley, Paul, ed. *Earthcare: Ecological Agriculture in Saskatchewan.* Indian Head, Sask.: Earthcare Information Center, 1980.

Harrington, Robert F., and Passmore, Richard C. *Learning About Environment.* Ottawa: Carlton-Green Publishing Company Ltd., 1972.

Hart, Roger. "The Questionable Practice of Slash Burning." Part 1. *NCAP News* 4 (Fall 1984), 17-21.

Hart, Roger. "The Questionable Practice of Slash Burning." Part 2. *NCAP News* 4 (Winter 1985), 19-24.

Haygarth, Henry W. "Recollections of Bush Life in Australia during a Residence of 8 years in the Interior." First published 1848. In W. K. Hancock. *Discovering Monaco —A Study of Man's Impact on His Environment.* London: Cambridge University Press, 1972.

Heilbroner, Robert. *An Inquiry Into the Human Prospect.* New York: W. W. Norton & Company, 1980.

Hepburn, Gail. "Pesticides and Drugs From the Neem Tree." *Ecologist,* vol. 19, no. 1 (January/February 1989), 31-32.

Herrera, Rafael. "Amazon Rain Forest Fires." In Peter Bunyard's "World Climate and Tropical Forest Destruction." *Ecologist,* vol. 15, no. 3 (1985), 125-136.

The High History of St. Benedict & His Monks. Compiled by a monk of Dubai Abbey. London: Sands and Co., 1945.

Hitti, P. K. *Lebanon in History.* London and Toronto: Macmillan & Co., 1967.

Hoffman, John S. "Carbon Dioxide and Future Forests." *Journal of Forestry,* vol. 82, no. 3, March 1984, pp. 164-167.

Hornaday, William T. "The Extermination of the American Bison with a Sketch of its Discovery and Life Story." In *Report of National Museum,* 1887. Reprint. Seattle: The Shorey Book Store, 1971.

Hutchins, Robert Mayne, ed. *Great Books of the Western World.* 54 vols. Chicago: Encyclopaedia Britannica, Inc., 1952.

Hyams, Edward. *Soil and Civilization.* Harper Colophon edition. London: John Murray, 1976.

Inglis, Rewey Belle; Stauffer, Donald A.; and Larsen, Cecil Evva. *Adventures In English Literature.* Canadian Edition. Agincourt, Ont.: W. J. Gage and Company Limited, 1952.

Jovanovich, Jovan. "Is Man Meddling?" *The Globe and Mail,* 10 January 1989.

Keats, John. "Letters to George and Georgiana Keats, February 14—May 3, 1819." In

The Norton Anthology of English Literature. 4th ed. New York: W. W. Norton & Company, Inc., 1979.

King, Thompson. *Water, Miracle of Nature.* New York: Collier Books, 1961.

King, Jonathan. *Troubled Water.* Emmaus, Pa.: Rodale Press, 1985.

Klemke, E. D.; Kline, A. David; and Hollinger, Robert, eds. *Philosophy, The Basic Issues.* New York: St. Martin's Press, Inc., 1982.

Lecky, William E. *The History of European Morals.* Vol. 2. London: Green & Co., 1910.

Lenssen, Nicholas. "The Ocean Blues." *Probe Post,* vol. 12, no. 2 (September 1989), 10-13.

Leopold, Aldo. *Sand County Almanac.* New York: Ballantine Books, Inc., 1966.

Lowdermilk, Inez Marks. *All in a Lifetime.* Berkeley, Calif.: Lowdermilk Trust, 1983.

Lucretius. *Of the Nature of Things.* Translated by W. E. Leonard. London: J. M. Dent and Sons Ltd., 1921.

Lull, Richard Swann. *Organic Evolution.* New York: The Macmillan Company, 1938.

Lundberg, C., ed. *The West Coast Environmental Law Research Foundation Newsletter* 13 (Fall 1987), p. 1.

Lynch, Wayne. "The Return of the Swift Fox." *Canadian Geographic,* August/September 1987, pp. 28-30.

MacEwan, Grant. *Tatanga Mani: Walking Buffalo of the Stonies.* Edmonton: Hurtig Publishers, 1969.

Mackay, Donald. *The Crisis in Canada's Forests.* Toronto: Macmillan of Canada, 1985.

Macrobius. *The Saturnalia.* Book 7, ch. 5. Translated by P. V. Davies. New York: Columbia University Press, 1969.

Marcus Aurelius. *Meditations.* Translated by Maxwell Staniforth. Harmondsworth, Middlesex, England: Penguin Books, 1964.

Marsh, George Perkins. *Man and Nature,* edited by David Lowenthal. First published in 1864. Cambridge, Mass.: Harvard University Press, Belknap Press, 1967.

Marsh, A. "Air Pollution." In *Technological Injury,* edited by J. Ross. New York: Fordon & Breach, 1969.

Mathiessen, Peter. *Wildlife in America.* New York: The Viking Press, 1959.

McLuhan, T. C. *Touch the Earth.* New York: Simon & Schuster, Inc., Pocket Books, 1972.

Mellanby, Kenneth. *Pesticides and Pollution.* London: Wm. Collins Publishers, 1967.

Michener, James A. *Chesapeake.* New York: Random House, Inc., 1978.

Miller, Jr. G. Tyler. *Living in the Environment: An Introduction to Environmental Science.* 4th ed. Belmont, Calif.: Wadsworth Publishing Co., Inc., 1985.

Monod, Th. "Conservation of Natural Resources in Africa." In *Man and Africa.* Edited by G. Wolstenholme and M. O'Connor. London: J. & A. Churchill Ltd., 1965.

Moser, B., and Taylor, D. *The Cocaine Eaters.* New York: Taplinger Publishing Co., Inc., 1964.

Mowat, Farley. *Sea of Slaughter.* Toronto: McClelland and Stewart, 1984.

Muir, John. *Steep Trails.* Boston: Houghton Mifflin Company, 1918.

Mumford, Lewis. *The Conduct of Life.* New York: Harcourt Brace Jovanovich, Inc., 1951.

Murray, Jacqueline. *The First European Agriculture: A Study of the Osteological and Botanical Evidence Until 2,000* B.C. Edinburgh: University Press, 1970.

Nash, Roderick. *Wilderness and the American Mind.* New Haven: Yale University Press, 1967.

Netboy, Anthony. *The Atlantic Salmon.* Boston: Houghton Mifflin Company, 1968.

Newton, Jan. M. "Herbicides and Economics." *NCAP News* 3 (1984): 10-11.

Packard, Vance. *The Hidden Persuaders.* New York: Simon & Schuster, Inc., Pocket Books, 1957.

Paine, Thomas. *The Rights of Man.* London: J. M. Dent & Son Ltd., Everyman's Library, 1915. Reprint 1969.

Pinchot, Gifford. *The Fight for Conservation.* Seattle: University of Washington Press, 1910.

Pinchot, Gifford. *Breaking New Ground.* New York: Harcourt, Brace and Co., 1947. Reprint. Washington, D.C., and Covelo, Calif.: Island Press, 1987.

Plato, *Critias.* Translated by Rev. R. G. Bury. Cambridge, Mass.: Harvard University Press, 1929.

Pliny, The History of the World. Translated by P. Holland and selected by Paul Turner. New York: McGraw Hill Book Co., 1962.

Pliny's Natural History. Compiled by Lloyd Haberly. Frederick Ungar Publishing Co., 1957.

Pollock, Cynthia. "Realizing Recycling's Potential." In *State of the World 1987.* New York: W. W. Norton & Company, 1987.

Postel, Sandra. *Worldwatch, Paper 71: Altering the Earth's Chemistry: Assessing the Risks.* Washington, D.C.: Worldwatch Institute, 1986.

Rienow, Robert, and Rienow, Leona Train. *Moment in the Sun.* New York: Ballantine Books, Inc. 1967.

Rifkin, Jeremy. *Entropy.* New York: The Viking Press, 1980.

Robinson, Gordon. *The Forest and the Trees.* Washington, D.C.: Island Press, 1988.

Roosevelt, Theodore. *Literary Essays.* New York: Charles Scribner & Son, 1926.

Roszak, Theodore. *Where the Wasteland Ends: Politics and Transcendence in Postindustrial Society.* Garden City, N.Y.: Doubleday and Company, Inc., Anchor Books, 1973.

Schneider, Stephen H. *The Genesis Strategy.* New York: Dell Publishing Co., A Delta Book, 1977.

Schneider, Stephen H. *Global Warming: Are We Entering the Greenhouse Century?* San Francisco: Sierra Club Books, 1989.

Schumacher, E. F. *Small is Beautiful: Economics as if People Mattered.* London: Blond & Briggs Ltd., 1973. Reprint. New York: Harper & Row Publishers, Perennial Libary, 1973.

Schweitzer, Albert. *Goethe, Five Studies.* Translated by Charles R. Joy. Boston: Beacon Press, 1961.

Schweitzer, Albert. *Civilization and Ethics.* London: Unwin Books, 1956.

Schweitzer, Albert. *The Decay and the Restoration of Civilization.* London: Unwin Books, 1956.

Sears, Paul. *Deserts on the March.* Norman, Okla.: University of Oklahoma Press, 1935. Reprint, with new foreword. Washington, D.C., and Covelo, Calif.: Island Press, 1988.

Service, Robert. *The Shooting of Dan McGrew and Other Poems.* Surrey, B.C.: Hancock House Publishers Ltd., 1989.

Seton, Ernest Thompson. *Lives of the Game Animals.* 8 vols. Boston: Charles T. Brantford Company, 1953.

Shaler, E. S. *Nature and Man in America.* New York: Charles Scribner & Son, 1906.

Simon Fraser University, Natural Resources Management Program, and Tourism Industry Association of British Columbia. "Tourism as a Generator for Regional Economic Development." Proceedings: First Annual Advanced Policy Forum on Tourism. Compiled and edited by Anne Popma and Ann Pollock. Whistler, B.C., May 1987.

Smuts, General, the Right Honorable J. C. *Holism and Evolution.* London: Macmillan and Co., Ltd., 1926.

Solomon, Lawrence. *The Conserver Solution: A Project of the Pollution Probe Foundation.* Toronto: Doubleday Canada Limited, 1978.

Solomon, Michel. *Future Life.* New York: Macmillan Publishing Company, 1983.

St. Barbe Baker, Richard. *My Life My Trees.* Forres, Scotland: Findhorn Publications, 1979.

Stegner, Wallace. *Beyond the Hundredth Meridian.* Boston: Houghton Mifflin Co., 1953.

"Swapping Debt for Nature." *Working for Wildlife,* Fall 1987, p. 5.

Swatek, Paul. *The User's Guide to Protection of the Environment.* New York: A Friends of the Earth/Ballantine Book, 1970.

Swift, Jamie. *Cut and Run.* Toronto: Between the Lines, 1983.

Sykes, Sir Percy. *A History of Afghanistan.* Vol. 1. London: Macmillan & Co., 1940.

Talman, J., ed. *Basic Documents in Canadian History.* Princton, N.J.: D. Van Nostrand Company, 1959.

Theophrastus. *Enquiry Into Plants.* Translated by Sir Arthur Hort. Cambridge, Mass.: Harvard University Press, 1916.

Thirgood, J. V. *Man and the Mediterranean Forest.* New York: Academic Press, 1981.

Thomas, M. L. H. "Effects of Bunker C Oil on Intertidal and Lagoonal Biota in Chedabucto Bay, Nova Scotia." *Journal of the Fisheries Research Board of Canada,* vol. 30, no. 1. (January 1973), 83-90.

Thucydides. *History of the Peloponnesian War.* Books 8 and 19. Translated by C. F. Smith. Cambridge, Mass.: Harvard University Press, 1918.

Tjahjad, Riza. "PAN Indonesia: A Grassroots Organization Moves Its Country Toward Alternatives to Pesticides." *Journal of Pesticide Reform,* vol. 9, no.2 (Summer 1989), 20-21.

Tolstoy, Leo. *The Kingdom of God is Within You: Or, Christianity Not As A Mystical Teaching But As a New Concept of Life.* Translated by Leo Wiener. Introduction by Kenneth Rexroth. New York: Farrar, Straus and Giroux, The Noonday Press, 1905.

Torrey, Bradford, and Allen, Francis H., eds. *The Journal of Henry David Thoreau.* 14 vols., bound as 2. Boston: Houghton Mifflin Co., 1906. Reprint. New York: Dover Publications, Inc., 1962.

Treakle, Kay, and Sacko, John. "Where There's a Will There's a Way: Indonesia, Rice and Alternatives to 57 Pesticides." *Journal of Pesticide Reform,* vol. 9, no. 2 (Summer 1989), 18-19.

U.S. Government Printing Office. *Annual Report of the Smithsonian Institution.* "Lessons from the Old World to the Americas in Land Use," 1943.

U.S. Department of Agriculture. Forest Service. *Methods of Managing Competing*

Vegetation. Report coordinator, Randall F. Perkins. May 1981.

Udall, Stewart L. *The Quiet Crisis*. New York: Avon Books, 1964.

Vergil. "The Joys of Farm Life." In *Latin Literature in Translation*. Translated by John Dryden. New York: Longman's Green and Co., 1954.

Vogt, William. *People!* In Philip Appleman. *The Silent Explosion*. Boston: Beacon Press, 1965.

Wallace, Alfred Russel. *Island Life*. London: Macmillan & Co., 1892.

White, Lynn. "The Historical Roots of our Ecological Crisis." In *The Everlasting Universe*. Edited by Lorne J. Forstner and John H. Todd. Lexington, Mass.: D.C. Heath and Company, 1971.

Whitman, Walt. *Leaves of Grass and Selected Prose*. Edited, with an Introduction, by John Kouwenhoven, Professor of English, Barnard College. New York: Random House, Inc., The Modern Library, 1950.

Whittaker, R. H., and Likens, G. E. "Carbon and the Biota." In *Carbon in the Biosphere*. Edited by George M. Woodwell and E. Pecan. Washington, D.C.: Technical Information Center, USAEC.

Whyte, R. O. *Grasslands of the Monsoon*. New York: Frederick A. Praeger Publisher, 1968.

Wilson, Carl, and Loomis, Walter E. *Botany*. New York: Holt, Rinehart & Winston, Inc., 1957.

Woodwell, George M. "Biotic Causes and Effects of the Disruption of the Global Carbon Cycle." In *The Challenge of Global Warming*. Edited by Dean Edwin Abrahamson. Washington, D.C.: Island Press, 1989.

The World Commission on Environment and Development. *Our Common Future*. New York: Oxford University Press, 1987.

The World Conference on the Changing Atmosphere. *Conference Statement: Implications for Global Security. Toronto, June 27-30, 1988*.

Index

294